Public Transport Planning and Management in Developing Countries

T0382730

Public Transport Planning and Management in Developing Countries

ASHISH VERMA

T. V. RAMANAYYA

CRC Press
Taylor & Francis Group
Boca Raton London New York

CRC Press is an imprint of the
Taylor & Francis Group, an **informa** business

CRC Press
Taylor & Francis Group
6000 Broken Sound Parkway NW, Suite 300
Boca Raton, FL 33487-2742

First issued in paperback 2020

ISBN-13: 978-1-4665-8158-6 (hbk)
ISBN-13: 978-0-367-73866-2 (pbk)

Dedicated
to
Lord Ganesha

Contents

1.0 General

1.1 Status of urban transport in India and developing countries

1.2 Status of public transport with respect to coverage, fleet strength, and utilization in urban areas

1.3 Sustainability and land use consideration

2.1 Introduction

2.2 Demographic changes of India since 1950

2.3 Gross domestic product (GDP)

2.4 Migration to urban areas

2.5 Growth of slums in urban areas

2.6 Accessibility and mobility issues for rural settlements

2.7 Transport infrastructure scenario in India

3.1 Mode of transport

3.2 Transport systems definitions and classifications

3.3 Intermediate public transport

3.4 Public transport modes

3.5 Classification of mass transit modes

3.6 Integrated transport infrastructure approach

3.7 A look ahead in public transportation

3.8 Comparative analyses

4.1 Current perception of PT

4.2 Current planning and operational practices

4.3 Issues of coordination and level of services

4.4 Funding pattern

4.5 Differences in scenario with respect to developed countries

5.1 Planning strategy

5.2 Network planning

5.3 Travel demand estimation

5.4 Stakeholder consultation and preferences

5.5 Public transport mode options

Contents

Preface

In the early stages of growth of any city, the vehicular trips are all road-based and are confined to modes like cycles, personalized cars, two-wheelers, and intermediate public transport (IPT) modes like cycle rickshaws, tongas, taxis, three-wheelers, tempos, etc. As the city's population and size grow further, commuter trips tend to get concentrated on particular sections and routes and call for a larger transport unit like a mini-bus or a standard bus, which forms part of the public transport system. In larger cities, public transport systems play an increasingly important role. In cities like Kolkata, Mumbai, Delhi, and Chennai, suburban rail services carry sizeable volumes of commuter trips. In Kolkata, tramways also play a noticeable role besides the metro rail operation. With the increase in city complexities and advancement in technology, new systems like automated guided transit (AGT) will soon be visible in metropolitan cities of India.

While making selection of a particular mode of mass transport for any Indian city, the criteria should essentially be the volume and pattern of travel demand. But, besides this, the systems should also be judged by their, suitability for Indian conditions; effectiveness and efficiency in dependably performing their designated role(s); flexibility of operation, with wide applicability; capital requirement; energy sources and consumption; environmental impact, from the point of view of pollution and noise; aesthetics, including image; available technology and indigenous capability; proven or nonproven technology; and future potential (especially in technological advancements).

This book attempts to cover various aspects of public transport planning and management particularly in the context of India and other developing countries, which have much different transportation issues and requirements as compared to developed countries. Many of the developing countries are attempting to expand and upgrade their public transport systems to create sustainable solutions for their cities and countries, however within the constraints of poor land use and urban planning, haphazard growth of settlements, high population and population density, growing income and travel demand, etc. Therefore it is quite timely to come up with this book that explains the principles of public transport planning and management that are relevant and suitable for developing countries' situations. The book covers both urban and rural public transport planning and management as well as, aspects of economics and finance related to public transport.

The highlight of the book is the use of rich data from Indian and developing countries con text and various examples from the research works of the authors to explain various aspect of public transport planning and management. In the opinion of authors, this book will be a good text/reference material for courses on public transport offered in various universitie at post-graduate and under-graduate levels.

Acknowledgments

The authors express their sincere thanks to Ms. Ganashree Shubhank for helping the authors in compiling references relevant for the book writing and also for typing and preparing book chapters in Latex. Due acknowledgement also to Dr. Gagandeep Singh from CRC Press whose continuous push and follow-ups helped the authors to complete the book in a reasonable time. The authors are grateful to their respective families for their constant support, encouragement, and help in completing this book and sparing us the time to write this book.

Ashish Verma
T. V. Ramanayya

About the Authors

Dr. Ashish Verma is a Ph.D. from IIT Bombay and currently serving as Assistant Professor of Transportation Engineering at the Department of Civil Engineer and the Center for Infrastructure, Sustainable Transportation, and Urban Planning (CiSTUP) at the Indian Institute of Science (IISc), Bangalore, India. Before joining IISc Bangalore, he served in IIT Guwahati and the Mumbai Metropolitan Region Development Authority (MMRDA). His research interests are in sustainable transportation planning, public transport planning and management, modeling and optimization of transportation systems, application of geoinformatics in transportation, driver behavior and road safety, intelligent transportation system (ITS), traffic management, etc. He has authored more than 70 research publications in the areas of sustainable transportation and road safety. He is an editorial board member of leading international journals of the American Society of Civil Engineers (ASCE) and other publishers. He has also been guest editor of special issues of leading journals of Elsevier, ASCE, and Current Science, focused on sustainable transportation in India and developing countries. He has received DAAD and CONNECT fellowships from the Humbolt Foundation in the past, for collaborative research with Germany. He has been involved in many national and internationally funded research projects related to sustainable transportation and road safety. He is the founding President of **Transportation Research Group of India** (TRG, www.trgindia.org), which is a registered society and has the mission to aid India's overall growth through focused transportation research, education, and policies in the country. He is also presently serving as Country Representative from India and Scientific Committee Member of the **World Conference on Transport Research Society (WCTRS)** based in Lyon, France. More details about him can be seen on his home-page http://civil.iisc.ernet.in/ashishv/.

Prof. T. V. Ramanayya holds a degree in Civil Engineering, a Master's in Transportation Engineering and a Ph.D. in Transportation Engineering, all from the Regional Engineering College (presently known as the National Institute of Technology) Warangal, Andhra Pradesh. He has four decades of experience (seven years in REC Warangal and 32 years at the Indian Institute of Management Bangalore) in teaching, training, research, and consultancy in the areas of transportation and urban infrastructure. He has guided a number of students for Master's degree and Ph.D. thesis. Some of the project assignments include: holistic organizational transformation strategies (HOTS) for APSRTC, sponsored by the government of Andhra Pradesh; development of strategic policymaking on bus passenger transport in India; design of internal control systems for KSRTC; rural transport infrastructure in entire South India; assessment of social and economic impact of rural roads component, sponsored by the government of Andhra Pradesh. He is involved in developing two new courses and taught them to Master's level students at IIM Bangalore, which includes: planning and management of urban infrastructure; computer applications including simulation programs for urban traffic and transportation.

Chapter 1

Introduction

1.0 General

The world is increasingly looking at the developing nations as potential markets and is eagerly waiting to see how the nations perform in the coming years. An efficient transportation system is essential for a country's development especially in urban areas that contribute to the majority of GDP of a country. The world today is increasingly urbanized. The challenge of growing population, and increase of vehicle ownership and usage casts a worrying shadow over projected emission of global greenhouse gases. It is roughly estimated that half the global population lives in cities. By 2030, it is projected that developing nations would have more vehicles than developed nations. Developing economies have been a prominent player in the game of rapid urbanization and its consequent irrevocable climate change impact. Booming economy, car manufacturers inflow to India, aspirations to own a car, increasing distances, comfort and safety, governments encouraging policies (open car market, easy loan schemes), etc. are a few reasons for increasing motorization at a rapid rate. In terms of an increase in motorization rates, India has registered a rapid growth, between 1997 and 2003, of two-wheeler contributing 40 percent of total vehicle population. The total number of motor vehicles in India has increased from 1.86 million in 1971 to 67 million in 2003. Motorized two-wheeler (motorcycles, scooters, mopeds) account for over 70 percent of the total registered fleet that will clearly impact carbon monoxide (CO) and hydrocarbon (HC) emissions. However, developing nations still posses the capacity for sustainable future in contrast to developed nations. Public and non-motorized transport still forms the major mode of traveling. Unfortunately, the quality of these modes is often quite poor with regard to level-of-service, security, comfort, and convenience. The sum effect of inadequate public transport and difficult conditions for walking and cycling implies that most developing-city citizens will move to private motorized vehicles as soon as it is economically viable for them to do so. The basic function of a transport system is to provide mobility, flexibility to people, and accessibility to places. A sustainable transport system must offer mobility and accessibility to all urban residents in a secure and eco-friendly mode of transport. Fundamentally more efficient and sustainable transport systems in developing nations should emphasize preservation, improvement of existing modes, encouraging modal shift towards sustainable modes, and implementing proper planning measures.

1.1 Status of urban transport in India and developing countries

1.1.1 Urban transportation status in developing countries

Taking as an example, China is one of the fastest growing countries of the world, and it is also one of the countries with the greatest development improvements in a short time. This development has important implications in terms of social, environmental, and economic

1

repercussions at a world level. In terms of transport, there are two major policy decisions that have to be acknowledged: the first is the decision as to the priorities of the automobile industry. The second is the decision to improve the urban public transport network. These two decisions, apparently contradictory, must be developed coherently to arrive at an optimum mix of improved public and private transport situation for its cities, while not hampering its industrial development. According to a World Bank study, the urban transport problems have been associated with globalization, urbanization, fiscal decentralization, and an economic transition. There are also growing concerns such as suburbanization of homes and consequent longer trips. Also, it should be noted that there is a lack of technical capacity and practical experience in strategic planning in transport. Finally, there is little public participation in planning processes, and there is a tendency towards technological improvements rather than modified policies, priorities of sustainable means of transport, or demand management techniques to improve transportation. The analysis of data and information available on developing countries clearly suggests that the current systems and trends of urban transportation, with respect to both mobility and safety, are not sustainable. The cities of developing countries are typically characterized by high-density urban areas, absence of proper control on land use, lack of proper roads and parking facilities, poor public transport, lack of road user discipline, etc. This results in the transportation problems, namely accidents, congestion, and pollution, taking a very different and much severe shape in developing countries than those in cities of developed countries.

1.1.2 Urban transportation status in India

The urban transport characteristics of India are proposed to be captured by studying the transport dynamics of 23 cities with million-plus population. As per 2001 census, these cities together account for about 33 percent of the Indian urban population and about 28.5 percent of the total vehicles in 2005. India's urban population is expected to increase from 286 million in 2001 to 534 million in 2026 (38 percent). The urban transport condition is shown in Fig (1.1).

Figure 1.1 has to improve its urban infrastructure to achieve the objectives of economic development. However, most of the cities in India have inadequate transport infrastructure. Urban transport is one of the major problem areas, affecting the mobility of people and accelerated economic growth of the urban centers of India.These problems are due to prevailing imbalance in modal split, inadequate transport infrastructure and its suboptimal use, and an absence of proper integration between land use and transport planning.

Figure 1.1: Glimpse of Transport Condition in India

In addition to million plus cities, India has more than 80 urban areas that are already grappling with many of the challenges mentioned above. These challenges arise because government and city planners have approached urban planning more as a knee-jerk reaction than from a strategic planning point of view to guide future growth. They have failed to understand the need to integrate urban transport development with city growth and as a result today we are faced with a huge challenge in providing a sustainable transport system to a population that is engaged in a variety of economic activities. Though an array of transport modes are available, Indian cities lack the necessary infrastructure to cater to an increased travel demand.

An associated problem has been the declining reliance on public transport. As a result the number of personal vehicles in Indian cities are growing at an unforeseen rate. Though significant improvements in public transport have been made in certain specified locations of some cities, these trends are still visible in many of the metropolitan cities including Delhi and its satellite towns like Noida, Gurgaon, and Ghaziabad. For instance the number of personal vehicles per 1000 population in Delhi has expanded by about 4 times in the last three decades where as the number of buses per 1000 population has increased only 2.3 times.

According to available data for all India, the share of public transport buses declined to 0.9 percent of total vehicle population in 2008 from 11.1 percent in 1951. Several urban transport studies also reveal that cities without good mass transit systems showed a higher growth rate in vehicular population as compared to those with mass transit systems. Average vehicular speeds in many of these cities were as low as 10 kilometers per hour during peak hours. The root cause of this problem is the failure to adapt the urban public transport system to the unique needs of these emerging cities. As a result, many cities in India today are faced with urban transport challenges like:

1. Mixed traffic flow and mixed land use

2. Severe congestion, pressure on existing public transport networks, and increased travel demand

3. Excessive delays, low speeds, and high travel times

4. Increased fuel consumption and air pollution

5. Safety issues

6. Exacerbation of problems due to rapid urbanization

7. Poor public transport and infrastructure deficiencies

8. Exponential growth in vehicle ownership

These problems are likely to intensify, if not multiply. With the transport sector already contributing to over 9 percent of India's total greenhouse gas (GHG) emissions, the increased use of private means of transportation will adversely impact energy use and environmental quality.

1.1.3 Urbanization

An urban area is an area with an increased density of human-created structures in comparison to the areas surrounding it. Urban areas may be cities, towns, or conurbations, but the term is not commonly extended to rural settlements such as villages and hamlets. The definition of urban varies from nation to nation and, as per the definition of India:

3

The towns (places with municipal corporation, municipal area committee, town committee, notified area committee, or cantonment board), all places having 5000 or more inhabitants, a density of not less than 400 per square kilometer, pronounced urban characteristics, and at least three fourths of the adult male population employed in pursuits other than agriculture, are treated as urban areas. As per 2011 census, India has 468 towns with a population more than 0.1 million. Also, during the second half of the last century, the number of cities in India with a population of one million and above has steadily increased from 35 in 2001 to 53 in 2011, which is expected to further increase to 70 by 2025. Observing the historical trends of population growth in India (Table 1.1), it can be seen that the annual average growth rate in every decade has been positive since 1931. Similar positive trends can be seen for the growth in percentage of urban population to the total population since 1921 and which is expected to increase from 28 percent in 2001 to 58 percent by 2025. From the trends of urban population, similar trends can be observed for developing countries compared to developed countries (Figure 1.2).

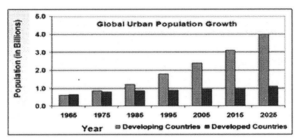

Figure 1.2: Population Growth in Developed and Developing Countries

Source: MOUD (2008)

Clearly, this growth of urban population in developing countries has a definite impact on travel demand and subsequently on urban mobility. It is clearly understood that cities are the economical contributors of the nation with its 50-60 percent contribution to GDP. But, the question is how an urban India can survive with the estimated population as indicated above?

Table 1.1: Historical Growth of Population Growth

Year	Population (in millions)	Density of Population per Sq.Km.	Average Annual Exponential Growth Rate	Percentage of Urban Population to Total Population
1	2	3	4	5
1901	238.40	77	-	10.85
1991	252.09	82	0.56	10.29
1921	251.32	81	-0.03	11.18
1931	278.98	90	1.04	11.99
1941	318.66	103	1.33	13.86
1951	361.09	117	1.25	17.29
1961	439.23	142	1.96	17.97
1971	548.16	177	2.22	19.91
1981	683.33	216	2.20	23.33
1991	846.42	267	2.14	25.70
2001	1028.61	325	1.95	27.83
2011	1210.19	382	-	31.80

Source: Census figures of different years

The most important factors common to India and other developing countries are population growth, increasing urbanization, rising motorization, and low per-capita income. The rapid growth of Indian cities has generated a correspondingly rapid growth in travel demand, overwhelming the limited transport infrastructure. The sharply increasing levels of motor vehicle ownership and use, in particular, have resulted in alarming levels of congestion, air pollution, noise, and traffic danger. For most segments of the population, mobility and accessibility have declined.

1.2 Status of public transport with respect to coverage, fleet strength, and utilization in urban areas

1.2.1 Fleet utilization (per) and fleet strength

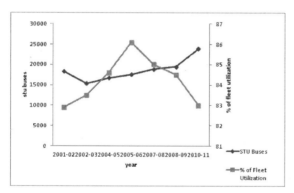

Figure 1.3: Fleet Strength of STUs from 2000-01 to 2010-2011
Source: State Transport Undertakings (Central Institute of Road Transport)

Fleet utilization is defined as the percentage of buses put on the road to the number of buses held. The overall fleet utilization of reporting state transport undertakings (STUs) is given in (Figure 1.3). It can be seen from the figure that the percentage of fleet utilization is decreasing from 2006 to 2011, whereas the number of STU buses is considerably increasing from 18,000 in 2001 to around 24,000 in 2011.

1.2.2 Public transport with respect to coverage

From Table 1.2, it is clear that the public transport coverage of STU buses in terms of effective kms, dead kms, and gross kms is going on increasing from 2001 to 2011. The next section discusses the sustainability and land use consideration.

Table 1.2: Public Transport with Respect to Coverage of STU Buses

Sl.no	Year	Effective Kms (in millions)	Dead Kms (in millions)	Gross Kms (in millions)
1	2001-02	1250.644	32.132	1282.776
2	2002-03	1054.966	30.932	1085.898
3	2004-05	1182.724	31.286	1214.010
4	2005-06	1273.293	40.4	1313.693
5	2007-08	1306.280	50.074	1356.354
6	2008-09	1404.215	51.768	1455.983
7	2010-11	1618.323	59.796	1678.119

Source: State Transport Undertakings (Central Institute of Road Transport)

1.3 Sustainability and land use consideration

Transport plays a significant role in the overall development of a nation's economy. However, this sector also accounts for a substantial and growing proportion of air pollution in cities. In addition, the sector contributes significantly to greenhouse gas emissions and is a major consumer of petroleum resources (petrol, diesel, etc.). In the recent past, the word sustainability has attained a prominent place in transportation planning, policy, and other documents. It can be broadly defined as development that meets the needs of the present without compromising the ability of future generations to meet their needs. In the context of transportation, sustainability would mean developing better transportation systems, options, and expectations consistent with the objective of securing future social and economic development within a sustainable environment that ensures community well-being. Sustainable transport can be achieved through measures pertaining to transportation system management, energy management, capacity management, and environmental management (Figure 1.4).

Sustainable transport is also important for developing countries from the perspective of climate change, i.e., to improve carbon foot print/ecological foot print (EF), etc. of transportation systems. As per some of the studies conducted in U.K and U.S., it has been found that road transport emits 22-25% of the total carbon dioxide emissions. These findings thrust the need for achieving sustainability in transport not just from mobility and safety perspectives but also from the perspectives of local and global environmental concerns.

1.3.1 Are current systems and trends in Indian cities sustainable?

Are current systems and trends in Indian cities sustainable? It is important to answer this question before discussing the problems with respect to the Indian scenario. For this, it is essential to first understand the present trends on aspects such as urbanization, motorization, modal share, and their impact on mobility, safety issues, and environmental issues.The urbanization trends are already discussed in a previous section.

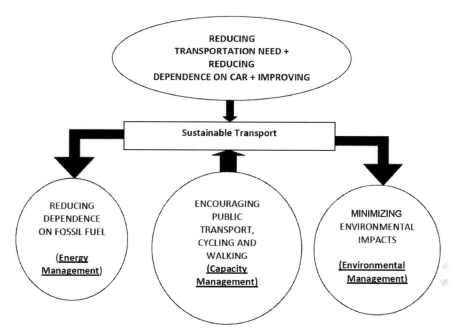

Figure 1.4: Components of Sustainable Transport

1.3.2 Motorization

Indian cities have registered an astronomical growth in registered motor vehicles in the last decade (Figure 1.5). Booming economy, aspirations to own a car, unmatched public transport (with respect to demand, comfort, or both), governments encouraging policies (open car market, easy loan schemes), etc. are few reasons for increasing motorization at a rapid rate. From 1981 to 2001, population increased in six major metropolises by 1.9 times, but motor vehicles increased by 7.75 times. Also, energy demand in the transport sector is projected to grow at 5-8 percent per annum. The estimates of vehicular growth are unimaginable and threatening. To give an example, Table 1.3 shows that cars and SUVs will increase 13 fold in 2035 with respect to 2005 statistics under a do-nothing scenario. Unfortunately, similar growth of vehicles has not been observed for bus fleets of major transport undertakings in India (Table 1.4). In fact, the size of bus fleets has been decreasing in most of the urban transport undertakings except in Bangalore where the annual growth is about 10%.

1.3.3 Modal share

Figure 1.6 shows mode split in selected cities of India. Also, Table 1.5 shows the existing modal split for different Indian cities based on population size. As a general trend, with the increase in the size of the city in terms of both area as well as population, the modal share on public transport has been increasing, but there is no evidence either for the reduction of private motorized transport (2w+car, etc.) share except for the 5 million plus cities.

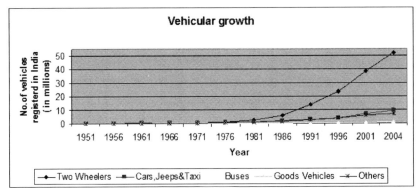

Figure 1.5: Growth of India's Motor Vehicle Fleet by Type of Vehicle from 1951-2004 (in millions)

Source: MORTH (1999, 2000, 2003), Handbook on Transport Statistics in India. Transport Research Office, Ministry of Road Transport and Highways, Delhi, India.

Table 1.3: Forecast of Vehicle Population in India

Population	2005	2008	2015	2025	2035
2-W	35.8	46.1	87.7	174.1	236.4
3-W	2.3	3.0	5.3	8.8	13.1
HCV	2.4	2.9	4.6	9.1	16.2
LCV	2.4	3.2	5.7	12.5	26.9
Car,SUV	6.2	8.8	18.0	41.6	80.1
Grand Total	49.1	63.9	121.3	246.1	372.7

Source: MOUD (2008)

Table 1.4: Growth of STU Bus Fleet in India

City	STU	year								AAGR (2000 -07)
		2000	2001	2002	2003	2004	2005	2006	2007	
Mumbai	BEST	3269	3155	3075	3075	3074	3069	3010	3143	-0.8
Delhi	DTC	4916	4330	4466	2496	2905	3010	3143	2814	-7.7
Chennai	CHII	2353	2314	2211	2270	2251	2187	2176	2087	-1.7
Kolkata	CSTC	814	821	856	800	769	707	659	635	-3.5
Ahmed abad	AMTS	752	729	630	410	382	371	545	727	-0.5
Pune	PMT	657	664	647	662	697	764	784	752	1.9
Chandig arh	DCHN TU	393	395	404	-	-	-	405	404	0.4
Banglore	BMTC	2110	2250	2446	2656	3062	3533	3802	3967	9.4

Source: MOUD (2008)

Note: Annual Average Growth Rate (%)

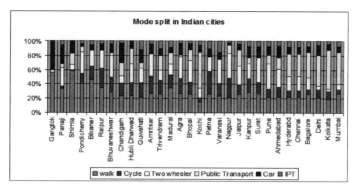

Figure 1.6: Mode Split in Indian Cities

Source: MOUD 2008

Table 1.5: Existing Modal Split in Indian Cities (as a % of Total Trips)

City Population (in millions)	Walk	Mass Transport	Intermediate Public Transportation ..Fast & Slow		Car	Two-Wheeler	Bicycle	Total
0.10-0.25	37.1	16.4	10.4	20.1	3.3	24.1	25.7	100.0
0.25-0.50	37.8	20.6	8.9	17.2	2.6	29.8	20.9	100.0
0.50-1.0	30.7	25.4	8.2	12.0	9.5	29.1	15.9	100.0
1.0-2.0	29.6	30.6	6.4	8.1	3.3	39.6	12.1	100.0
2.0-5.0	28.7	42.3	4.9	3.0	5.0	28.9	15.9	100.0
5.0+	28.4	62.8	3.3	3.7	6.1	14.8	9.4	100.0

Source: MOUD (1998)

One of the important reasons for considerable PT mode share is the presence of a substantial percentage of captive riders in most of the Indian cities. But, at the same time, the modal share on nonmotorized transport (walk and bicycle) is also considerable; however, the policy, infrastructure, and facility support is extremely poor for NMT modes in India. Moreover, if we compare the existing modal split with the desired modal split given in Table 1.6, it is clear that we still have an imbalance in modal split particularly in terms of desired share of public transport and NMT. From a recent study by MOUD (2008), during 1994 to 2007, the average public transport share has been reducing for the cities with above 2 million population (Table 1.7) and if the PT share is projected further (Table 1.8) considering the present trend of urbanization and motorization, it is further going to decrease aggravating the imbalance in the modal split. From the same MOUD study, it is also highlighted that the major portion of vehicular composition during peak hour on important corridors in the metropolitan cities consists of cars, two-wheelers, and IPT (even though their mode share is less compared to PT), which clearly indicates the reason for extreme congestion on Indian urban roads during peak hours (Table 1.9). After understanding the trends of urbanization, motorization, and modal share, it is now important to understand how they are affecting the mobility and safety, which are the two main goals of transportation, as well as the environment.

Table 1.6: Desirable Modal Split for Indian Cities (as % of Total Trips)

City Population (in millions)	Mass Transportation	Bicycle	Other Modes
0.1-0.5	30-40	30-40	25-35
0.5-1.0	40-50	25-35	20-30
1.0-2.0	50-60	20-30	15-25
2.0-5.0	60-70	15-25	10-20
5.0+	70-85	15-20	10-15

Source: MOUD (1998)

Table 1.7: Change in Public Transport Share

City Category	City Population Range (in million)	WSA Study, 2007 %	RITES Study, 1994 %
1	<0.5	0.0-15.6	14.9-22.7
2	0.5-1.0	0.0-22.5	22.7-29.1
3	1.0-2.0	0.0-50.8	28.1-35.6
4	2.0-4.0	0.2-22.2	35.6-45.8
5	4.0-8.0	11.2-32.1	45.8-59.7
6	above 8.0	35.2-54.0	59.7-78.7

Source: MOUD (2008)

Table 1.8: Projected Change in Public Transport Share and Estimated Mode Share for Different City Categories

Year		2001			2011			2021			2031		
City Category	Population (in millions)	PT	PV + IPT	NMT	PT	PV + IPT	NMT	PT	PV + IPT	NMT	PT	PV + IPT	NMT
1a	<0.5 population with plain terrain	5	57	38	4	59	36	3	66	31	2	72	26
1b	<0.5 population with hilly terrain	8	34	58	7	37	56	5	47	48	3	57	40
2	0.5-1.0	9	39	53	8	42	50	6	51	43	5	58	36
3	1.0-2.0	13	43	44	12	46	43	10	52	38	9	57	34
4	2.0-4.0	10	47	43	9	49	42	8	51	41	8	52	40
5	4.0-8.0	22	42	36	21	45	35	15	51	34	12	54	34
6	>8.0	46	24	30	42	28	30	31	40	29	26	46	28

Source: MOUD (2008) Note: PT - Public Transport, PV - Personal Vehicle, IPT - Auto Richshaw NMT - Nonmotorized transport including walk and cycle

1.3.4 Effects on mobility

Mobility can be assessed in terms of speed, travel times, delays, etc. along the important corridors in the city. According to GMMN report, the average journey speeds in 2007 on important city corridors is in the range of 15-20 kmph, which is considerably low as compared to design speeds for the same roads. Considering the do-nothing scenario, these speeds are expected to fall to single digits by 2031 (refer to Table 1.10). Also, as per an interesting finding from MOUD report on calculating congestion index of 30 cities of India (Figure 1.7), it is concluded that 0.25 is the average congestion index on a scale of 0-0.6 where 0 indicates good and 0.6 indicates poor index value, and most of the major metro cities fair very badly on the congestion index with its value much higher than the average. Here, the congestion index is calculated as (1- x/y), where x is observed speed and y is expected speed. As per the same report by MOUD, the average volume to capacity (V/C) ratio on major corridors within cities (in 2007) has already reached values closer to or exceeding 1, indicating extreme congestion conditions during peak hour (Table 1.11). This V/C ratio is expected to reach a value of up to 2 by 2031, under the do-nothing scenario.

Table 1.9: Average Peak Hour Vehicle Composition at Locations within City%

City Category	Population (in million)	Std bus	Mini Bus	Cars /Jeep / Van	Two Wheelers	Auto Rickshaws	Commercial Vehicles	SMVs	Total
1a	<0.5 with plain terrain	9	4	17	30	14	9	17	100
1b	<0.5 with plain terrain	6	15	40	33	0	5	0	100
2	0 .5-1.0	7	2	17	32	20	6	16	100
3	1.0-2.0	6	4	19	33	20	5	14	100
4	2.0-4.0	6	2	23	36	16	4	13	100
5	4.0-8.0	9	2	20	37	21	4	7	100
6	>8.0	12	3	31	23	23	3	4	100

Source: MOUD (2008)

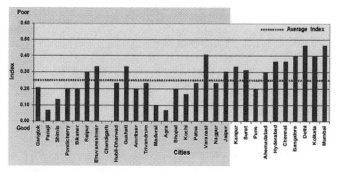

Figure 1.7: Congestion Index of Selected Indian Cities

Source: MOUD (2008)

Table 1.10: Anticipated Average Journey Speed (KMPH) on Major Corridors

Sl no	City Category	Population (in millions)	2007	2011	2021	2031
1	1	<0.5	26	22	15	8
2	2	0.5-1.0	22	18	13	9
3	3	1.0-2.0	18	13	10	7
4	4	2.0-4.0	22	18	12	9
5	5	4.0-8.0	19	15	10	7
6	6	>8.0	17	12	9	6

Source: MOUD (2008)

Table 1.11: Average V/C Ratio on Major Corridors under Do-Nothing Scenario

Sl.No	City Category	2007	2011	2021	2031
1	1	0.24	0.33	0.69	1.48
2	2	0.73	0.78	1.2	1.64
3	3	0.81	1,24	1.8	1.97
4	4	0.97	1.05	1.16	1.32
5	5	1.12	1.51	2.01	2.54
6	6	1.21	1.79	2.4	2.9

Source: MOUD (2008)

1.3.5 Effects on environment

If we consider the current state of sectorwise carbon emissions as shown in Figure 1.8, it can be observed that transport sector carries a major share of 12.6% of total carbon emissions as compared to other sectors like, energy, manufacturing, residential, commercial, etc. Also, within the emissions from transport sector, road transport has the major share of 87% as compared to rail, air, and water transport (Figure 1.8a). Certainly, these facts are closely related to the present trends of urbanization, motorization, and modal share. Table 1.12 and Table 1.13 show the fuel consumption per day in kiloliters and emissions per day in tonnes, respectively, by different types of vehicles for different city categories and it can be seen that the major share of fuel consumption as well as emissions is by cars and two-wheelers as compared to buses, except for cities of Category-6, i.e., population more than 8 million, where the fuel consumption is higher for buses but still the emission is less compared to cars. This scenario clearly comes from the prevailing imbalance in modal split (as mentioned in section 1.3.3), which is not just affecting the mobility but also the environment.

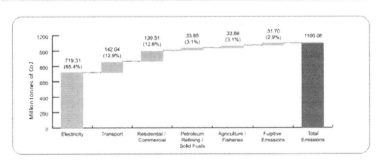

Figure 1.8: Sectorwise Carbon Emissions

Source: INCCA (2007)

12

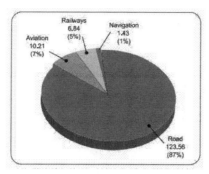

Figure 1.8a: Carbon Emissions by Transport Sector in 2007

Source: INCCA (2007)

Table 1.12: Fuel Consumption per Day in Kilo-liters

City Category	Car	TW	AR	Bus	Total
1	36	8	5	6	55
2	603	414	362	280	1659
3	1003	1058	602	376	3039
4	436	393	393	140	1362
5	921	901	553	833	3208
6	4782	1605	2869	7442	16697

Source: MOUD (2008)

Table 1.13: Emissions per Day in Tonnes

City Category	Car	TW	AR	BUS	Total
1	6	3	0	0	10
2	90	133	24	21	268
3	158	342	125	27	652
4	64	127	37	9	238
5	143	300	143	60	647
6	556	365	451	375	1747

Source: MOUD (2008)

As per Asian Development Bank (ADB): Sustainable Working Paper Series, No. 9. (2009), transport-related CO2 emissions from developing countries will contribute in increasing proportion to global CO2 emissions unless mitigating measures are implemented soon. This phenomenon can be understood by referring to Figure 1.9 (assuming a datum of 100 for all regions and/or countries in 1980 under reference scenario) which shows that the maximum growth in CO2 emissions would be in the developing countries of Asia. This projection is closely related to projected growth in personalized vehicles, namely cars and two-wheelers as observed in the previous section.

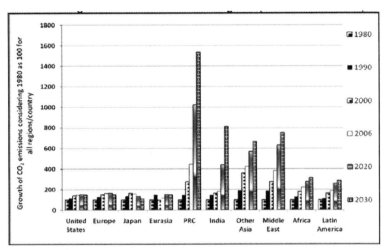

Figure 1.9: Transport Sector Energy-Related CO2 Emissions Growth
Considering 1980 Value as 100 for All Regions

Source: PRC = People's Republic of China

To summarize this section, most of the Indian cities today are typically characterized by high-density urban areas, absence of proper control on land use, lack of proper roads and parking facilities, poor public transport, lack of road user discipline, etc. This level and type of urbanization in India has caused many problems, especially with regard to its impact on the demand for infrastructure facilities. Urban transport systems have come under heavy strain and this has adversely affected the quality of life of urban dwellers. Mass transport facilities in the cities are grossly inadequate for providing fast, comfortable, and convenient travel. This has resulted in heavy shift of commuter patronage from mass transportation to private and intermediate transport and consequently, a huge increase in the number of intermediate and private vehicle ownership. The introduction of small cars, in the Indian market is further adding to the complexity of the transportation situation in the Indian cities. The resultant effects are increased traffic congestion and transport-borne pollution, heavy fuel consumption, poor level of service to the commuter, etc. So, it can be clearly said that the current systems and trends in Indian cities are not sustainable.

Summary

This chapter presents the status of urban transport in India and developing countries, mainly the terms of inefficient transportation system, urbanization, specter of growing population, myriads of vehicle ownership, and usage which casts a worrying shadow over projected emission of global greenhouse gases. This chapter also discusses the condition of urban public transport with respect to coverage, fleet strength, and fleet utilization with respect to the state transport undertakings (STU). It also discusses the sustainability in terms of environment, energy, economic, and land-use perspectives by considering the trends of motorization, vehicle growth, modal share, effects on mobility and environment, and transport energy consumption and emissions in India.

Chapter 2
Demography and Settlement Patterns

2.1 Introduction

India is a country located in South Asia that is home to the 2nd largest population in the world (behind China) estimated at 1.2 billion as of the year 2011. India is the largest democracy in the world, its official form of government being a federal constitutional republic. It also has the 7th largest geographical area in the world at 3,287,263 sq.km. It became an independent nation on August 15, 1947 by gaining freedom from the British Empire that was won by a peaceful resistance led by Mahatma Gandhi. For thousands of years previous to that time, the Indus Valley civilization was located in India. Currently, India is comprised of 29 states, 7 union territories, and 640 districts. In terms of religion, Hinduism is the one with the most followers at 817,112,705 or 72.03% of the country. As for language, Hindi is the most spoken first language with 180,764,791 speakers. India is a big continent, it accounts for about 2.4 percent of the total surface area of the world. India is nearly twenty times as large as Great Britain. Many of the Indian states are larger than several countries of the world. Figure 2.1 indicates the Indian subcontinent with administrative boundaries of different states. India is predominantly rural, but it also has many densely populated metropolitan areas. Most of the land is inhabited except for the higher regions of the Himalayan mountains. Since the time of the Indus Valley civilization, the key factor that settlers have considered in deciding where to live in India has been the ability to have continuous cultivation. This is mainly determined by water availability and soil fertility.

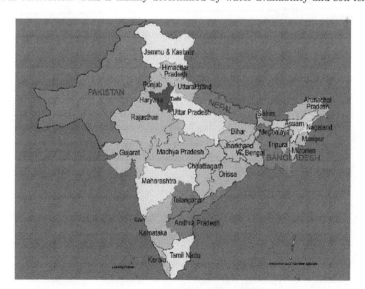

Figure 2.1: Map of India Indicating Different States

Source: www.mapsofindia.com

2.1.1 Definition of urban areas

In the case of India, census authorities adopted the following criteria for defining urban areas:

a. All places with a municipality, corporation, cantonment board, notified town area committee, or other such places

b. All places which satisfy the following criteria:

i) A minimum population of 5000

ii) At least 75 percent of male working population engaged in nonagricultural pursuits

iii) A density of population of at least 400 persons per sq. km.

c. Besides the major project colonies, areas of industrial development, railway colonies, and important tourist destinations were also treated as urban though they might not fulfill the above criteria strictly.

2.1.2 Urban development in India

Only 25% of India's population during 1981 lived in the 4500 areas of India that are classified as urban. Most of these urban areas are located in places where there is prosperous agriculture which is in western, southern, and northwestern India though that is starting to change. Urban growth is surprisingly faster than India's rural growth even though there is a high amount of congestion in most cities. The reason for this exponential urban growth is due to the commercialization of the agricultural industry as well as the expansion of various other industries such as manufacturing and services. Some urban areas were comparable to major cities of the world in terms of urban population and density of population. The top five major urban centers of India are:

1. Mumbai, 12,478,447

2. Delhi, 11,007,835

3. Kolkata, 4,486,679

4. Chennai, 4,681,087

5. Bangalore, 8,425,970

All these cities are experiencing traffic congestion during most of the day time in one locality or another. Figure 2.2 illustrates a typical traffic jam in the city of Mumbai.

Figure 2.2: A Typical Traffic Jam in Mumbai

2.1.3 Rural settlement pattern

75% of India's population lives in small villages with a few hundred people in a settlement.

These villages normally follow caste based clusters, an old social class system that is not exhibited in most urban areas. The forward caste people belonging to top of the caste system live in the central part of the village and the people of the backward caste live on the outskirts.

Most forward caste people are rich and better educated compared to people belonging to backward caste. Figure 2.3 depicts a typical village setting in India.

Figure 2.3: A Typical Village in India

2.2 Demographic changes of India since 1950

The population of the country as per 2011 census is 1.2 billion. This population is distributed in 580,000 rural settlements and 4500 urban centers of different sizes. The country is experiencing rapid growth in population. The growth of population since 1951 is presented in Table 2.1 and Table 2.2. The population of the country as per 2011 census has crossed 1.2 billion, compared to 0.361 billion during 1951. Figure 2.4 provides the pictorial presentation of urban and rural population from 1951 to 2011. The annual compounded growth rate (CAGR) during the last 6 decades works out to be 2.04 percent. However, there are variations in growth rates of urban and rural populations.

The CAGR of rural areas during last 6 decades is about 1.73%.
The CAGR of urban areas during last 6 decades is about 3.05%.

Table 2.1: Growth of Population Since 1951

Year	Total Population (in billions)	Decadal % Growth of Total Population	Total Rural Population (in billions)	% of Rural Population	Total Urban Population (in billions)	% of Urban Population
1951	0.361	13.31	0.298	82.71	0.062	17.17
1961	0.439	21.64	0.360	82.03	0.079	17.97
1971	0.548	24.80	0.439	80.09	0.109	19.91
1981	0.683	24.66	0.523	76.66	0.159	23.34
1991	0.846	23.87	0.628	74.28	0.217	25.72
2001	1.03	21.54	0.742	72.17	0.286	27.83
2011	1.21	17.64	0.833	68.84	0.377	31.16

Source: Census of India for different years

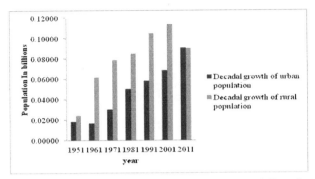

Figure 2.4: Decadal Growth of Urban and Rural Population

Source: Census of India 1951 to 2011

Table 2.2: Decadal Growth Rates of Population

Year	Total Population (in billions)	Urban Population (in billions)	Decadal Growth of Urban Population	Rural Population (in billions)	Decadal Growth of Urban Population
1951	0.361	0.062	0.01829	0.298	0.02414
1961	0.439	0.079	0.01649	0.36	0.06165
1971	0.548	0.109	0.03018	0.439	0.07875
1981	0.683	0.159	0.05035	0.523	0.08482
1991	0.846	0.217	0.05815	0.628	0.10483
2001	1.03	0.286	0.06851	0.742	0.13380
2011	1.21	0.377	0.09099	0.833	0.9060

Source: Census of India 1951 to 2011

It may be noted from the above table that urban population is increasing at a faster rate compared to rural population. It is further observed as presented in Table 2.2 that during the last decade (i.e., 2001-2011), the net addition of the urban population (90,986,071) has exceeded the net addition of the rural population (90,597,023) by 389,058. This trend is likely to continue in the future. Demographers estimate that the percentage of people living in urban areas is likely to touch 50% of the total population by the year 2050.

2.2.1 Growth of urban settlements

Urban areas could be classified into different cities as per population. In India many researchers for purposes of infrastructure planning has divided them into '6' categories. The urban population in each category as per 2011 census is presented in Table 2.3.

Table 2.3: Distribution of Population in Urban Settlements

Population Classes	1991	2011	% Decadal Growth
less than 5000	663	668	0.75
5000-9999	5650	6658	17.84
10,000-19,999	17,074	19,458	13.96
20,000-49,999	28,688	35,155	22.54
50,000-99,999	23,629	27,832	17.79
more than 100,000	140,067	196,345	40.18
All classes	215,772	286,120	32.6

Source: Census of India (2011)

For the purposes of providing an efficient public transport infrastructure, the urban centers are classified into category I to category V depending upon population. The growth of 23 million plus cities from 1951 to 2001 is presented in Table 2.4.

Table 2.4: Million Plus Cities in India

Rank	City	Population (in millions)				Per Increase in the Last Decade
		1951	1971	1991	2001	
1	Bombay	2.97	5.97	12.57	16.37	30.23
2	Kolkata	4.67	7.42	10.92	13.22	21.06
3	Delhi	1.44	3.65	8.38	12.79	52.63
4	Madras	1.54	3.17	5.36	6.42	19.78
5	Hyderabad	1.13	1.80	4.28	5.53	29.21
6	Bangalore	0.79	1.66	4.09	5.69	39.12
7	Ahmadabad	0.88	1.75	3.30	4.52	36.97
8	Pune	0.61	1.14	2.49	3.75	50.60
9	Kanpur	0.71	1.28	2.11	2.69	27.49
10	Nagpur	0.48	0.93	1.66	2.12	27.71
11	Lucknow	0.50	0.81	1.64	2.27	38.41
12	Surat	0.24	0.49	1.52	2.81	84.87
13	Jaipur	0.30	0.64	1.52	2.32	52.63
14	Koch i	0.18	0.51	1.14	1.35	18.42
15	Coimbatore	0.29	0.74	1.14	1.45	27.19
16	Vadodara	0.21	0.47	1.12	1.49	33.04
17	Indore	0.31	0.56	1.10	1.64	49.09
18	Patna	0.32	0.56	1.10	1.71	55.45
19	Madurai	0.37	0.71	1.09	1.19	9.17
20	Bhopal	0.10	0.38	1.06	1.45	36.79
21	Vishakapatnam	0.11	0.36	1.05	1.33	26.67
22	Varanasi	0.37	0.64	1.03	1.21	17.48
23	Ludhiana	0.15	0.40	1.01	1.40	38.61

Source: Government of India Ministry of Statistics and Programme Implementation Central Statistics Office Social Statistics Division. Census 2001.

2.2.2 Growth of rural settlements

The information on the growth of population in rural settlements is presented in Table 2.5; it may be noted that for settlements with population less than 2000 (4 settlement sizes), the growth rates are negative or negligible. Settlements sizes 5000 to 10,000 and above generate higher growth rates.

Table 2.5: Distribution of Population in Rural Settlements

Population classes	Rural (population class in millions)		
	1991	2001	% Change
less than 200	10.52	9.2	-12.55
200-499	48.45	43.96	-12.55
500-999	104.38	105.3	-9.27
1000-1999	160.31	183.35	0.88
2000-4999	185.59	239.19	14.37
5000-9999	69.81	98.1	28.88
>10,000	43.721	63.49	45.22
Total	622.81	742.62	19.24

Source: Government of India Ministry of Statistics and Programme Implementation Central Statistics Office Social Statistics Division. Census 2001.

2.2.3 Variation in economic status of urban and rural population

Rural households main occupation is agriculture with 75 to 80 percent deriving a large part of the income through agricultural related activities. About 10 to 15 percent of rural households generate secondary income through dairy (milk) related activities. About 10 to 15 percent of households only generate income through other means such as employment, manufacturing, trade, etc.

2.3 Gross domestic product (GDP)

GDP is the market value of all officially recognized final goods and services produced within a country in a given period of time. GDP per capita is often considered an indicator of a country's standard of living.

Urban areas contribute to the national income at a much higher rate compared to rural population. Contribution to national wealth by urban as well as rural population in last 5 decades is presented in Table 2.6 and Figure 2.5.

Table 2.6: Percentage Contribution of GDP by Rural and Urban Areas

Year	1951	1981	1991	2001	2011
GDP of India (in billion USD)	NA	196.1	274.8	492.4	1873
Percentage Contribution of Urban Area	30	48	55	60	70
Percentage Contribution of Rural Area	70	52	45	40	30

Source: GDP of India (1951-2011)

It may be noted that the contribution of urban population per million is increasing at a faster rate compared to the contribution made by rural population. Currently a million of urban population contributes 2.5 times that of rural population. This underlines the need and rationale for providing adequate transport infrastructure to enhance its contribution to GDP of the nation. Figure 2.6 shows the GDP values of India in millions of Indian Rs from 1950 to 2011.

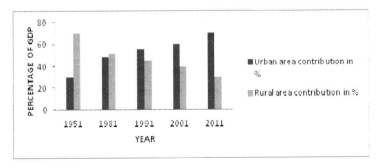

Figure 2.5: Percentage GDP Contributions by Urban and Rural Areas
Source: GDP of India (1951-2011)

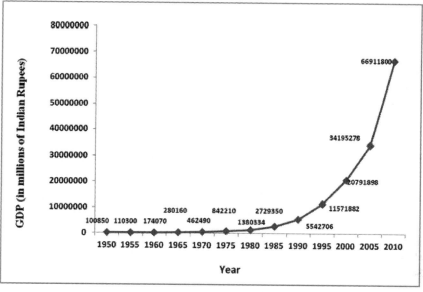

Figure 2.6: GDP Values of India from 1951 to 2010

Source: GDP of India (1950-2010)

2.4 Migration to urban areas

Urban centers provide better opportunities for education, health, employment, and social interaction. Due to these better opportunities, migration to urban areas is unstoppable and this fact needs to be considered while planning transport infrastructure in an appropriate manner. This migration has led to slums in various cities. This slum population is also increasing in almost all urban centers. Table 2.7 provides migration details to urban areas. A common perception is that explosive rural to urban migration is the primary cause for the state of India's cities. This is not borne out by the evidence. For the last 30 years, migration has contributed about a fifth of the urban population, natural urban population growth contributed about 60 percent, and the rest about equally split between new town formation because of reclassification and urban boundary expansion or sprawl. One important facet of study on population is the study of migration arising out of various social, economic, or political reasons. For a large country like India, the study of movement of population in different parts of the country helps in understanding the dynamics of the society better. At this junction in the economic development, in the country, especially when many states are undergoing faster economic development, particularly in areas, such as, manufacturing, information technology, or service sectors, data on migration profile of population has become more important.

Table 2.7: Migration Details from Rural to Urban

Year	Migration from Rural to Urban Areas (in millions)	Decadal Percent Growth
1951	NA	-
1961	66	-
1971	68.2	3.33
1981	81	18.77
1991	80.9	-0.12
2001	98.3	21.51
2011	NA	-

Source: Ministry of Urban Development

2.5 Growth of slums in urban areas

The census of India defines a slum as "residential areas where dwellings are mostly unfit for human habitation" because they are dilapidated, cramped, poorly ventilated, unclean, or "any combination of these factors which are detrimental to the safety and health," as per 2011 figures, roughly 13.7 million households or 17.4 percent of urban Indian households lived in slums in 2011. The new data is difficult to compare with previous years, because the 2011 census covers all 4,041 statutory towns in India, as compared to 2001 when only statutory towns with populations over 20,000 were covered. The 2001 data had set India's slum population at 15% of the total population. More than one in five urban households in the states of Andhra Pradesh (combined), Chhattisgarh, Madhya Pradesh, Odisha, West Bengal, and Maharashtra lives in the slum. In absolute terms, Maharashtra has the highest number of slum blocks compared to any state—over 21,000 (21%) out of a total of just over 0.1 million slum blocks for the whole country. Table 2.8 gives the slum population of 2001.

Table 2.8: Population Living in Slums in Different Categories of Urban Areas in India in 2001

Class	Population Size	2001	
		No of Cities and Towns with Slums	% of Slum Population
I	>4 million	5	26
II	2-4 million	8	8.8
III	1-2 million	14	6.8
IV	5000000-1 million	42	13.7
V	100000-500000	309	32.7
VI	<100000	262	12
All classes	Total	640	100

Source: Census of India, 2001(slum details)

The number of towns reporting the existence of slums is on the increase. As per census information the number of towns in the year 2000 were 1743 and this number increased to 2613 as per census records of 2011. From this it is clear that due to migration the rate of slums in urban towns is increasing at a faster rate. Table 2.9 compares the million plus cities slum population to their total population in 2001. Figure 2.7 shows the typical slums in urban centers. Over a third of India's slum population lives in its 46 million-plus cities. Of the metros, Mumbai has the highest proportion of slum-dwelling households 54.06% of its population). Kolkata is next at nearly 30% with Chennai at 19%. Delhi has 14.6% of its households living in slums while Bangalore is the best off of the five metros at about 10%.

Table 2.9: Total and Slum Population of Million Plus Cities in India, Census 2001

Million Plus Cities	Total Population (in 000s)	Slum Population in (000s)	Percent of Slum to Total Population
Great Mumbai	11978	6475	54.06
Delhi M.Corp	9879	1851	18.74
Kolkata	4573	1485	32.48
Banglore	4301	431	10.02
Chennai	4344	820	18.88
Ahmedabad	3637	474	13.46
Hyderabad	3520	627	17.23
Kanpur	2551	368	14.42
Pune	2538	492	19.39
Surat	2433	508	20.89
All India	7334	17697	24.13

Source: Census of India 2001

Figure 2.7: Urbanization and the Increase of Slums in Urban Centers.

2.5.1 State share of slum population to total slum population of India

Figure 2.8 gives the changes in the rate of slum population in the states of India during 2001 to 2011, it may be noted that some states show increases in slum population like Andhra Pradesh (combined), Karnataka, Madhya Pradesh, etc. while some states show decreases in rates like Maharashtra, West Bengal, etc.

2.6 Accessibility and mobility issues for rural settlements

The population of India is distributed in 580,000 settlements of different categories spread across the country. For the purpose of planning, the settlements are divided into '7' categories based on the population size of the settlements. Most of the settlements are not linked with all-weather roads almost four decades after independence. Accessibility is considered a prerequisite for economic development. The initiation of (Pradhan Mantri Gram Sadak Yojana) PMGSY during 2000 has provided impetus for providing all-weather roads to different categories of rural segments. Rural road connectivity is not only a key component of rural development by promoting access to economic and social services and thereby generating increased agricultural incomes and productive employment opportunities in India, it is also as a result, a key ingredient in ensuring sustainable poverty reduction. Notwithstanding the efforts made, over the years, at the state and central levels, through different programs, about 40% of the habitations in the country are still not connected by all-weather roads. It is well known that even where connectivity has been provided, the roads constructed are of such quality (due to poor construction or maintenance) that they cannot always be categorized as all-weather roads. With a view to redressing the situation, the government has launched the PMGSY on 25th December, 2000 to provide all-weather access to unconnected habitations. The PMGSY is a 100% centrally sponsored scheme. 50% of the cess on high speed diesel (HSD) is earmarked for this program.

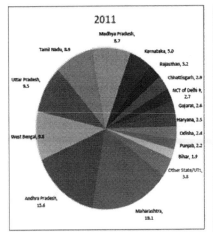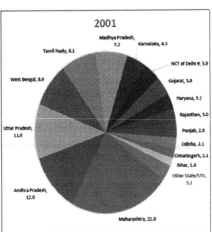

Figure 2.8: State Share of Slum Population to Total Slum Population of India

Source: Primary census abstract for slum 2011,Office of the Registrar General and Census Commissioner, New Delhi India

2.6.1 Pradhan Mantri Gram Sadak Yojana or PMGSY

PMGSY is a nationwide plan in India to provide good all-weather road (AWR) connectivity to unconnected villages. It is under the authority of the Ministry of Rural Development. The objectives of PMGSY are to connect all villages by AWR in a time bound manner as given below:

1. With a population of 1000 persons and above by 2003

2. With a population of 500 persons and above by 2007

3. In hill states, tribal, and desert area villages with a population of 500 persons and above by 2003

4. In hill states, tribal, and desert area villages with a population of 250 persons and above by 2007

The PMGSY will permit the up gradation (to prescribed standards) of the existing roads in those districts where all the eligible habitations of the designated population size have been provided AWR connectivity. However, it must be noted that up gradation is not central to the program and cannot exceed 20% of the state's allocation as long as eligible unconnected habitations in the state still exist. In up gradation works, priority has been given to through routes of the rural core network, which carry more traffic.

Due to nonavailability of AWRs, many of these rural populations are unable to generate resources for comfortable living, sending their children for higher education, etc. A recent study indicates that the benefit stream due to improved accessibility improves different areas such as health, education, banking, and other services.

The improvement in accessibility during the decade 2000 to 2010 by AWRs in different groups of rural settlements in percentage terms is presented in Table 2.10.

Table 2.10: Percentage Change in Accessibility by All Weather Roads (AWR) 2000-2010

Population Ranges	2000	2010
0-249	57.1	59.6
250-499	58.9	64.2
500-999	62.6	73.4
More than 1000	73.5	83.7
Total	62.8	70.2

Source: PMGSY site

However, the number of settlements unconnected in different states of southern India vary widely across different states. The percentage of settlements unconnected by AWR and the status of a state in terms of economic development are highly interrelated. The distribution of unconnected villages by population size in the year 2000 is given in Table 2.11.

Table 2.11: Distribution of Unconnected Villages by Population Size in the Year 2000

Subregion	up to 1000	percent of total	1000 to 1500	percent of total	More than 1500	Percent of total
Andhra Pradesh	9334	67.21	1533	40.7	339	3.49
Goa	0	0.0	0	0.0	25	19.84
Karnataka	12178	65.36	877	25.34	684	13.86
Kerala	0	0.0	0	0.0	0	0.0
Madhya Pradesh	49491	77.87	1492	33.7	166	5.7
Maharashtra	18609	74.27	281	5.46	20	0.32
Orissa	28902	70.27	562	13.11	4	0.15
Tamil Nadu	7802	39.27	0	0	2	0.05

Source: Ramanayya and Anantharamaiah (2003)

2.6.2 Achievements made by PMGSY

The primary source of funding for the program is from the cess on high speed diesel, 50% of which is earmarked for rural roads. The PMGSY has been formulated as an anti-poverty Program, focusing on providing connectivity to unconnected rural habitations in order to enable access to economic and other essential services. The program is executed by state government agencies in a project mode. Detailed guidelines have been issued for the PMGSY scheme and a separate rural roads manual has also been published on the technical aspects of rural roads construction. Up to November 2010, an additional rural road network of 418,991 kms have been cleared out of which 298,810 kms have already been constructed under the scheme. Table 2.12 and Figure 2.9 gives the information of the yearly achievement of PMGSY.

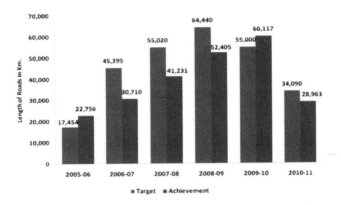

Figure 2.9: Pradhan Mantri Gram Sadak Yojana (PMGSY) Road Works

Source: Ministry of Rural Development

http://rural.nic.in/netrural/rural/index.aspx

Table 2.12: Yearly Sanction Details of PMGSY

Sl. No.	Year	Total Number of Package	No. of Roads	No. of Habitation Covered	Pavements	
					Length in Kms	Cost rs in millions
1	2000-01	2719	13272	13271	12342	296695.6
2	01-02	3226	10557	10557	14177	318087.57
3	03-04	3095	8478	13413	30124.05	46348.3
4	04-05	2885	7651	11838	11838	291718.3
5	05-06	4956	11713	23364	49986.55	101235.1
6	06-07	8015	15171	31541	72231.25	168342.1
7	07-08	9586	15988	33762	76545.98	208634.1
8	08-09	12881	18730	24892	82660.65	246622.8
9	09-10	1912	3123	6400	14905	39792.8
10	10-11	772	1078	1141	3047.21	8568.1
11	11-12	4420	7506	10590	25480.84	73934.6
12	12-13	9082	14216	25052	48738.779	169579.7

Source: PMGSY site (project details year wise report)(data taken on 10-30-2013)

2.7 Transport infrastructure scenario in India

Many research studies and administrative reports emphasized the need for better transport infrastructure for accelerated economic development of India. Both urban India as well as rural India is experiencing inadequacies of transport infrastructure.

Urban areas mainly suffer from a shortage of capacity of transport network to meet the ever increasing demand. This is reflected in volume to capacity ratio (v/c) exceeding more than one in most of the urban corridors in India. This problem is much more severe in almost all the cities with a population more than 5 million. A recent study by the Indian Institute of Management Bangalore (IIMB) revealed that in all the eight important corridors of Bangalore city the v/c ratios are more than one. The impact of these high v/c ratios are reflected in terms of congestion, delay, accidents, and economic losses. Currently, the Ministry of Urban Development (MOUD) is involved in improving the urban mobility through dedicated funding under JnNURM to selected cities.

In respect of rural areas the problem is quite opposite, i.e., many settlements do not enjoy AWR connectivity. In India we use the term AWR to provide accessibility throughout the year including monsoon season. If a settlement is accessible during part of a year especially during nonmonsoon period, then it is considered to have been accessible by fair weather roads (FWR).

During the decade 1975-85, Ministry of Transport, Ministry of Rural Development, and the Planning Commission initiated a number of rural road studies in a number of districts to assess the socio-economic scenario of FWR and AWR connectivity patterns. I.I.M. Bangalore has entrusted the Ratnagiri district in Maharashtra to quantify the socio-economic impacts of AWR and FWR in that district. Ratnagiri is a land locked district in the state of Maharashtra. As per census information 98% of settlements were provided with AWR systems. However, the geographical distribution of houses in a village in Ratnagiri district is quite different from other districts of India. A normal village consists of 6 to 8 wadies (wadi is part of a village) separated by 3 to 5 km between wadies.
In the census, it is normally recorded as having an AWR if the main wadi is connected by an AWR. However, all the wadis might not have been really enjoying an AWR. The comprehensive study undertaken by IIMB revealed the following patterns.

1. The average income of a household in a wadi (part of a village) connected by an AWR is statically higher than the household which enjoys FWR accessibility.
2. At the taluk (part of a district with a number of settlements) level also, this hypothesis was noticed and statistically proved.
3. This study was repeated in other districts of Maharashtra. Even at the district level, districts with a higher percentage of settlements connected by AWRs, enjoy higher per capita income.

Thus the study clearly brought out that settlements connected to AWRs enjoy statistically higher income at the macro level, i.e., district level, submacro level, i.e., at taluk level and at micro level, i.e., at the settlement level as well as submicro level, i.e., household level in a settlement.

IIM Bangalore was also involved in another rural road study sponsored by the Ministry of Road Transport and the Ministry of Rural Development across southern part of India covering 8 states. The study was conducted during three time periods: first time in 1976-78, second time in 1986-87, and finally third time during 1996-97. Many important findings were observed. For proper comparison, in all three studies the same sample frame was (the same settlements) used.

The sample could be broadly divided into.

1. Villages remain as they were in the first study until the end of the third study, i.e., FWR as FWR and AWR as AWR.
2. Change of accessibility from FWR to AWR.
3. Change of accessibility from AWR to improved connectivity to class 1 roads during this 20 year period, i.e., major district roads or state highway system.
4. Settlements with multiple connections to class 1 category of roads.
The results of all these studies indicate that during the 20 year period (1976-96) locations with category 1 mentioned above saw a quantum of change both in passenger demand as well as freight demand at the least. The changes are more pronounced (quantum jump) in the case of category 2. Exponential growth was recorded in categories 3 and 4.

The freight movement pattern also exhibited many major changes. There is a gradual shift from bullock carts (which account for more than 75 percent of the total tonnage) nonmotorized transport movement during 1976 study to mechanized models in 1996 (accounting more than 80 percent of the total tonnage). The shift also is more pronounced in the settlements with improved connectivity patterns.

Many international agencies are also providing funds to improve the rural accessibility in India. The state of Andhra Pradesh received assistance from World Bank under the Andhra Pradesh economic reconstruction project in three districts of Andhra Pradesh. At the end of the project, World Bank insisted that an impact study needed to be undertaken by a third agency. IIM was again roped in to undertake this task.

The main objectives of the study were:
a. To assess the direct and indirect socio-economic impacts/benefits of the rural roads
b. To study the impact of these new roads on the travel characteristics of the rural population
c. To carry out an economic analysis comparing the costs and benefits of these roads
d. The assess whether the expectations of the village communities and local users are met.
The sample details for the study are presented in Table 2.13 and Table 2.14 below.

Table 2.13: Summary of Sample Data Collected

Description	Number
Total No. of Districts Represented	3
Total No. of Villages Considered	37
Total Road Users	903
Total Households	620
Total Banks	6
Total Schools	32
Total Health Care Centers	20

Source: censusindia.gov.in

Table 2.14: Distribution of Sample Villages by Population

Population Ranges	Warangal	Karimnagar	Adilabad	Total	Percentage of Villages Selected
<1000	0	0	2	2	5.4
1001–1500	3	4	2	9	24.3
1501–2000	1	2	2	5	13.5
>2000	9	6	6	21	56.8
Total	13	12	12	37	100

Source: censusindia.gov.in

The responses reveal that there are considerable improvements in many areas of socio-economic indicators as presented in Table 2.16 below.

The results clearly show that all sections of the household are satisfied. However, there are variations among districts, road type, and settlement size.

The results clearly indicate that education, health, and banking sectors are positively impacted by the changes in accessibility pattern. Other benefits include:

a. Travel cost savings due to laying roads

b. Travel time saved per day by the road users

c. For calculating monetary value of travel time savings, 25 working days in a month and Rs.90/day wage are used. Thus an hourly rate of Rs.9 is used.

d. Average monthly travel cost savings on an average is: Rs 127.50, and travel time saved is about 22.61 minutes.

Table 2.15: Number of Road Users before and after Laying Roads by Mode of Transport

No.	Mode of Transport	Before	After
1	Pedestrian	399	123
2	Public Transport	53	133
3	Private Transport	6	20
4	Auto / Taxi	82	174
5	Freight Transport	13	31
6	Bullock Cart	13	18
7	Cycle	184	195
8	2 - Wheeler	43	202
9	4 - Wheeler	1	7
10	Others	54	0
11	Boat	1	0
12	Not Specified	54	0
	Total	903	903

The distribution of sample trips by mode before and after improvements are presented in Table 2.15.

Table 2.16: Benefits Recorded (%) by Settlement Size

Sl No.	Benefits	All	Population of Villages			
1	Women	All	501-1000	1001-1500	1501-2000	¿2000
	Transport facilities are good and increased	42.41	25	51.79	13.33	47.54
	Ease of travel between villages	9.38	0	10.71	6.67	10.66
	Good for women to travel during maternity period	17.86	31.25	10.71	36.67	14.75
2	Children					
	Good / increase in transport facilities	26.11	20	17.07	13.04	33.02
	Good facilities for school children	51.11	60	56.1	47.83	49.06
3	Aged					
	Good / increase in transport facilities	29.17	22.22	31.71	4.35	34.74
	Convenient to go to hospital	35.12	33.33	31.71	52.17	32.63
4	Students					
	Good for higher education / further studies	26.35	28.57	27.5	27.78	25.3
	Easy transport facilities for college going students	43.24	28.57	37.5	44.44	46.99
5	Sick Persons					
	Good for emergency service / treatment	22.4	20	18.75	15.79	26.09
	Convenient to go to hospital	48.8	60	43.75	52.63	49.28

The benefit stream consists of three components: Benefits accrued to cultivators for better yields and prices as informed by them, savings to road users in their travel costs, Travel time saved converted into monetary values. This travel time savings was considered in two ways. In Case A, whatever travel time is saved, only 10% of it could be converted into earning additional wages. Thus an individual who gains 10 hours in a month may be able to earn additional wages for one extra hour only in a month. In Case B, it is possible to utilize the savings fully in realizing additional wages. The costs and benefits for the study villages as a whole are presented in Table 2.17 and Table 2.18.

Table 2.17: Cost - Benefit (Case A) - All Districts (Rs. Millions)

Year	Cost	Benefit	Net Benefit
0	360	65.75	-294.25
1	370.8	132.82	56.27
2	381.92	201.22	57.28
3	393.38	271	58.32
4	405.18	342.17	59.37
5	417.34	414.76	60.44
6	429.86	489.17	61.89
7	442.75	565.06	63
8	484.84	642.48	35.33
9	498.52	721.44	65.28
10	512.61	801.98	66.45
11	527.12	884.94	68.44
12	542.07	970.39	70.5
13	557.47	1058.4	72.61
14	573.33	1149.05	74.79
15	589.67	1242.42	77.03
Internal Rate of Return:			18.71%

Table 2.18: Cost - Benefit (Case B) - All Districts (Rs. Millions)

Year	Cost	Benefit	Net Benefit
0	360	105.55	-254.45
1	370.8	213.21	96.86
2	381.92	323.03	98.69
3	393.38	435.04	100.55
4	405.18	549.29	102.45
5	417.34	665.82	104.38
6	429.86	785.27	106.93
7	442.75	907.11	108.94
8	484.84	1031.38	82.19
9	498.52	1158.14	113.08
10	512.61	1287.44	115.2
11	527.12	1420.61	118.66
12	542.07	1557.78	122.22
13	557.47	1699.07	125.89
14	573.33	1844.59	129.66
15	589.67	1994.48	133.55
Internal Rate of Return:			39.39%

The analysis clearly shows that for Case A, the EIRR is about 18.71 % per and for Case B it is about 39.39%. It may be noted from the figures, the payback period is just 3 years for Case B and 6 years for Case A.

Summary

This chapter discussed the demography and urban and rural settlements in India and how they have changed over time. The chapter also throws some light on how these changes have impacted transportation and how programs like PMGSY have improved connection, accessibility, and the well being of rural settlements.

Chapter 3

Different Modes and Their Characteristics

3.1 Mode of transport

Modes of transport or transport modality is a term used to describe the substantially different ways of transportation. The ability of people and goods to move from one place to an other is fulfilled through the use of one or an other modes of transport.

The most dominant modes of transport are air transport, land transport and water transport. Land transport includes road, rail, and off-road transport. Off-road transport consists of pipelines, cable transport, etc. Animal and human powered transport are sometimes regarded as modes in itself, but these normally also fall into the above mentioned categories. Each mode of transport has a fundamentally different technological solution, and some require a separate environment. Each mode has its own infrastructure, vehicles, and operations, and often has its unique regulations. Each mode also has separate subsystems like propulsion, suspension, control, guidance, structure, and support. Transport using more than one mode is described as intermodal. Transportation that carries around many people and can be used by the public is known as mass transportation.

3.2 Transport systems definitions and classifications

Urban transportation modes and operational concepts can be classified in different ways. Some of the classifications are interdependent. For example, modes are often identified with system technology only, but the same is strongly influenced by the characteristics of rights-of-way and operations. The following subsections discusse these classifications.

3.2.1 Classification by type of usage

There are three basic categories of transportation by type of operation and usages. They are

i. Personal or private transportation

ii. For hire or intermediate public transportation

iii. Public or mass transportation

The main characteristics, typical modes, and operating domains of these categories are shown in Table 3.1 and Table 3.2.

Table 3.1: Classification of Urban Passenger Transportation by Type of Usage

Characteristics/ Usage Type	Personal	Intermediate	Public
Common designation	Private transportation	Para transit	Transit
Service availability	Owner	Individuals, group	Public
Service supplier	User	Carrier	Carrier
Route determination	User (flexible)	User (carrier)	Carrier (fixed)
Time-schedule determination	User (flexible)	User (carrier)	Carrier (fixed)
Cost price	User absorbs	Fixed rate	Fixed fare

Source: V. R. Vuchic, 2005 - Urban Transit

Table 3.2: Classification of Urban Passenger Transportation by Carrier Type

Carrier type	Individuals				Group
	Personal		Intermediate		
Modes	Walking Bicycle Motorcycle Automobile	Carpools Van-pools	Rental car Cars, Sharing taxi Autorick-shaws, Cycle-Rickshaw, Hand-Pulled Rickshaw, Horse-Pulled Carriages	Dial-a-ride Charter bus	Street-transit (bus, trolleys, streetcar), Semi rapid-transit (bus-rapid-transit, light rail transit), Rapid transit (rail and met-ros), specialized modes
Optimum (but not exclusive) domain of opera-tion area density	Low-medium	Origin: low; Destination: high;	Any		High-medium
Routing	Dispersed	Radial	Dispersed		Concentrated (radial), ubiqui-tous
Time	Off-peak	Peak only	All times		Peak, daily hours
Trip pur-pose	Recreation, shopping, business, other	Work only	Business spe-cial services		Work, school, business, social, other emergency

Source: V.R. Vuchic, 2005 - Urban Transit

3.2.2 Personal transport modes and their characteristics

Personal transportation consists of privately owned vehicles operated by owners for their own use, usually on publicly provided and operated streets. Private automobiles are the most common mode in the category of personal transport, but motorcycles, bicycles, and of course, walking also belong to this category. The following subsections discuss different personal transport modes and their characteristics.

3.2.3 Walking or jogging

Walking is the most energy efficient, healthy, and sustainable mode of transport. It is also the most universal mode. Everyone is a pedestrian for part of their trip even if they are driving or using a bus or rail transit. Hence, walking needs to be the primary focus of any plan or policy related to urban transport in India cities; it has been observed that people do not prefer walking or cycling even for short distances. This is predominantly because of lack of pedestrian infrastructure and walkable street networks.

Currently, the share of public transport trips in major urban areas in India is between 25-30 percent. Since every public transport user is also a pedestrian at the time of access and egress, walking trips may constitute 50-60 percent of total trips. Despite the high share of walk trips, transport infrastructure does not include any facilities for this mode. With the exception of a few cities, street networks in most cities do not provide even minimum width (2m) foot paths.

If our cities are to sustain walking as a viable mode of transport (even for short/medium trips between 1-3 kms), provision of pedestrian infrastructure needs to be an immediate priority. Safety and comfort of pedestrians is equally important. People will not walk in unsafe environments which are often the after effects of automobile oriented street designs. Hence, designing streets where walking is prioritized is important along with building regulations that also prioritize access and egress by pedestrians. As per Rastogi (2007), the per hour per meter capacity of public transports modes like busways, suburban rail, and surface rapid rail ranges between 4000 and 8000. It is 3500 for walking and 1500 for cycling. The similar values for other motorized vehicles usually range between 100 and 400.

3.2.4 Bicycles and motorcycles

Figure 3.1: Glimpse of a Cycle

After walking, cycling (Figure 3.1) is the second most efficient and effective mode of transportation for short to moderate distances. There are many health as well as environment related benefits of walking and cycling. The bicycle, which is also known as green transport, is often an important consideration to improve the urban transport problems. Many countries recognize the potential of cycling to grow as a mode of transport and act as an alternative to car use to create more sustainable urban futures.

Currently in India cycling is considered to be the mode of transportation that is used by lower income groups of society who cannot afford any other means of transport. Higher income groups of people prefer using cars or two wheelers even for short distances. This reality needs to change and use of these modes needs to be brought into the day-to-day lifestyle of all sections of society if our future is to be sustainable.

Currently, most of the street space allocation and provision of infrastructure caters to private vehicle users. In order to make cycling an urban transport priority, one of the most important tasks is to create a high quality cycling infrastructure. This means providing dedicated and segregated cycle lanes on all major arterials along with proper cycle crossing, cycle parking, and other facilities at regular intervals.

A number of cities in the world have been successful at promoting the use of cycling by having a strong public bicycle sharing program. Such programs have been implemented in many cities including, New York, Washington DC, Guangzhou, Hangzhou, London, Paris, etc. Some cities in India (Bangalore, Delhi etc) have initiated pilot projects along similar lines. Public bicycle sharing not only helps promote bicycling, it also helps sensitize users of other modes to the needs of cyclists. Moreover, integrating provision of cycling infrastructure with the existing and planned public transport modes is important to link the trip chains. It also allows a larger group of people to access public transport at a very low/no cost and use it for longer trips.

As per Rastogi (2007), the comparative overview of space requirements by different modes with respect to the bicycle requirements indicate that only LRT and walk consumes less bicycle space equivalent, whereas, in the case of cars it is quite high. In terms of per person, the road space required by a car is 120 sq. m., for a bus is 12 sq. m., by rail is 7 sq. m., for a bicycle is 9 sq. m, and by pedestrian is 2 sq. m.

3.2.5 Automobiles

An automobile, auto car, motorcar, or car is a wheeled motor (Figure 3.2) vehicle used for transporting passengers, which also carries its own engine or motor. Most definitions of the term specify that automobiles are designed to run primarily on roads, to have seating for one to eight people, to typically have four wheels, and to be manufactured principally for the transport of people rather than goods.

Figure 3.2: Glimpse of an Automobile

The year 1886 is regarded as the year of birth of the modern automobile - with the Benz Patent-Motorwagen, by German inventor Carl Benz. Motorized wagons soon replaced animal-drafted carriages, especially after automobiles became affordable for many people when the Ford Model T was introduced in 1908.

The term motorcar has formerly also been used in the context of electrified rail systems to denote a car which functions as a small locomotive but also provides space for passengers and baggage. These locomotive cars were often used on suburban routes by both interurban and intercity railroad systems.

It was estimated in 2010 that the number of automobiles had risen to over 1 billion vehicles, up from the 500 million of 1986. The numbers are increasing rapidly, especially in China and India.

3.2.6 Automobile resources

The automobile sector is divided into four segments: two-wheelers (mopeds, scooters, motorcycles, electric two-wheelers), passenger vehicles (passenger cars, utility vehicles, multi-purpose vehicles), commercial vehicles (light and medium-heavy vehicles), and three wheelers (passenger carriers and good carriers).

The automobile industry is one of the key drivers of economic growth of the nation. Since the delicensing of the sector in 1991 and the subsequent opening up of 100 percent FDI through automatic route, the Indian automobile sector has come a long way. Today, almost every global auto major has set up facilities in the country.

The world standings for the Indian automobile sector, as per the Confederation of Indian Industry, are as follows:

i. Largest three-wheeler market

ii. Second largest two-wheeler market

iii. Tenth largest passenger car market

iv. Fourth largest tractor market

v. Fifth largest commercial vehicle market

vi. Fifth largest bus and truck segment

3.3 Intermediate public transport

Commonly designated as para-transit, it is transportation service provided by an operator and available to all parties who meet the conditions of a contract for carriages (i.e., pay prescribed fares or rates), but which is adjustable in various degrees to the individual user's desires. Most para-transit modes do not have fixed routes and schedules. Taxi, dial-a-ride, and auto-rickshaws are major modes.

Para-transit is an alternative mode of flexible passenger transportation that does not follow fixed routes or schedules. Typically minibuses are used to provide para-transit service, but share taxis and jitneys (in China) are also important providers.

Para-transit modes routes and schedules that change with request to individual users are called as demand-responsive. When the difference is pointed out and transit is pointed, that transit is described as fixed-route or fixed-schedule service.

Para-transit services may vary considerably on the degree of flexibility they provide their customers. At their simplest they may consist of a taxi or small bus that will run along a more or less defined route and then stop to pick up or discharge passengers on request. At the other end of the spectrum of fully demand responsive transport, the most flexible para-transit systems offer on-demand call-up, door-to-door service from any origin to any destination in a service area. Para-transit services are operated by public transit agencies, community groups, not-for-profit organizations, and for-profit private companies or operators.

3.3.1 Taxicab

A taxicab, also known as a taxi or a cab, is a type of vehicle for hire with a driver, used by a single passenger or small group of passengers often for a non-shared ride. A taxicab conveys passengers between locations of their choice.

Figure 3.3: Glimpse of a Taxi Cabs

In modes of public transport, the pick-up and drop-off locations are determined by the service provider, not by the passenger, although demand responsive transport and share taxis provide a hybrid bus/taxi mode. There are four distinct forms of taxicab, which can be identified by slightly differing terms in different countries:

i. Hackney carriages also known as public hire, hailed, or street taxis, licensed for hailing throughout communities

ii. Private hire vehicles, also known as minicabs or private hire taxis, licensed for prebooking only

iii. Taxi-buses, also known as jitneys, operating on preset routes typified by multiple stops and multiple independent passengers

iv. Limousines, specialized vehicle licensed for operation by prebooking.

Although types of vehicles and methods of regulation, hiring, dispatching, and negotiating payment differ significantly from country to country, many common characteristics exist.

3.3.2 Auto rickshaws

Auto rickshaws are a common means of intermediate transportation in many countries in the world. Also known as a three wheeler, samosa, tempo, tuktuk, trishaw, auto rickshaw, autorik, bajaj, rick, tricycle, mototaxi, babytaxi, or lapa in popular parlance, an auto rickshaw is a usually three-wheeled cabin cycle for private use and as a vehicle for hire.

It is a motorized version of the traditional pulled rickshaw or cycle rickshaw. Auto rickshaws are an essential form of urban transport in many developing countries, and a form of novelty transport in many Eastern countries.

Figure 3.4: Glimpse of an Auto-Rickshaw

3.3.3 Airport taxi

Airport taxi is one of the IPT modes in major cities which provide good services for the people to travel from their origin to an airport or from an airport to a destination. There are many private cab services in major cities; as we consider Bangalore there are Meru cabs, Easy cabs, and Hire cabs which play an important role as the paratransit modes.

Figure 3.5: Glimpse of Taxis

3.3.4 Hand pulled rickshaws

Around 1880, rickshaws appeared in India, first in Shimla. At the turn of the century it was introduced in Kolkata (Calcutta), India and in 1914 was a conveyance for hire. A pulled rickshaw (or rickshaw) is a mode of human-powered transport by which a runner draws a two-wheeled cart which seats one or two persons. In recent times the use of human-powered rickshaws has been discouraged or outlawed in many countries due to concern for the welfare of rickshaw workers. Pulled rickshaws have been replaced mainly by cycle rickshaws and auto rickshaws.

Figure 3.6: Hand Pulled Rickshaws

3.3.5 Horse pulled carriage

A carriage is a wheeled vehicle for people, usually horse-drawn; litters (palanquins) and sedan chairs are excluded, since they are wheelless vehicles. The carriage is especially designed for private passenger use and for comfort or elegance, though some are also used to transport goods. It may be light, smart, and fast or heavy, large, and comfortable. Carriages normally have suspension using leaf springs, elliptical springs (in the 19th century) or leather strapping. A public passenger vehicle would not usually be called a carriage terms for such include stage coach, char banc, and omnibus. Working vehicles such as the (four-wheeled) wagon and (two-wheeled) cart share important parts of the history of the carriage, as a fast (two-wheeled) chariot.

Figure 3.7: Horse Pulled Rickshaws

3.3.6 Ox-wagon

An ox-wagon or bullock wagon is a four-wheeled vehicle pulled by oxen (draught cattle). It was a traditional form of transport, especially in Southern Africa but also in New Zealand and Australia. Ox-wagons were also used in the United States. The first recorded use of an ox-wagon was around 1670, but they continue to be used in some areas up to modern times.

Figure 3.8: Glimpse of an Ox-wagon

3.3.7 Cycle rickshaw

The cycle rickshaw is a small-scale local means of transport; it is also known by a variety of other names such as bike taxi, velotaxi, pedicab, bikecab, cyclo, beca, becak, trisikad, or trishaw. As opposed to rickshaws pulled by a person on foot, cycle rickshaws are human-powered by pedaling. They are a type of tricycle designed to carry passengers on a hire basis. Cycle rickshaws are widely used in major cities around the world, but most commonly in cities of south, southeast, and east Asia.

Figure 3.9: Cycle Rickshaws

3.4 Public transport modes

Mass transportation, or transit is a common type of urban transport, these are transport systems with fixed routes and schedules, available for use by all persons who pay the established fare. The most common representatives are bus, light rail transit, and rapid transit or metro, but there are a number of other modes.

Public transport (North American English: public transportation or public transit) is a shared passenger transport service which is available for use by the general public, as distinct from modes such as taxicab, car pooling, or hired buses which are not shared by strangers without private arrangement.

Public transport modes include buses, trolleybuses, trams, trains, rapid transit (metro/subways/undergrounds, etc). Public transport between cities is dominated by airlines, coaches, and intercity rail. High-speed rail networks are being developed in many parts of the world.

Most public transport runs to a scheduled timetable with the most frequent services running to a headway. Share taxi offers on-demand services in many parts of the world and some services will wait until the vehicle is full before it starts. Paratransit is sometimes used in areas of low-demand and for people who need a door-to-door service.

Urban public transport may be provided by one or more private transport operators or by a transit authority. Public transport services are usually funded by government subsidies and fares charged to each passenger. Services are normally regulated and possibly subsidized from local or national tax revenue. Fully subsidized, zero-fare (free) services operate in some towns and cities.

For historical and economic reasons, there are differences internationally regarding use and extent of public transport. While countries in the world tend to have extensive and frequent systems serving their old and dense cities, many cities of the new world have more sprawl and much less comprehensive public transport.

3.4.1 Transit modes

A transit mode is mainly considered on three basic characteristics
i. Right-of-way(ROW) category
ii. System technology
iii. Type of service
Transit modes vary with each one of these characteristics. Contrary to the common belief that technology mostly determines modal characteristics, the ROW category has a major influence on both performance and costs of modes.

3.4.2 Right-of-way (ROW) category

A transit way or ROW is the travel way or strip of land on which the transit vehicles operate. There are three basic ROW categories distinguished by the degree of their separation from other traffic.
i. Category C represents surface streets with mixed traffic. Transit may have preferential treatment, such as reserved lanes separated by lines or special signals or travel mixed with other traffic.

ii. Category B includes ROW types that are longitudinally physically separated by curbs, barriers, grade separation, and the like from the other traffic but with grade crossings for vehicles and pedestrians, including regular street intersections. This category is most frequently used for LRT system.

iii. Category A is a fully controlled ROW without grade crossings or any legal access by other vehicles or persons. It is also referred to as grade-separated, private or exclusive ROW, and it can be a tunnel, an aerial structure, or at grade level.

3.4.3 System technologies

Technology of transit modes refers to the mechanical features of their vehicles and ways. The four most important features are defined here:

i. Support is a vertical contact between vehicle and riding surface, which transfers the vehicle weight and traction force. The most common types are rubber tire on concrete, asphalt, or other surface and steel wheel on steel rail.

ii. Guidance refers to the means of lateral vehicle guidance. Highway vehicles are steered (by the driver) and their lateral stability is provided by wheel/support adhesion. Rail vehicles are guided by flanges and the conical form of the wheel surfaces.

iii. Propulsion refers to the type of propulsion unit and method of traction, or transferring acceleration/deceleration forces. Its major components are type of propulsion unit, method of transferring tractive forces.

iv. Control is the means of regulating the travel of one or all vehicles in a system. The most important control is for longitudinal spacing of the vehicles, which may be manual-vision, manual-signal, fully automatic, or various combinations of these.

3.4.4 Types of service

There are many different types of services. They can be classified into groups by three characteristics:

i. By the types of routes and trips served

ii. By stopping schedule or type of operation

iii. By time of operation

Table 3.3: Classification of Urban Public Transportation Modes by ROW Category and Technology

ROW/ Technology	Highway Driver Steered	Rubber-Tired Guided, Partially Guided	Rail	Specialized
C	Paratransit Shuttle bus Regular bus (on street)	Trolley bus	Streetcar/Tramway/ Cable car	Ferryboat Hydrofoil
B	Bus rapid transit (BRT)	Guided bus	Light rail transit	(cog railway)
A	Bus on bus bay only	Rubber-tired metro Rubber-tired monorail Automated guided transit (AGT) PRT	Light rail Rapid rail Rapid transit/ metro regional/ commuter rail monorail schwebe-bahn	Cog railway funicular Aerial tramway

Source: V.R. Vuchic, 2005 - Urban Transit

3.5 Classification of mass transit modes

Common-carrier urban passenger transport mode is known as transit, mass transit, or mass transportation. These are transport systems with fixed routes and schedules, available for use by all persons who pay the established fares. Transit is described as fixed route, fixed schedule service. The best known classification of transit modes is into three generic classes based mostly, but not entirely, on right-of-way (R/W) type [Gray et.al. (1979)]. They are street transit or surface transit, semi rapid transit, and rapid transit or mass rapid transit systems.

The capacity of these public transport modes can be calculated as follows:

For Bus:

Passenger/hr./dir=

$$\frac{Buses}{hr}\left[\frac{seats}{buses}*\frac{passengers}{seat}+\frac{standingArea(m^2)}{bus}*\frac{standees}{m^2}\right] (1)$$

For Rail Systems:

Passenger/hr./dir=

$$\frac{Trains}{hr}*\frac{Cars}{Trains}\left[\frac{seats}{car}*\frac{passengers}{seat}+\frac{standingArea(m^2)}{bus}*\frac{standees}{m^2}\right]. (2)$$

3.5.1 Street transit or surface transit

Street transit modes are operated on streets with mixed traffic (i.e., R/W category C); its reliability is often low because of various interference and its speed is lower than the speed of traffic flow, owing to the time lost at passenger stops. This class includes the following modes:

1. Mini bus: These are smaller diesel or petrol driven buses, and have their present use largely in private operation. They are useful for narrow, crowded streets, where large buses have a problem in maneuvering, and also for low demand routes where provision of large buses may prove to be uneconomical.

Figure 3.10: Mini Bus

2. Regular bus (RB): It consists of single-decker buses operating along fixed routes on fixed schedules. Buses comprise by far the most widely used transit mode. The more travel demand is concentrated along corridors, the more advantageous the regular bus becomes. The most typical bus services are street transit routes, which may represent the entire transit network (small and most medium size cities) or supplementary and feeder services to rail networks.

Figure 3.11: Regular Bus

3. Double-decker bus: This is a higher capacity bus, with a design capacity of about 114 and crush capacity of 130. The bus is of similar size to a regular bus, though of course higher, with a more powerful engine. It is however slower for two reasons, namely power-to-weight ratio and longer stop times. It is not as economical (mainly due to its high capital cost) as a regular bus.

Figure 3.12: Double-decker Bus

In addition, it has a disadvantage that all flyovers, elevated rights-of-way, bridges, etc. need clearance of 5.5m instead of 4-4.5m.

4. Articulated bus:

Figure 3.13: Articulated Bus

These buses are usually 55 feet or more in length with two connected passenger compartments that bend at the connecting point when the bus turns a corner (Figure 3.13). It is not recommended, though it has a higher capacity because its extra length creates its own problems under Indian traffic conditions. The driver cannot be as aware of the rear of the bus and cornering is more difficult. As important is the fact that at stops the driver is not able to pull in correctly even with the standard, and takes up 2 lanes. In addition the bus stop lengths would need to be altered.

5. Express bus: Express bus service is provided by fast, comfortable buses on long routes with widely spaced stops. Its reliability of service is dependent on traffic conditions along the route (Figure 3.14).

Figure 3.14: Express Bus

6. Trolley bus (TB):

Figure 3.15: Trolley Bus

Trolley buses are the same vehicles as buses except that they are propelled by an electric motor and obtain power from two overhead wires along their route. The advantages the trolley bus offers include higher riding quality (smooth vehicle motion) and excellent environmental features (extremely low noise, no exhaust). It is always more expensive than the standard bus because at low demand levels its infrastructure cost makes it more expensive and at high demand levels, it cannot meet the demand, being limited to 2 lanes. However, since these factors are not reflected in the operators revenues, financial problems of transit agencies have often led to substitution of buses for trolley buses.

7. Streetcar (SCR) or tramway SCRs are electrically powered rail transit vehicles operating mostly on streets as shown in Figure 3.16. Their tracks and distinct vehicles give transit service a strong identification. When compared with buses, the streetcars have: more comfortable ride, quieter and pollution free operation, better vehicle performance, higher labor productivity (large vehicles), higher line capacity, but higher investment cost, less reliable street operation unless transit enjoys priority treatment, less flexible operation, higher maintenance, and greater impedance of other traffic. A tram is by far the most expensive street transit mode, as well as with very low capacity.

Figure 3.16: Tramway

8. Guided bus: Guided buses free the driver from the task of steering the bus while operating in a section of route equipped with guided-bus infrastructure (Figure 3.17). The guidance could be lateral, central, or electronic. The theoretical maximum capacity quoted for guided buses is 12,000 pphpd, but the realized capacity of the guided busway system as observed in Adelaide, Australia is around half the theoretical capacity just quoted.

Figure 3.17: Guided Bus

9. Battery operated bus: Battery operated buses (Figure 3.18) have low range and speed capability, and cannot be used on a large scale in a city. However, they offer the following advantages as a low capacity (500-1000 pphpd) people mover in a congested area:
i. Economic at low speeds with frequent start/stops
ii. Low noise
iii. Small in size, so easy to manoeuvre.
They should be considered seriously for short routes and low demand routes in city areas.

46

Figure 3.18: Battery Operated Bus

The Tables 3.4.a and b give the system Parameters for street transit and capacity of street transit system.

Table 3.4.a: Systems Parameters for Street Transit

	Mini Bus	Standard Bus	Double Decker Bus	Trolley Bus	LRV (Tram)
L*W(m)	6.6*2.3	9.7*2.5	9.1*2.4	11*2.5	11*2.5
Turning Radius(m)	7	11	12	22	15
Design (Seats)	30(20)	76 (35)	114 (70)	75(40)	75(40)
Crush	40	100	130	110	110
PCU	2	3	3.5	4[1]	5[1]
Acceleration (m/s2)	0.8	0.4	0.4	1.2	0.6
Cruising Speed (kmph)	60	60	50	60	50
Average Speed (kmph)[2]	20	17	15	20	15
Life(yrs)	8	8	8	18	30
Cost (Rs million) 1986 Level	0.2	0.3	0.6	0.7	0.7
Energy Source	D/P	D	D	E	E
Pollution (kg/000veh.kms at avg.speed)	35	38.05	38.05	0	0

(1) for reason of length as well as lack of maneuverability (2) at average congestion

Compiled from GOI(1987)

Table 3.4.b: Capacity of Street Transit System

No. of lanes per direction	1(Single)	1	1	2(double)	2
Bus type	Large urban single-decker	High capacity double-decker	Articulated	Large urban single-decker	High capacity double-decker
Overtaking possible	No	No	No	Yes	Yes
Buses/hr/dir. (normal breaking)	85 (headway 42 sec.)	85 (headway 42 sec.)	80 (headway 40 sec.)	240 (headway 15 sec.)	240 (headway 15 sec.)
Pphpd (normal load)	6460	9690	9440	18240	27360
Pphpd (crush load)	8500	11050	12000	24000	31200

Compiled from GOI(1987)

3.5.2 Semi rapid transit

Semi rapid transit consists of modes utilizing mostly R/W category B [i.e., R/W types which are longitudinally physically separated (by curbs, barriers, grade separation, etc.) from other traffic, but with grade crossings for vehicles and pedestrians, including regular street intersections]. This class includes the following modes:

1. Semi rapid buses (SRBs): SRBs are regular or high-performance buses operating on routes that include substantial sections of R/W categories B. Performance of such systems depends greatly on proportion and locations of separated R/W sections, R/W types, and types of operation.

2. Light rail transit (LRT): LRT is a mode utilizing predominantly reserved, but not necessarily grade-separated R/W. Its electrically propelled rail vehicles operate singly or in trains.

Figure 3.19: Light Rail Transit

LRT provides a wide range of level-of-service (L/S) and performance characteristics. LRT compared with SRB on the corresponding alignments is characterized by: easier securing of B or A R/W, stronger image and identity of lines (rail technology), more spacious vehicles, higher passenger attraction, low noise, no exhaust, better vehicle performance due to electric traction, higher system performance, ability to operate in tunnels, ability to upgrade into rapid transit, but lower frequency for a given demand due to larger vehicles, a need to introduce new facilities for a different technology in case of a new application, lower ability to branch out and hence requiring more transfers, and a longer implementation period. Figure 3.19 shows the picture of the LRT and the capacity of LRT is given in Table 3.5.

Table 3.5: Capacity of LRT 1

	Normal Load($5p/m^2$)	Crush Load($8\ p/m^2$)
Seats	65	65
Standees	160	256
Vehicle Capacity	225	321
2-vehicle Train Capacity	450	642
Line Capacity(h-60sec.)in pphpd	27000	38520

(Source: Verma and Dhingra 2001)

3.5.3 Rapid transit or mass rapid transit system

These modes operate exclusively on category A R/W (i.e., a fully controlled R/W without grade crossings or any legal access by other vehicles or persons) and have high speed, capacity, reliability, and safety. All existing rapid transit systems utilize guided technologies (rail or rubber tire), that permit operation of trains (high capacity) and automatic signal control (high safety). This class includes the following modes:

1. Rubber-tired rapid transit (RTR): RTR (Figure 3.20) consists of moderately large vehicles (gross floor areas between 36 and 53 mm^2- 380 and 570 ft$2m^2$) supported and guided by rubber tires, running on wooden, steel, or concrete surfaces in trains of 5 to 9 cars.

Figure 3.20: Glimpse of a Rubber-Tired Rapid Transit

2. Rail rapid transit (RRT): RRT typically consists of large four-axle rail vehicles (area up to 70 mm^2-750 ftm^2) which operate in trains of up to 10 cars on fully controlled (A) R/W which allows high speed, reliability, capacity, rapid boarding, and fail-safe operation (in the case of drivers error or disability, the train is stopped automatically). The capacity of RRT is shown in Table 3.6.

Figure 3.21: Glimpse of a Rail Rapid Transit

Table 3.6: Capacity of Rapid Rail Transit (RRT)

	Normal Load	Crush Load
Seats	98	98
Standees	300	480
Vehicle Capacity	398	578
3 Twin-Vehicle capacity (6 vehicles)	1194	1734
Line capacity (h-90sec.)	47,760	69,360

(Source: Verma and Dhingra, 2001)

3. Regional rail (RGR): RGR usually operated by railroads, has high standards of alignment geometry. It utilizes the largest vehicles of all transit systems (up to 80mm^2-860ftm^2) which operate in trains, on longer routes, with fewer stations, at higher speeds than typical for RRT. Thus, RGR functionally represents a large-scale RRT which serves most efficiently regional and longer urban trips. Capacity of RGR is shown in Table 3.7.

As per Verma and Dhingra (2001) the following are the capacity ranges, within which a particular mass transit system is suitable for operation in Indian cities:

Street transit system = Up to 12,000 pphpd

(Mini-bus, single-decker standard bus, double-decker, and articulated)

LRT1 = 12,000 to 36,000 pphpd

LRT2 = 36,000 to 50,000 pphpd

RRT (Metro) = 50,000 to 69,000 pphpd

RGR = 59,000 to 89,000 pphpd

Figure 3.22: Regional Rail

The above ranges can be taken as the basis for determining the suitability of transit systems for Indian cities of different population sizes and forms based on the peak hour passenger per direction (pphpd) count on major corridors within the city. Further Table 3.8 (Verma and Dhingra, 2001) shows the recommended combination of mass transit modes for Indian cities of different population size and structure.

Table 3.7: Capacity of Regional Rail Transit (RGR)

	Normal Load	Crush Load
Seats	60	60
Standees	270	432
Vehicle Capacity	330	492
Train Capacity (6 vehicles)	2970	4428
Line Capacity (h-3min.)	59,400	88,560

(Source: Verma and Dhingra, 2001)

Table 3.8: Recommendation of Mass Transit Systems for Indian Cities

Population (M)	Activity Structure	Recomended Mass Transit System		
		Circular City	Semi-circular City	Linear City
13	PNU	RGR+LRT1/LRT 2+ST	RGR+LRT1/LRT 2+ST	RGR+RRT+LRT 1/LRT2+ST
	PU	RGR+LRT1+ST	RGR+LRT 1/LRT 2+ST	RGR+RRT+LR T1/LRT2+ST
	M	-	-	-
6	PNU	RRT+LRT 1/LRT2+ST	RRT+LRT 1+ST	RGR+LRT 1/LRT2+ST
	PU	RRT+LRT 1/LRT2+ST	RRT+LR T2+ST	RGR+LRT 1/LRT2+ST
	M	-	-	-
3	PNU	LRT1+ST	LRT2+ST	RRT+LRT1 /LRT2+ST
	PU	LRT1+ST	LRT2+ST	RRT+LRT1 /LRT2+ST
	M	LRT1+ST	RRT+LRT1+ST	RRT+LRT1 /LRT2+ST
1.5	PNU	ST	LRT1+ST	LRT1+ST
	PU	ST	LRT1+ST	LRT1+ST
	M	LRT1+ST	LRT1+ST	LRT1+ST
0.75	PNU	ST	ST	ST
	PU	ST	ST	ST
	M	ST	ST	ST
0.375	PNU	ST	ST	ST
	PU	ST	ST	ST
	M	ST	ST	ST

(1)RGR=Regional Rail Transit, RRT=Rail Rapid Transit, LRT1=Light Rail Transit1, LRT2=Light Rail Transit2, ST=Street Transit
(2)PNU=Polynuclear Nonuniform, PU=Polynuclear Uniform, M=Mononuclear

(Source: Verma and Dhingra 2001)

3.5.4 Special transit

Specialized transport systems are those which may have a role to play in a specific part of a city, without in any way forming a substantial part of the urban transport network. These are:

1. Magnetic levitation: In levitation systems the coach is suspended in air by magnetic levitation or by air cushion. The reason for the development of these technologies was to overcome the problems of vibration and resonance, which make it virtually impossible for normal trains to exceed 300 kmph. The air cushion system is still experimental and is not seriously considered. Until now, only small systems have been constructed at low capacities of 2000-5000 pphpd. Under Indian overloading patterns, the magnets may need to be augmented and may need remagnetizing more often.

2. Monorails: They have been designed for their low guide way cost, but have three main drawbacks:

i. Low capacity (up to 15-20,000 pphpd)

ii. No form of emergency evacuation, so a low safety factor

iii. Complicated guide wheel system. Figure 3.23 shows a picture of monorails.

Figure 3.23: Monorails

Primarily since the monorail is designed for low capacities, and cannot meet the necessary demand levels in India, it has not been seriously considered, until now.

3. Water borne transport: Water borne transport should be taken more seriously since most cities are either by the sea or on a river, and water transport may be able to take some of the load if traffic demand is across or along water.

4. Automated guided transit (AGT): AGT (Figure 3.24) modes are a low capacity rail based system of lightweight construction and totally automated. They consist of two groups: personal rapid transit (PRT), with small vehicles serving individual parties only, and group rapid transit (GRT), also known as people mover systems (PMS), with somewhat larger vehicles (15 to 50 spaces) designed mostly for short-haul medium capacity lines. AGT is classified as special transit, together with other proposed and specialized modes. This class of transit contains both supported and suspended types of technologies. These modes basically provide service in such areas as shopping centers, commercial areas, airports, etc. as an enhancement to the areas activities.

Figure 3.24: Automated Guided Transit

Table 3.9: System characteristics of Some Selected Rail Based Transit Systems

	Heavy Rail			Medium Capacity				
	EMU	Metro	Heavy Rail Recommended	LRT	Purpose De-signed Lin. Mtr.	Mag. Lev.	Mono-rail	Sky Bus
Gauge (M)	1.667	1.667	1.667	1.435	1.435	1.435	N/A	1.435
Coaches/ train	9	8	9	3	6	4	4	4
Length* Width (m)	20* 3.66	20* 2.74	20* 2.74	29*2.5	16*2.65	12*2.3	10*2.5	8*2.8
Tare Weight (T)	350	300	244	123	99	36	40	N/A
Payload/ Tare Ratio	0.5	0.52	0.64	0.585	0.73	0.88	0.75	N/A
Axle Load (T)	19	16.5	16	8	8	N/A	6	N/A
Acc./Dec/ (m/s^2)	1.1/ 1.2	1.1/ 1.2	1.0/ 1.3	1.0/ 1.3	1.0/ 1.3	1.0/ 1.3	1.4/ 1.5	1.3
Max. Speed (Kmph)	80	80	80-120	80	80	80	80	100
Min. Radius (m)	200	200	200	20	20	20	20	100
Max. Gradient (per)	2	2	2	7	10	10	10	1.3
Power Supply	25KV AC	750V DC	750V DC	750V DC	750V DC	1KV AC	750V DC	750V DC
Enerrgy Consumption (W hr/Ton. km)	40	52	40	34	40	35	40	N/A
Min. Headway (Mts)	3	1.5	1.5	1	1	1	1.5	1

Source: Compiled from GOM (2000)

3.6 Integrated transport infrastructure approach

Consider an intermodal trip between any given origin (O) and destination (D), as shown in Figure 3.25. The same can be made using various mode options and their corresponding infrastructure, in such a way that it optimizes the complete journey of travelers from origin to destination. While we plan the integrated transportation infrastructure to improve mobility and accessibility for all, it is important that we consider various scenarios consisting of combinations of different modes and infrastructure options and adopt the one that is most sustainable in terms of both mobility/accessibility and safety.

Cities like, London, Zurich, Berlin, Paris, Munich, Hong-Kong, Bogota, etc. provide good examples of well integrated multi-modal transport systems that provide, seamless O-D connectivity through sustainable mode options.

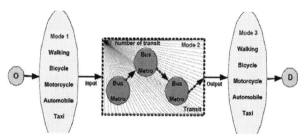

Figure 3.25: An Intermodal Trip

3.6.1 Various transport modes and their roles

In order to create different scenarios for integrated transport infrastructure planning, it is important to understand the role of various modes possibly available, and which can be broadly categorized as public or private modes. Public modes are generally the ones that are available to all on fixed route and fixed schedule basis and on payment of established fares and will include; bus, commuter rail, metro rail, light rail, ferry, etc. The best known classification of public transit modes is into three generic classes based mostly, but not entirely, on right-of-way (R/W) type. They are street transit or surface transit, semi-rapid transit, and rapid transit or mass rapid transit systems.

Private modes are at the disposal of the individuals and can be used as per requirement and discretion of the individual concerned. They include private cars, motorcycle/scooter, etc. Figure 3.26 shows a comparison between private or individual vehicle (IV) and public transport with respect to various parameters and on the scale of sustainability. Walking and cycling are also the other and very important sustainable mode options. Figure 3.27 depicts how with change in settlement size the transport needs and role of various modes changes. Figure 3.28 shows the variation in speed (mobility) and accessibility for different modes. Further, Figure 3.29 depicts how an integrated multi-modal transport system helps in balancing access and speed (mobility).

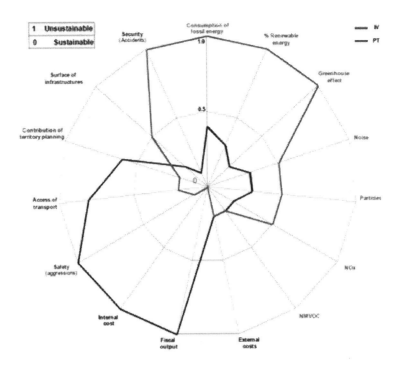

Figure 3.26: Comparison between Private Vehicle and Public Transport

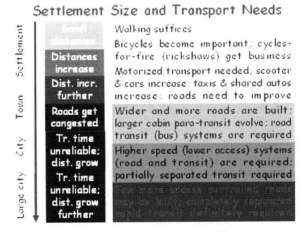

Figure 3.27: Settlement Size and Transport Needs (Ref: Chakroborty, 2009)

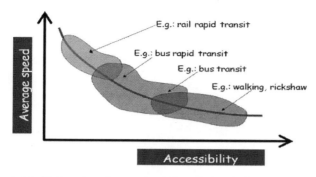

Figure 3.28: Balancing Access and Speed (Ref: Chakroborty, 2009)

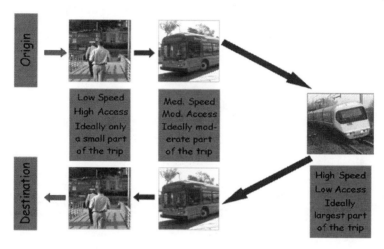

Figure 3.29: Mobility vs. Accessibility for Different Modes (Ref: Chakroborty, 2009)

3.6.2 Cost of the metro project and corridors

Taking the Bangalore Metro project 2005, as far as rail systems are considered, it is not always possible in present urban conditions to go for any particular (surface, underground, or elevated) type of construction, hence, a network should not be thought of as solely elevated or surface or underground, but rather the three should complement each other in a network, and fit in with the requirement of each individual section. Table 3.10 shows the details of the two corridors approved by the government of India for Bangalore City and Table 3.11 gives the estimated cost of the project approved by the government of India based on April 2005 prices.

Table 3.10: The Details of the Two Corridors Approved by the Government of India for Bangalore City

Corridors	East/West		North/South	
	Length(Km)	Stations	Length(Km)	Stations
Elevated	14.35	13	11.3	10
Underground	3.4	4	3.3	3
Surface	0.35	1	0.3	1
Total	18.1	18	14.9	14

Source: DMRC (2003)

Table 3.11: Cost Detail of the Bangalore Metro Rail Project

Construction cost in billions	50.80(59.12)*
Interest during construction	3.48(4.49)*
Financing charges and preoperative expenses	0 .25(0.29)*
Total current cost	54.53(63.95)*

Source: DMRC (2003)

* Figures in brackets refer to completion cost which is the current cost plus an annual escalation of 5 percent per year for the likely duration of the project.

3.7 A look ahead in public transportation

In the dispersed regional city of future, public transportation will be needed to carry out five essential functions:

1. To guarantee city wise mobility for the growing number of people who are nondrivers by choice or necessity.

2. To supply the exclusive means of travel in high-density areas where cars are prohibited.

3. To complement the services rendered by the automobile on trips that requires both methods.

4. To provide local extensions of the intercity and global public transportation networks.

5. To help create a more satisfying, manageable, pollution-free, and sustainable urban environment that maximizes the ability to move while minimizing the necessity for movement.

Harman (1988) outlined the major advances anticipated in the different forms of public transportation. These included:

Buses: There will likely be production of a bus that has two methods of propulsion in one coach, a diesel engine for use on suburban streets and electric power for city streets and in tunnels. Some innovations can be expected in alternative forms of access to the vehicle, in particular for the elderly and handicapped. Although some concepts are currently being developed that would make the bus-road interface much more intelligent in terms of navigation and vehicle control, such programs are not likely to see widespread implementation in the early part of the twenty-first century.

Heavy and Light Rail: The major source of innovation will likely come in the means of providing propulsion and in automatic system control.

Commuter and Intercity Rail: There were possible major advances that could be anticipated in the application of linear induction motor, magnetic levitation technology, and other forms of providing high-speed passenger transportation.

Automated Guide way: The technology for implementing automated guide way transit, group rapid transit, or personal rapid transit systems is already available. The key issue is now to find the appropriate applications.

Harman then suggested that perhaps the greatest technological innovations will come in the areas of transit user information systems, automatic vehicle monitoring, and in revisiting already tested applications such as high-occupancy vehicle facilities.

3.8 Comparative analyses

The procedure for the comparative analysis and selection of transportation modes follows these major steps:

Step 1: Based on urban transportation policy, develop goals for the transit system.

Step 2: Define conditions for the area to be served.

Step 3: Utilizing results from preceding steps, define specific requirements and standards for the planned system.

Step 4: Select ROW type for candidate modes.

Step 5: Select technologies and type of operation for candidate modes.

Step 6: Develop functional designs for candidate modes.

Step 7: Evaluate candidate modes.

Step 8: Compare evaluation results (based on capacity, cost, environmental impact, etc.) and select the optimal mode.

From the results obtained (Table 3.8), it can be seen that in cities with population up to 0.75 million (also circular PNU and PU cities of population 1.5 million), the street transit can fully cater to the peak hour passenger travel demand, as the maximum peak hour public transport demand is within the capacity of the street transit, (Table 3.12). But for cities with population above these values, a rail-based system along with a street transit system is required to cater to increased passenger travel demand. Also, it can be seen from Table 3.8 that cities with population greater than 6 million probably require the highest order mass transit systems like regional rail transit to meet the heavy passenger travel demands (Table 3.12) on major corridors within the city.

Finally, Table 3.13 shows in tabular form, some of the more frequently encountered relationships involved in translating system goals into design objectives and, in turn, into design methods and technology attributes. For example, to meet the goal of minimizing construction cost, the designer must choose the objective of maximizing the use of shared facilities, seeking to run on HOV lanes and transit ways open to carpools and vanpools. In this case, bus rapid transit (BRT) would be the favored technology, being capable of operation in all types of HOV configurations, LRT would be the second choice, being appropriate for limited running in arterial HOV lanes only, and the last choice would be RRT and AGT with their requirements for exclusive guide ways.

The authors feel that the chapter would strongly help planners in selecting a suitable mass transit system for Indian cities of different sizes and forms.

Table 3.12: Maximum Peak Hour Public Transport Demand in pphpd for Indian Cities

Population (M)	Public Transport Share Factor	Activity Structure	Maximum Peak Hour pphpd		
			Circular City	SemiCircular City	Linear City
13	0.84	PNU	1,68,840	2,52,000	3,88,080
		PU	1,20,960	2,97,360	3,83,040
		M	-	-	-
6	0.74	PNU	66,600	1,00,788	1,55,400
		PU	57,720	1,19,880	1,50,960
		M	-	-	-
3	0.64	PNU	27,264	38,400	61,440
		PU	24,192	49,920	62,208
		M	33,408	65,280	65,280
1.5	0.58	PNU	10,440	16,356	24,360
		PU	9,744	19,488	24,360
		M	13,224	26,796	26,796
0.75	0.55	PNU	3,960	5,940	8,910
		PU	3,300	6,930	8,910
		M	4,620	9,900	9,900
0.375	0.53	PNU	477	859	1,272
		PU	636	954	1,272
		M	700	1,272	1,272

Table 3.13: Some Relationships between Design Goals and Technology Attributes

Goal/Design Objective	Design Method	Technology Suitability Rank			
		RRT	AGT	LRT	BRT
Maximize ridership:					
Locate station within easy walk of	Locate system underground to allow unobtrusive/no disruptive high capacity entry into high density areas	1	2	2	3
Many major centers	Locate system in surface streets/malls of major centers,with first-floor-level stops	2	2	1	1
	Use high line mileage and many stations system wide	1	1	1	1
Provide high frequency service	Use short trains or single-vehicle trains with short headed ways	3	1	2	1
Maximize scheduled speed	Provide grade separation and high speed alignment for entire system	1	2	3	4
	Provide skip-stop and express service	2	2	2	1
Reorganize transit service system wide	Remove radial bus service; provide focus to reorient bus route into community/cross town operation	1	2	3	4
Maximize development impact:					
Stress accesibility and permanence	Use fixed guide way with substantial stations centers to areas of potential development/redevelopment	1	2	3	4
Minimize construction cost:					
Use of existing ROW to avoid under-	Use freeway medians, rail road/power-line right-of way though these may be distant from activity centers	1	1	1	1
Ground/elevated construction	In lower density areas let system run on streets/ highways mixed with other traffic	3	3	2	1
Maximize use of shared facilities	Run on HOV lanes and other facilities open to carpools/vanpools	2	2	2	1
Reduce total construction required	Reduce system milege, number of stations	1	1	1	1
	Use shorter,simpler stations,low platforms,etc.	2	2	1	1
	Use smaller horizontal and vertical clearances, lighter structures	2	1	2	2
Reduce system complexity	Elimate power distribution and control system	3	3	2	1
Minimize operating cost:					
Reduce operating personnel	Use long trains to reduce personnel/passenger ratio	1	2	2	3
	Use more complex system affording greater automation	2	1	3	4
	Use short trains in off-peak	3	1	2	1
Reduce maintenance personnel	Use simpler system with less electronics and hardware	3	4	2	1
Maximize public support:					
Provide service to widest possible area	Use low cost/ mile systems, maximum use of at-grade, nonexclusive right-of-way	4	3	2	1
File predispositions of public	Use rail/fixed guide way systems; avoid bus systems	1	1	1	2

Summary

This chapter mainly deals with the different transport modes and their characteristics which are mainly classified into 3 modes, i.e., personal, intermediate, and public transport modes. The transit modes are classified into street, semi rapid, and special transit. These transit modes consist of different types and their characteristics. This chapter also covers the: detailed capacity assessment of some selected technologies, and integrated transport infrastructure approach, besides information about the various transport modes and their role with specified figures and graphs.

Chapter 4

Current Scenario of Public Transport (PT) in Developing Countries

4.1 Current perception of PT

Public transport service plays a vital role in the overall development of a country. The living standard in many developing countries is changing. While developing cities are showing improvements in economic growth in terms of GDP, middle class people are no longer attached to the particular transport services; higher income society is going to the higher car ownership and higher expectations in terms of better mobility and better quality of services. Public transport systems are known to be sustainable modes in terms of space and energy efficiency, and environmental and social benefits. A good networked public transportation system with time-bound schedules, reliable services, comfort, competitive travel times, and affordable prices, are some of the required traits for providing sustainable transport services and commuter satisfaction. Passenger transportation has an impact on all aspects of mobility and is an important part of overall economic development. Improving the performance of public transport undertakings is becoming more and more critical due to the paucity of public funds, increased demand on transport services, and expanding social needs. Of late, the performance measurement and evaluation systems have been gaining importance (Kittelson Associates et. al. 2003, Sulek and Lind 2000). Increased urbanization has increased the number of passenger vehicles in the cities in developing countries such as India. The Road Transport Corporations Act came into effect in India in 1950 and led to various state governments setting up respective State Road Transport Corporations with an objective of providing affordable transport services within the state as well as across states. Over the years, most of these corporations have become loss making. The trade-off between commercial objectives and social responsibility goals of these state owned corporations became an issue of major concern.

In the work of Verma et al. (2013), the SERVQUAL framework, which is a multi-item instrument used for measuring service quality, is used to measure gaps between commuters expectations of urban bus transport services and the actual service quality provided by the Bangalore Metropolitan Transport Corporation (BMTC), this is among the few profit-making urban public bus transport organizations in India. While the services of BMTC are very competitive among any other urban public bus transport organization in the country, they are still to reach the desired level of passenger mode share that will enable them to provide sustainable mobility solutions to the commuters in Bangalore.

The results of this study may help organizations like BMTC to bridge the gap between commuters expectations and actual service quality and to work towards developing sustainable services.

4.1.1 Working process

The objective of the study is to measure gaps between commuters expectations of urban bus transport services and the actual service quality provided. The SERVQUAL framework is used to measure gap between customers (commuters) expectations of public transport services and the actual service quality provided. SERVQUAL is a multi-item instrument for measuring service quality. This instrument was first developed by Parasuraman et al. (1985) through an exploratory study of marketing academics. The outcome was a 22-item scale that has received widespread application in the research of service quality. The 22-items are essentially framed around the following five dimensions of service quality:

i. Tangible: Physical facilities and equipment

ii. Reliability: Ability to perform the promised service dependably and accurately

iii. Responsiveness: Willingness to help customers and provide prompt service

iv. Assurance: Knowledge and courtesy of employees and their ability to inspire trust and confidence

v. Empathy: Caring and individual attention the firm provides to customers

Using the above five dimensions of service quality, parameters related to the case study were identified under each of the five dimensions. Accordingly a survey questionnaire was developed to obtain the required data for analysis. Finally, statistical analysis using a paired t-test was done to identify, measure, and interpret the gaps between perception and expectation. The next section discusses the case study application.

4.1.2 Case study Bangalore

Bangalore Metropolitan Transport Corporation (BMTC), which is among the very few profit-making urban public bus transport organizations in India, is taken as the case study for applying the proposed approach. BMTC operates about 6000 routes in Bangalore city and has a fleet of more than 6100 buses with a considerable number of luxury (Volvo and Mercedes-Benz) buses to its credit. It carries about 4.5 million passengers every day and has a very efficient bus staff ratio of 5.3. While the services of BMTC are very competitive among any other urban public bus transport organization in the country, they are still to reach the desired level of passenger mode share that will enable them to provide sustainable mobility solutions to the commuters in Bangalore city. Also, while BMTC is currently modernizing the bus fleet, to improve its services and mode share, through funding under Jawaharlal Nehru National Urban Renewal Mission (JnNURM) scheme, there is still very little focus on improving overall service quality to improve commuter patronage. The outcome of the study may help BMTC to bridge the gap between commuters expectations and actual service quality and to work towards developing sustainable services.

4.1.3 Data collection and analysis

4.1.3.1 Sampling

The main intent of this study is to measure gaps between commuters expectations of urban bus transport services and the actual service quality provided. The empirical data were collected using a questionnaire. 196 samples of bus commuters were selected from different regions of Bangalore, using snow ball sampling technique. The questionnaires were distributed personally and also by using the social media networks like Facebook. An online version of the questionnaire was also distributed using Google Docs. to the potential respondents. Out of 196 responses, 186 were usable, since 10 questionnaires received were partially filled and cannot be used for analysis. This shows 94.87% response rate. Thus the actual sample size used for analysis was 186.

4.1.3.2 Variable measurement

A total of 50 questions were used to measure the service quality of bus services in Bangalore based on five dimensions defined by Parasuraman et al. (1985). All questions were designed as closed ended questions using 7-point Likert scale varying from strongly disagree (1) to strongly agree (7).

4.1.3.3 Sample profile

The demographic and travel profile of the respondents is shown in Table 4.1 to Table 4.3 which includes gender, age group, marital status, education profile, income range per month, occupation of respondents, and various types of buses used by the respondents and frequency of bus travel on an average.

4.1.4 Survey results

4.1.4.1 Demographic profile of respondents

There is a notable difference in the genders using urban bus services from the respondents. 63% of the total respondents were male commuters and 36% were female. 67.74% of the users were in the age group of 20-25 which shows that the commuters (among the respondents) are mostly the young generation, i.e., the students & the neo-working class.

4.1.4.2 Service quality gaps

The questionnaire which was developed consisted of 2 sets of items each set had 25 questions. The first set was used to measure the perceived levels of service quality (P). The same set of questions were reframed/rephrased to inquire the users expectations of the service quality (E). The questions under each dimension were rated using a 7 point Likert scale.

Table 4.1: Demographic Profile of the Respondents

Characteristics		No. of Respondents	Percentage of Respondents
Gender	Male	115	62%
	Female	71	38%
Age	Below 20	12	6%
	20-25	123	66%
	25-30	34	18%
	35-45	6	3%
	45 & above	11	6%
Marital Status	Married	35	19%
	Unmarried	151	81%
Education	Under-graduate	26	14%
	Graduate	68	37%
	Post-graduate	92	49%
Income Range/Month	Below 5000	52	28%
	5000-10,000	30	16%
	10,000-20,000	48	26%
	20,000 & above	56	30%
Occupation	Student	125	67%
	Government employee	4	2%
	Own business	7	4%
	Private company employee	38	20%
	Others	12	6%

Table 4.2: Types of Buses Used by the Respondents

Bus Type	No. of Respondents	Percentage of Respondents
Vajra	46	25%
BIG 10	5	3%
Suvarna	12	6%
Ordinary	101	54%
Pushpak	10	5%
Others	12	6%

Table 4.3: Frequency of Bus Travel

Frequency of Bus Travel	No. of Respondents	Percentage of Respondents
Daily	58	31%
Occasionally once in a while	72	39%
Rarely	56	30%
Never	0	0%

A gap analysis was conducted on each dimension of the SERVQUAL (Parasuraman et. al., 1988) taking averages of individual items under each dimension and subtracting the expectations from the perceptions (P-E). The average of the perceptions score and the expectations score results are tabulated in Table 4.4. The comparison of average of each of these dimensional scores is shown in Figure 4.1, which clearly shows that the perceptions of the commuters are below the expectations of the services provided by the BMTC in almost all the dimensions, and the gap is much wider in case of the empathy dimension.

Table 4.4: Comparison of Perceptions and Expectations of Respondents

Dimensions	Average Perception Score (P)	Average Expectation Score (E)	Difference (P-E)
Reliability Dimension			
Bus information schedule and route maps are available and reliable	3.806452	5.451613	-1.64516
Buses are available on time during peak hours	3.704301	5.715054	-2.01075
Buses are available to every area in the city	3.994624	5.682796	-1.68817
Frequency of buses is very high on every route	3.456989	5.526882	-2.06989
Computerized ticketing system leaves little scope for cheating and bribing	5.021505	5.682796	-0.66129
Tangible Dimension			
Buses are clean and well maintained	4.064516	5.827957	-1.76344
Buses are a safe mode of transport	5.016129	5.887097	-0.87097
Buses are the best mode for advertising and campaigning	4.478495	4.930108	-0.45161
Eco-friendly buses are used	4.016129	5.822581	-1.80645
Bus stops are well maintained	3.301075	5.860215	-2.55914
Responsiveness Dimension			
Bus tickets are affordable and buses are a real value for money	4.634409	5.763441	-1.12903
Bus routes are not lengthy	4.021505	5.306452	-1.28495
Bus stops are conveniently located	4.489247	5.548387	-1.05914
Response time to resolve complaints is very low	4.344086	5.365591	-1.02151
Bus information is easily available through calls, SMS and on the Internet	3.844086	5.811828	-1.96774
Assurance Dimension			
Drivers and conductors are courteous	3.860215	5.715054	-1.85484
There is a lot of safety measures against crime on buses	3.913978	5.741935	-1.82796
There are very little accident damage caused by buses	4.086022	5.682796	-1.59677
Drivers are well trained and safety measures are taken care of	4.225806	5.88172	-1.65591
Fire and emergency exits are available on all buses	4.268817	5.865591	-1.59677
Empathy Dimension			
Bus is user friendly for handicapped	3.543011	5.973118	-2.43011
Seats are available on every bus	3.11828	5.44086	-2.32258
Buses are safe for young mothers	3.403226	5.860215	-2.45699
There is first aid available on every bus	3.096774	5.827957	-2.73118
Destination displays systems are useful for visually impaired and aged	4.33871	5.930108	-1.5914

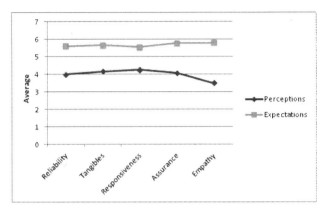

Figure 4.1: SERVQUAL Dimension Gaps between Expectations and Perceptions

Interpretation of the Gap Analysis

Following are three possible outcomes and their interpretation, for the gap analysis done in Table 4.4:

P-E >0, this implies that the users are satisfied with the level of service being provided.

P-E = 0, this implies that the satisfactory levels are just being touched or reached.

P-E <0, this implies that the satisfaction levels are low.

An average of the perception and expectation scores of each of the dimensions in the questionnaire is taken and the respective difference is sought out in Table 4.4. The differences can be a positive or negative value. A positive value indicates that the perceptions of the users have exceeded their expectations and have resulted in a satisfied customer, whereas a negative value shows that the expectations of the users have not been met by the service provider, and there is a scope of improvement in services.

Quite clearly, all the values in Table 4.4 are negative, i.e., the service quality at present levels is not satisfactory to the commuters, which implies that there is a gap in the service quality offered and the expectations of the users. Analysis indicates that the bus services provided within the Bangalore region have to improve in all the 5 dimensions of reliability, tangibility, responsiveness, assurance, and empathy dimensions as all the dimensions have negative scores. Commuters indicate the biggest overall service quality gap in the empathy dimension where commuters are asking for safety for young mothers, seat availability on the buses, provision for the disabled, availability of first aid and destination display systems for the visually impaired and aged. Each of the five dimensions is discussed in detail below.

4.1.4.3 Reliability dimension

The reliability dimension elaborates the ability of the BMTC buses to perform the promised service dependably and accurately. This dimension elaborates the availability of service during peak traffic hours, reliability of public transport in all areas of the city as well as the trustworthiness of the computerized ticketing system which has been recently introduced. The negative scores on all these areas of focus show that the expectations are higher than the perceptions and that the BMTC bus services should improve in all the areas of focus such as timely availability of buses during peak traffic hours, providing reliable transport to all areas of the city, and providing more of buses for the convenience of commuters.

4.1.4.4 Tangible dimension

The tangible dimension expounds the physical facilities and equipment of the BMTC buses in terms of safety, cleanliness, and maintenance of the buses as well as the bus stops. All the values in the gap analysis shows negative values indicating that the BMTC bus service scores low again on the tangible dimension. Commuters expectations are not met by the BMTC services, buses and bus stops are neither clean nor well maintained; the safety of the commuters is not taken care of as expected by the public.

4.1.4.5 Responsiveness dimension

The responsiveness dimension elaborates on the willingness of service providers to help customers and provide prompt services. The gap analysis shows the values are negative, and the expectations are not met in this case either. Overall, it shows that bus stops may not be conveniently located, bus routes are lengthy, and the response time to resolve complaints is high according to the perceptions of the commuters.

4.1.4.6 Assurance dimension

This dimension accesses the knowledge and courtesy of employees and their ability to inspire trust and confidence in their services. The gap analysis shows all the values on the negative scale which implies that the overall BMTC service quality in the assurance dimension falls below the expectations of the commuters. Also, the wide gap with respect to all parameters of this dimension (refer to Table 4.4) shows that this dimension fairs second worst after the empathy dimension. The overall interpretation of this gap will be that drivers and conductors are not well trained to behave courteously with the public, fire and emergency exits are not available on all buses, and there are instances of theft and crime that takes place on the buses.

4.1.4.7 Empathy dimension

The empathy dimension expounds on the care and individual attention the firm provides to customers by improvising and adding new features to the services which are user friendly to the differently abled, young mothers, and the safety of the passengers/commuters.

4.1.5 T-Test analysis

To statistically validate the results, a paired sample t-test was conducted for all the dimensions to evaluate the statistical significance of gap between expectations, and perceptions and the results are shown in Table 4.5. The null hypothesis for each dimension is defined as:

H0 : There is no significant difference in commuters perception and expectation of BMTC bus service quality in Bangalore.

As the sample size is large, the t-value corresponds to probabilities for a standard normal distribution. The t values for all 5 dimensions, i.e., tangibility, reliability, responsiveness, assurance, and empathy dimensions were found to be significantly high as shown in Table 4.5. At 5 % level of significance, all the values above 1.96 in the t - table are considered as not satisfactory. Hence there is not enough evidence to accept the null hypothesis. The results presented in Table 4.5 show that the t-values fall out of the upper limit considering 95% confidence limits and this implies that the expectations of the commuters fall above the services that is offered by the Bangalore Metropolitan Transport Corporation.

Table 4.5: t-test

Dimensions	Paired Differences					t-value	Degree of Freedom ((df)
	Mean of (P-E)	Standard Deviation	Standard Error	95% Confidence Interval of the Differences			
				Lower	Upper		
Reliability	1.6150	2.022091	0.1482669	1.324451	1.905657	10.892	185
Tangibles	1.4903	1.956503	0.1434578	1.209145	1.7715	10.388	185
Responsivenes	1.2924	1.998823	0.1465610	1.00521	1.57973	8.818	185
Assurance	1.7064	2.198294	0.1611870	1.390523	2.022377	10.586	185
Empathy	2.3064	2.259601	0.1656820	2.631187	2.631187	13.921	185

The overall results of this study also explains some of the reasons for the unsustainable trend in Indian cities, including Bangalore, of exponential growth of car ownership and its usage and the corresponding transport externalities resulting from this trend. Due to overall higher levels of expectations than perceptions from bus transport and particularly a wider gap on the empathy dimension, commuters shift to cars as soon as they are able to afford it. Also, Indian cities have higher levels of two-wheeler usage, which is cheaper and more flexible to use than buses.
This case study of BMTC from Verma et.al. (2013) demonstrares an effective methodology for measuring current perception and service quality of public bus services.

4.2 Current planning and operational practices

In most large cities in developing countries, buses continue to be the public transport option of choice, carrying a large share of urban travelers. However, transit bus companies in these countries are often cash-strapped. In many cases, the operating cost per bus kilometer exceeds revenues and bus fares are often kept low irrespective of the cost of providing service. Many cities are dominated by old and fuel-intensive buses with high operating costs. Transit systems are also often plagued by overcrowded and undependable service, congested roadways, and chaotic operating environments. Across the board, city officials in developing countries are under strong pressure to improve the efficiency and enhance the attractiveness of bus transportation.
To understand the process of planning and operational practices of a developing country like India, one of the cities of India, Bangalore is taken as an example for the case study like Bangalore.

4.2.1 Transportation in Bangalore

The Bangalore Metropolitan Transport Corporation (BMTC) is the sole provider of public transport in the city. Bangalore has one of the most extensive networks of public bus transport in India. BMTC do not use private contractors currently and have no plans to use them in the future. They have 30 depots spread throughout their region so there are minimal dead kilometers in getting to and from the bus starting and terminal point. BMTC owns their bus fleet.

They even have their own bus body building centers. Their Shantinagar workshop performs body building and reconditioning of assemblies. Their innovations in body building have improved aesthetics and resulted in fuel savings with better KMPL and EPKM.

BMTC, just like most public transport corporations in India, do not have a transportation planning and modelling divisions. Most of the decisions are taken via demand-response techniques. Travel demand analysis is seldom used for planning present or future operations. Government of India is trying to change this scenario by the creation of UMTA (Unified Metropolitan Authority) that will include all major stakeholders. UMTA will be responsible for developing comprehensive mobility plans using reliable demand estimates.

Bangalore has the youngest fleet for a city transport corporation. They have many new Volvo buses which lead the industry in terms of vehicle design and comfort. The Vajra buses are tracked using GPS and real time arrival and departure information is displayed at the bus stops. The BIG10 buses also have GPS and can be tracked online at the www.btis.in website. Other than these services, about 1000 buses have GPS fitted into them, but they are still working on setting up systems to download, analyze, and distribute that information. Most of the buses are diesel or petrol. There are no plans to convert to CNG until 2012. BMTC has planned to construct 45 Traffic and Transit Management Centers (TTMCs) as a part of the development of urban infrastructure stated in the Comprehensive Traffic and Transportation Plan (CTTP) for Bangalore and vision plan under JnNURM. These TTMCs are conceived as transport infrastructure for the urban renewal project aimed at providing one stop travel to commuters. The TTMCs comprised of state of the art bus terminals, maintenance facilities, public amenities, park and ride facilities, and they provide intermodal connectivity. In turn, they also directly impact traffic congestion and address environment concerns in the long run.

4.2.2 Published schedules and route searches

One of the very basic facilities that are missing in most Indian public transport systems are the lack of published bus routes and schedules. Information can be gathered anecdotally, but there is very little information available at the bus stops or on the internet. This causes difficulties to passengers who are new to the city or those that are new to public transport. Bangalore has made many improvements in this area. The BMTC website now has a 'Route Search' page where you can enter your origin and destination stop or look at pull down menus of bus routes and look up the list of stops and timings.

4.2.3 BMTC bus system performance

BMTC is one of the few public transport corporations in the world that are profitable.

They have been consistently increasing the number of buses and kilometers run every year and also the profit every year since 2005. Table 4.6 below shows the detailed statistics from 2004 to 2009.

Table 4.6: BMTC System Performance Indicators, 2004 - 2009

Parameter	2004-05	2005-06	2006-07	2007-08	2008-09
Fleet Size	3925	4106	4606	4891	5542
Bus Kilometers	2974	3163	3334	3767	4062
Operational Costs(INR)	49218	58852	66327	79958	94545
Fare Revenue(INR)	50619	62334	70744	80149	90750
Other Revenue(INR)	6601	8006	18015	13831	9313
Ridership	-	3480000	3853184	4258989	4704689
Passengers/Bus	-	848	848	848	848

4.2.4 Operational statistics

Annual bus kilometers increased by 36% while fleet size increased almost 40% from 2004 to 2009. Ridership increased 35% and revenue went up 45% in the last 5 years. As can be seen from the graphs below bus services have been increasing gradually every year resulting in increased ridership every year.

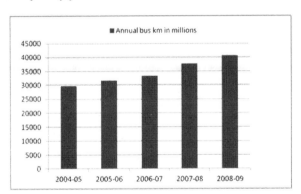

Figure 4.2: BMTC Annual Bus-Kilometers Operated, 2004 - 2009

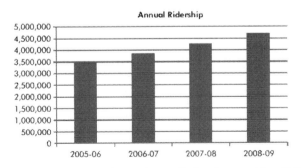

Figure 4.3: BMTC Annual Bus Ridership, 2005 - 2009

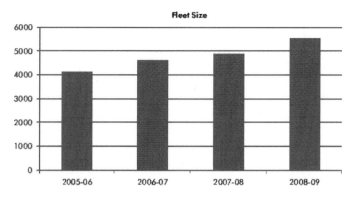

Figure 4.4: BMTC Bus Service Fleet Size, 2005 - 2009

4.3 Issues of coordination and level of services

Infrastructure is the basic physical and organizational structure needed for the operation of services and facilities of a system. For a transportation system, the infrastructure will mean roads and highway network, mass transit system, railways, walking and cycling facilities, waterway network and facilities, airways, etc. Here, a service is nothing but an intangible commodity provided to facilitate the movement of people and goods from one place to the other using the available transportation infrastructure. Presence of integrated transportation infrastructure is a key requirement to ensure provision of effective, smooth, reliable, and safe services.

Decisions about transport systems, the form of urban development, and how land is used impact each other. It is therefore important to take a holistic or in other words a systems approach to transportation infrastructure planning wherein we treat all individual transportation facilities or projects as part of a single interrelated system and thus provide for both safe and fast movement of people and goods from point A to point B in a given physical space. The present state of transport externalities that Indian cities are experiencing today are a result of negligence towards the need for such an approach. Various projects pertaining to individual modes or infrastructure categories are planned and executed in isolation and without understanding their impact over the whole network and system. For example, often flyovers are planned over junctions to improve local conditions but without understanding its impact over the whole citywide network flows. Further alternative analysis with various feasible options is seldom done to ensure provision of the best solution within the given practical constraints. Similarly, master plans are never prepared for integrated public transport systems, rather individual and separate studies are done for introducing say, metro rail or BRTS system without effectively treating them as a single system and considering their impact on each other. Typically, the various infrastructure components have interlinkages and inter-dependencies between each other, for example; the planning for road network expansion has to go hand-in-hand with planning the locations of junctions/roundabouts/flyovers, or planning the locations of drains along with planning of roads is important to avoid digging of roads later, which is quite a common feature in India. Similarly, location of bus or rail terminals require good access and which is dependent on careful planning of other infrastructure. Therefore, it is essential to have integrated planning of transport infrastructure that takes account of and connects all these considerations and helps ensure development of the transportation network and land use in a coordinated manner. In this way, it ensures the most efficient use of public funds and avoids creating unintended impacts. To achieve integration, we need to consider a range of factors for both current and future demand, including:

A. interaction of the transport network and land use

B. performance of the transport system

C. affordability

D. value for money

E. urban design

F. demand management

G. behavioral change

H. accessibility

I. safety

J. network management

K. balance of small-scale and large-scale improvements

L. different modes of transport, e.g., cars, trucks, buses, rail, walking, cycles

M. key stakeholders involved in planning, operating, and using transportation networks

N. sequencing of works.

The benefits of an integrated approach to transport infrastructure planning are:

A. improved transport efficiency and lower costs to deliver on economic growth and productivity goals

B. better management of environmental and social impacts to enhance quality of life.

C. enhancements to the public realm to generate employment and community well-being.

D. efficient use of public funds

E. transport strategies and packages of activities are developed alongside land use strategies and implementation plans.

While there are larger benefits of integration, we also need to be aware of limitations associated with it:

A. the planning exercise becomes more complex and requires use of advanced tools and technologies to do it

B. it requires substantial efforts in bringing various agencies together and develop consensus to do something, which is always very challenging at least in India.

The following are the areas of transit integration so as to achieve successful integration of transport infrastructures.

1. Institutional Integration: Institutional Integration refers to the creation of an organizational framework within which joint planning and operation of transit services can be carried out. Four types of organizational arrangements for implementing institutional integration can be made:

a. Tariff Association: A Tariff Association is suitable only in situations where the partners do not compete and share no territory but rather make end-to-end connections. For instance, the suburban rail system in Mumbai is an example of intraurban transport. A passenger can purchase a single ticket covering western and central railways and pays no penalty for moving between the two railways.

b. Transit Communities: Transit Communities not only bind themselves to a common traffic but co-ordinate routes and schedules and, if appropriate, pool or exchange some rolling stock. The railroads in the United States have long operated under such an arrangement.

c. Transit Federations: Transit Federations establish a formal federated agency and delegate to it certain powers related to planning, tariffs, revenue distribution, and so on. The Munich (Germany) Transit Federation is an example.

d. Mergers: Mergers are portions of companies that are merged into one firm, within which the companies either operate as subsidiaries or lose their identity altogether. Examples are transit services in London and Paris.

Of the several organizational alternatives, mergers appear to be the most effective in achieving a high degree of transit integration. A single authority is able to function more effectively and with greater flexibility than are associations of essentially independent public and private transit operators. Institutional arrangement in India for urban transport infrastructure has been extremely poor and still it is divided among multiple organizations in most of the Indian cities without any umbrella organization to control the quality and quantity of services. A few states have accepted and adopted to create the urban transport authorities with insignificant levels of success. The present level of institutional arrangements provide for competition across modes and infrastructure, whereas it should generally be among the providers of services under same mode. The individual institutions of different modes are stronger in existing set ups than the umbrella organization, and it does not meet the objectives. Also, in many cases, para-transit and other unconventional service supply and operations are not safe and in violation of every rule and which are not seen and controlled by any institution. A massive overhaul of the institutional and management set up with significant innovations in the institutions with defined tasks and targets are required. Qualified land use and transport planners are required to be at the helm of affairs to provide the direction in the institutions, which is grossly lacking at this time. Multi-modal integration is the key for efficiency in urban transport.

Complementaries of modes should be adopted as the first principle of planning multi-modal transport for urban India. Seamless travel with the highest efficiency will be possible only when all the modes share the same objective and urban transport vision. Of course, they would have to be totally transparent in their business model so as to collectively adopt fair division of responsibilities and revenues. In such a system, all effort of marketing, PIS, scheduling, etc. must be a coordinated effort so as to maximize the total business for the benefit of all partners. For a successful multi-modal integration to be achieved, integrated infrastructure, terminal facilities, etc. will have to be developed jointly by all the partner organizations to maximize the integration and the business.

4.3.1 Case example - Mumbai

Currently the Mumbai region's traffic and transportation is managed by different agencies in a fragmented approach (Table 4.7). Though the ultimate aim is to provide an improved level of service, there is no coherent integrated approach in providing transportation services and infrastructure. Further, the necessary investment in the transport sector is not forthcoming due to financial constraints of respective organizations.

Issues, policies, and projects related to urban transport are handled at different levels by several departments and agencies in the region. Railways (central and western) are a central subject whereas public transport by bus/ferry are provided by municipal corporations as part of their mandate and in few places by Maharashtra State Road Transport Corporation (MSRTC). However, the present Motor Vehicle Act enforces certain restrictions on state carriages. The passenger interrelation facilities are poor and seamless travel through integrated ticketing is still a dream.

Table 4.7: Institutional Arrangements in Mumbai Metropolitan Region (MMR) and Their Responsibilities

Agencies	Responsibilities
Mumbai Metropolitan Region Development Authority (MMRDA)	Overall Transportation and Urban Planning in MMR
Municipal Corporation of Greater Mumbai (MCGM)	Road and Other Infrastructure within Greater Mumbai Jurisdiction
Public Works Department	Express Highways
Traffic Police Department	Traffic control and Enforcement
Western/Central Railways	Suburban Rail System
Brihanmumbai Electric Supply and Transport (BEST)	Road Based Public Transport in MCGM
Navi Mumbai Municipal Transport (NMMT)	Road Based Public Transport in Navi Mumbai
Thane Municipal Transport (TMT)	Road Based Public Transport in Thane
Kalyan-Dombivil Municipal Transport (KDMT)	Road based Public transport in Kalyan Dombivili
Maharashtra Maritime Board	Water Transport
Maharashtra State Road Development Corporation	Urban Transport Infrastructure
Maharashtra State Road Transport Corporation	Road Based Public Transport in Maharashtra

Apart from the above, various municipal organizations (corporations/councils), City and Industrial Development Corporation of Maharashtra, Ltd. (CIDCO), have their own jurisdiction to maintain their local roads. Similarly in Bangalore, the Bangalore Metropolitan Land Transport Authority (BMLTA) has been set up to coordinate the transport programs in the Bangalore metropolitan region. However, it has been set up by an executive order of the government. It needs the legislative power to control and act as an apex agency under whose umbrella all projects are coordinated and evaluated as per the benchmarks.

2. Physical Integration: Physical Integration refers to the provision of jointly used facilities and equipment. There are various techniques of physical transit integration, some of them are:

a. Intermodal Terminals: Transfer between modes of transit service is facilitated by intermodal terminals, often described as transportation centers. The most highly developed of these facilities accommodate commuter rail lines, rail rapid transit lines, light rail and streetcar lines, and bus services, with facilities of transfer between themselves or from dial-a-ride or circulation feeder services, taxis, or private vehicles. Parking accommodation is provided to encourage park-and-ride travel, and loading areas permit passengers to be dropped off by car (kiss-and-ride). Appropriate provisions for bicycles and pedestrians are also provided at the terminals. Where single-fare systems for all transit modes have been established, passengers move freely among different services without being stopped by barriers or turnstiles.

b. Transit Shelters: Transit shelters range from simple weather-protection structures on surface transit routes to mini-terminals at important stops and transfer points. The more complex facilities may provide automatic ticket vending machines, free direct-line telephone connections to a centralized information service, locater maps, posted routes and schedules, and promotional material on reduced-fare multiride passes or special excursions.

3) Network Integration: Network integration involves application of management techniques to optimize the allocation of transit resources and coordinate services. The techniques of operational integration include (among others):

a. Coordinated Routing and Scheduling: Routing and Scheduling for high-capacity, long-haul modes, such as commuter rail and rail rapid transit, are considered as the main system and buses act as a feeder to the rail system. Accordingly, the integrated route network is planned by generating feeder bus routes for each rail station. Also, the schedules of trains and buses are coordinated to minimize transfer time between the two modes.

b. Rationalization of Redundant Services: The wasteful duplication of transit service by competing systems is eliminated and resources are redeployed to reduce headways on existing routes and extend services into new areas.

c. Information Integration: Information on routes, schedules, fares, and transfer points for all transit modes and services throughout the urban area is provided by a centralized source. Information services include route maps, timetables, fare schedules, promotion materials, uniform street signs, vehicle identification, displays at stops, transfer points, and major stations, and telephone inquiry answering service. Providing integrated information during every leg of the journey is important to make them attractive (Figure 4.5).

d. Fare Integration: A single, areawide fare structure is established that permits riders to purchase one ticket at the beginning of the trip and transfer freely among all modes or lines of service within the system. For example, in Berlin, Germany (Figure 4..6) one can buy a transit ticket and travel seamlessly between metro (surface as well as underground), bus, tram, and ferry.

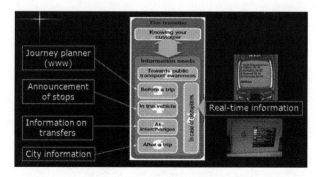

Figure 4.5: Information Integration

Figure 4.6: Fare Integration in Berlin, Germany

4.4 Funding pattern

The development of public transport has been widely recognized to achieve environmental, social, and economic sustainability in cities in developed and developing countries (Cervero, 1998; Vuchic, 2005). However, the emphasis on environmental and social sustainability of public transport is frequently compromised due to a focus on financial sustainability (Buehler & Pucher, 2011). Comprehensive public transport infrastructure is expensive to build and costly to operate (White, 2002; Ubbels and Nijkamp, 2002). Moreover, the costs to public transport agencies have increased significantly with the broadening of policy goals, and, therefore, many public transport systems are struggling for funding.

Traditional methods of funding, such as public sector funding, subsidies, and revenue from fares are not sufficient to make improvements to public transport infrastructure and innovative funding mechanisms are, therefore, demanded. This problem is made more challenging because public transport is generally not a profitable investment for the private sector. Often public transport systems use low fares as a means of promoting their use which require government subsidies. There are different methods of funding options, and they are mentioned below:

a. Traditional public transport funding options

b. Innovative options to fund public transport.

4.4.1 Traditional public transport funding options

Traditional options used to fund PT includes: subsidies, government funding, and fare box revenue.

4.4.1.1 Subsidies

Subsidies are very simple, a government allocates funds paid in income or corporate taxes to public transport systems that usually run at a financial loss the subsidies ensure that the systems can continue to operate even if they cannot be profitable (Ubbels and Nijkamp, 2002; Ubbels et al., 2001). Subsidies have been used to increase public transport use in order to reduce environmental externalities like air and noise pollution, greenhouse gas (GHG) emissions, and congestion. In this situation, benefits are broadening to those who do not even use the public transport services (Serebrisky, 2009). Although subsidies create social and environmental benefits, the economic costs are progressively increasing. For example the provision of low fares through subsidies on public transport in Madrid has decreased the amount of revenue from users yet operational costs are increasing (Manuel et al., 2009). Subsidies can also lead to inefficiencies and are viewed as an inferior good.

In summary, subsidies have an important role in public transport, but it is not sustainable to expect long-term funding from subsidization to increase or even remain at the same level. This is due to increasing competition for government funding from the priority areas of education and health.

4.4.1.2 Fares

The collection of fares allows public transport operators to reclaim the cost of operating the system. However, the fare box revenue is usually insufficient to pay for both the capital cost and running expenses of a modern mass transit system (Wetzel, 2006). For example, in the U.S., fares pay for an average of only 35-42 percent of operating costs (but not capital costs) of public transport, while in Europe fares cover an average 45-48 percent of total operating costs (Pucher et al., 1983; van Reevan, 2008). Despite these trends, efficient public transport systems perform very well. The Hong Kong and Singapore public transport systems operate at profit while German cities cover two thirds of their operating costs from fare box revenue.

In order to plan fares for a given transit system, it is necessary to define what the fares should achieve. The basic objectives for a fare system may be the following:

a. to attract the maximum number of passengers

b. to generate the maximum revenue for the transit agency

c. to achieve specific goals, such as increasing the mobility of the labor force, students, or seniors, improving access among certain areas, promoting the use of a more efficient transit mode, etc.

The common requirements and constraints that must often be considered in setting up fares include the following:

1. Elasticity of demand may limit the choice of fare level and structure; the quality of service and price of competing modes play a major role in passengers willingness to use transit at a given fare level.

2. Equality among transit travelers in terms of value of services (trip length, local or express, comfort level, safety, and security), versus the fare paid by different users groups. This may be an important factor for individual users, as well as for groups of population.

3. Social and political aspects or the need for service and the ability to pay by different population groups often play an important role.

4. Fares should be understandable and convenient for passengers to pay.

5. Fare type should allow easy and low-cost collection and control by the agency.

The process of fare collection—the locations and methods of collecting fares and control of payments by passengers—has a major impact on passenger convenience, on vehicle standing (dwell) times at transit stops, and on the cost of collecting revenue. Street transit mostly bus operations are particularly affected by the delays fare collection may cause at transit stops. When fares are collected in stations usually rail, fare collection has no impact on boarding, but the cost of collection may be high if it involves personal or complicated equipment. Self service systems and the use of smart cards may avoid most of these disadvantages when they can be applied.

4.4.1.3 Fare structure

Fare structures are classified on the basis of the relationship between fare amount and distance traveled on a transit line. Using this criterion, there are two main structures: flat fare and graduated fare. The latter can be further subdivided into zonal and sectional fare. Flat fare is a constant amount independent of trip length. In contrast, zonal and sectional fares change with distance traveled on the transit network. The three types of fare structures are shown schematically in Figure 4.7.

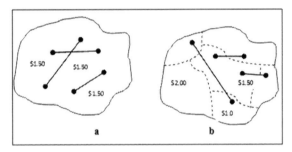

Figure 4.7: Schematic Presenting of Alternative Fare Structures a) Flat Fare; b) Zonal Fare

4.4.1.4 Flat fare

As the name implies, a flat fare is constant regardless of the distance a passenger travels on a single vehicle or throughout the transit network. The flat fare is the simplest possible fare; therefore, it is easy for passengers to understand and use. If it is used for individual lines, it is usually collected at fare gates in a station or upon boarding the transit vehicle. Thus, supervision of payment is easy, the work of fare collectors or vehicle operators is simple, and the boarding process is rather fast.

The basic disadvantage of a flat fare is that it is a fixed amount that does not in any way reflect the quantity of service that the rider receives: a passenger traveling three street blocks pays the same amount as a passenger traveling 8 or 10km.

4.4.1.5 Graduated fares

To avoid the inherent limitation of the flat fare, the inequity of short-distance riders actually subsidizing long distance riders and inability to collect additional revenue from the latter group, graduated fares can be used. Graduated fares can include many variations, but as noted above, there are two basic types: zonal fare and sectional fare. They are described in the following two sections.

4.4.1.6 Zonal fare

The simplest method for charging graduated fares proportionally to the lengths of passenger trips is achieved by dividing the city or urban area into fare zones, sometimes two (central and outlying), sometimes more. Then one fare applies to passenger trips wholly within a single fair zone, a higher fare applies to passenger crossing from one zone to another, an even higher applies to passengers whose trip is across two fare zone boundaries, etc.

The main advantage of a zonal fare structure is that it provides a uniform base fare for a given small geographic area, as well as a correspondingly higher amount of revenue from longer trips. In comparison with a flat fare, a zonal fare has the advantage of charging increasing amounts for longer trip lengths. This makes the fare more equitable and acceptable to the users. Consequently, zonal fares usually result in both attraction of higher patronage and collection of greater revenue than flat fares.

4.4.1.7 Sectional fare

Another way of making fares related to travel distance is obtained by dividing transit lines into sections. The fares then increase with the number of sections traveled. Since sections are usually shorter and fare increments smaller than zone diameters, sectional fares are even more closely related to travel distances than zonal fares. On the other hand, sectional fares are correspondingly more complicated to compute, collect, and control than zonal fares. Consequently, sectional fares often result in longer fare collection times, require more personnel, and allow greater opportunity for evasion of full fare payment. The fare system of most of bus operators in India like BMTC is based on the sectional fare system.

To recapitulate, both zonal and sectional fares have amounts that vary with trip lengths, but they are computed differently: zonal fares are determined on the basis of geographically defined zones, while sectional fares are based on the distance traveled in a single transit line.

4.4.1.7.1 Comparison of the three basic fare structures

The preceding description of the three basic types of fare structures shows that each has its advantages and shortcomings. In general, there are major differences between flat and graduated fares and minor differences between the two types of graduated fares, zonal and sectional. The main differences can be summarized in the below Table 4.8.

4.4.1.8 General taxes

General taxation is the most widely used traditional form of funding for public transport (Mills, 1991; Ubbels and Nijkamp, 2002). Although, subsidies are typically funded from general taxation, it is important to recognize that general taxes are also used for wider infrastructure development (ibid). The most widely used general taxes include income tax rates (property taxes) and goods and services taxes.

On the other hand, general tax has been perceived to be an appropriate approach to mitigate unsustainable transport behavior as this form of funding message is effective in discouraging private car use. This is because, using taxes to fund public transport means that the majority of people, regardless of whether or not they use public transport are paying for and making the service cheaper for patrons (Buehler and Pucher, 2011).

Table 4.8: Comparison of Trade-offs among Alternative Fare Structure Types and Their Optimal Applications

Characteristics		Types of Fares		
		Flat	Zonal	Sectional
Important Characteristics	Equity	Poor	Good	Very good
	Passenger attraction	Good	Very good	Very good
	Revenue collection	Variable	Good	Very good
	Simplicity of collection	Excellent	Fair - good	Poor
	Simplicity of control	Excellent	Fair	Poor
	Simplicity for passengers	Excellent	Fair - good	Poor
Desired Conditions	Line length	Short (<5km)	Medium	Long
	Network type	Ubiquitous	Dividible in zones	Long line
	Travel distance	Short	Variable	Variable

4.4.2 Innovative options to fund public transport

Increasingly, fare box revenue, subsidies, and government funding are not enough to build public transport infrastructure and operate the system. Therefore, local based innovative charges and taxes have been introduced where some or all of the revenue is directed to public transport (Enoch et al., 2005; Tsukada and Kuranami, 1994; UITP, 2003). These innovative funding options for public transport are assessed under four headings: beneficiary pays development taxes/funds; polluter pays carbon taxes/funds; public transport operation taxes/funds; and private sector and other transport taxes and/or funds. Under each category a variety of options are discussed.

4.4.2.1 Beneficiary pays development taxes/funds

Beneficiary pay for public good taxes have traditionally been used to fund services such as police, fire services, and ambulances which cannot be provided on a market-exchange basis. Many projects and some elements of public transport are also funded on this basis (Enoch et al., 2005). Within this beneficiary pay category a number of options are available, many with their own subcategories. These are:

1. Property taxes/rates
2. Land acquisition along public transport routes
3. Smart tax
4. Off-set charges
5. Student surcharges

4.4.2.2 Polluter pays carbon taxes/funds

1. Fuel charges
2. Regional fuel tax
3. Road pricing
4. Parking charges and fines
5. Fee on parking buildings
6. Vehicle registration fee
7. VKT taxes
8. Emission charges

4.4.2.3 Public transport operational and infrastructural taxes/fund

There are a number of options available to increase funds from public transport operations and infrastructure. These include:

1. Reprioritizing transport funding
2. Public transport trust fund
3. Railway development fund
4. Improving public transport network
5. Multimodal passes
6. Higher usage through modern services
7. Leasing public transport workshops
8. Advertising
9. Naming of routes and bus stops (naming rights)
10. Tourism
11. Fee on HOV lane use

4.4.2.4 Private sector taxes/funds

A number of options are available to increase funds from private sector organizations. These are:

1. Public-Private Partnership (PPP)
2. Privatization
3. Competitive tendering

4.4.2.5 Other taxes/funds

1. Visitor tax
2. Payroll tax
3. Cross-utility financing
4. Consumption tax
5. Luxury car tax

4.5 Differences in scenario with respect to developed countries

An efficient transportation system is essential for a country's development especially in urban areas that contribute to the majority of GDP of a country. The past decade saw enormous developments in the transportation infrastructure in India. This section evaluates the current state of mobility between developing (India) and developed countries based on the aspects of demography and economy, transportation policy and transport costs, and transport demand and transport supply.

For the comparative analysis, the recent history, status quo, and future prospects of mobility patterns in the BRIC countries (Brazil, Russia, India, and China), the USA and Germany is taken, the network aims at overcoming barriers for making existing information on transport and mobility useful for decision makers.

The analysis of developing countries, taking India as example and the following 5 cities comparative analysis is made, i.e., Delhi, Bangalore, Lucknow, Indore, and Guwahati. The main points are listed below.

a. A comprehensive analysis of the current mobility trends in five Indian cities and the variations observed between the already saturated cities like Delhi and Bangalore and the rapidly developing tier 2 cities of Lucknow, Indore, and Guwahati.

b. The relationship between the observed mobility trends and the underlying factors responsible for the tends.

c. The implications of these trends to provide a base for planning and policy level decisions. India is urbanizing at a fast pace. As per the census of India, in 2011, there were a total of 53 cities with a population of more than a million and this number is expected to rise to 68 by 2030 (McKinsey and Company, 2008). To keep pace with this rapid growth in the cities, the Indian government has launched massive urban infrastructure development schemes like Jawaharlal Nehru National Urban Renewable Mission (JNNURM), National Urban Transport Policy, etc. and has allocated an investment of 12,04,172 crore INR (221 billion US$) for transport sector up to 2018 (Planning Commission, 2013). These schemes are aimed at improving the overall urban development in India with a special focus on transportation.

India has traditionally been a transit and NMT oriented country, but is now seeing a sharp growth in private vehicle ownership, especially in urban areas. The public transportation systems in most of the cities are not enough and are encouraging the use of private vehicles. The cities have a peak hour travel speed of 15-20 kmph and the heterogeneous traffic makes the condition worse. With inadequate provisions for cycle and foot paths, and the congestion levels this high, the Indian roads have become practically unusable for cycle and walking. Due to this, people have no choice but to use private modes of travel. Along with all these, the number of fatalities due to road transport accidents is increasing year after year.

4.5.1 Comparative analysis

To enable comparative analysis the overall data collected should be correlated with the trends observed in the key indicators with the underlying factors responsible for them, as shown in Figure 4.8. Relationships were also derived based on the basic understanding of the region and its behavior. Comparisons have been made between India and other developing countries like China and Brazil and some of the developed countries like Japan, Germany, the UK, and the USA. This has been done in order to provide an understanding about how similar is India's growth path with other developing countries and where India stands with respect to some of the developed countries.

4.5.2 Data collection process in India

Data collection made in Indian cities is based on the following indicators as shown in Figure 4.8.

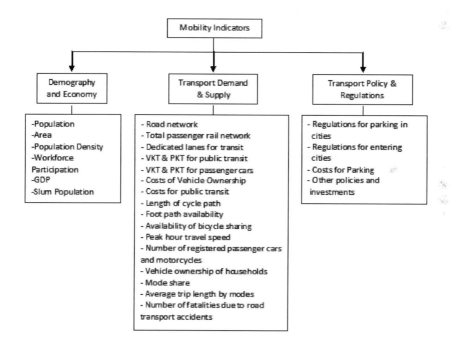

Figure 4.8: Categories of Mobility Indicators

Source: Census of India 1981-2011

4.5.2.1 Demography and economy

India has been one of the fastest growing countries in the world in terms of population. It has 3 of the 10 most populated cities in the world (United Nations, 2011) and unlike some of the developed nations like Japan or Germany where the annual growth rate of population is close to zero, the population in India is growing at a rate of 1.4% annually. Figure 4.9 shows the population for the five cities from 1971 to 2011. The population of the cities vary from almost a million in Guwahati to more than 16 million in Delhi. There has been a steep growth in population since 1991, especially in the cities of Bangalore, Delhi, and Indore where it has almost doubled in two decades. The sudden population growth in these cities has posed a high demand for transport. It has also caused unplanned development in these cities leading to an increased need for travel. Such growth, if not supplemented by an equivalent growth in transport supply, leads to reduced mobility levels impacting the social and economic growth in the cities.

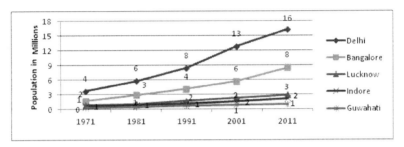

Figure 4.9: Population of Sample Cities 1981-2011
Source: Census of India 1981-2011
Note: The 1981 data for Guwahati has been extrapolated as census data was not collected in 1981; for Delhi, only national capital territory area has been included.

Table 4.9 shows the area, density, workforce participation, and the per capita GDP for the study cities. There is high variation in the size as well as density, with Delhi being more than five times as big and thrice as dense as Guwahati. Size and density are two of the most basic factors that have an impact on the mobility behavior. The size of a city directly influences the trip lengths and subsequently the choice of mode for travel whereas the density plays an important role in determining the transport demand like the capacity of public transit and road infrastructure required. For instance, a small but dense city requires greater supply of public transit in terms of its capacity but not necessarily longer trip lengths.

The workforce participation, i.e., percentage of population working depicts the need for work based trips and a higher workforce participation implies higher mobility demand especially in peak hours. At a national level, India has a workforce participation rate of 39%, which is much lower compared to most of the developed countries like the U.S., Japan, and Germany or even developing countries like China and Brazil where this percentage is more than 50% (World Bank, 2011). Among the study cities, Bangalore leads with a rate of 38.5%, followed by Guwahati and Delhi. In terms of per capita GDP, India scores very low (1,509 USD) compared to the developed countries of Germany (44,021 USD), U.S. (48,112 USD) or even developing nations like China (5,445 USD) (World Bank, 2011). The GDP indicates the purchasing power of the people and cost of travel as a proportion of GDP decides the choice of modes available. The per capita GDP for the five cities is slightly higher for the cities compared to the national average. The values are reflective of the trend observed in workforce participation for the five cities. It has been established that the per capita GDP is directly proportional to the per capita mobility (Schafer, 1998). Higher income enables more leisure based travel. In India, with GDP on the lower side, and most of the fuel imported, the proportion of income spent on travel is much higher than many of the countries. People are hence compelled to use public transport due to affordability issues.

Table 4.9: Demographic and Economic Indicators for Sample Cities

City	Area(sq km)	Density(persons per sq km)	Workforce Participa-tion(2001)	Per Capita GDP*(2008-09)
Delhi	1,483	11,014	32.8%	Rs. 101,381
Bangalore	1,241	6,851	38.5%	Rs. 147,250
Lucknow	530.4	5,470	27.6%	Rs. 39,534
Indore	505.3	4,290	32.1%	Rs. 65,782
Guwahati	264	3,669	35.1%	Rs. 45,813**

Source: Census of India (2011); RITES (2011); LDA (2005); MP Town and Country Planning Office (2008); Guwahati City Development Plan (2006); Government of NCT of Delhi (2009); Government of Uttar Pradesh (2006); Business Standard (2013); Directorate of Economics and Statistics, Karnataka; Directorate of Economics and Statistics, Uttar Pradesh; Directorate of Economics and Statistics, Madhya Pradesh; Directorate of Economics and Statistics, Assam (2013).

Even though the per capita GDP is slightly higher for the cities, the income is distributed unevenly. There is a lot of disparity between rich and poor in India and the cities have a high percentage of their populations living in slums (Figure 4.10). The urban poor are often deprived of the basic means of mobility. For most of them, the low public transportation cost is also not affordable, and they rely on cycle/walk trips. The trip lengths are hence limited to short distances. This further reduces the economic opportunities available to them and hinders their economic growth.

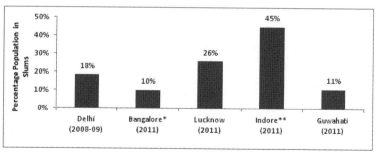

Figure 4.10: Percentage of Population Living in Slums

*Source: Directorate of Economics and Statistics, Delhi (2009); RITES (2011); Lucknow Municipal Corporation, DUDA; DMG Consultancy Services (2011); Guwahati Metropolitan Development Authority. *Although reported as 10%, according to Bruhat Bengaluru Mahanagar Palike, this percentage is more than 30% **Though reported as 45%, the actual percentage of slums for Indore are around 20-25% as many of the designated slums have now been rehabilitated.*

4.5.3 Transport demand and supply

4.5.3.1 Mode choice behavior

Indian cities differ significantly from their counterparts in developed countries in terms of traffic composition. India has mixed traffic comprised of vehicles of various sizes and speeds sharing the same right of way. Public transit and NMT together constitute the majority of trips in Indian cities. Also, unlike most of the developed countries, two wheelers are a very popular mode of travel in Indian cities. Figure 4.11 shows the modal split in the five study cities. Bigger cities of Delhi and Bangalore have a higher transit usage while the smaller cities have a higher two wheeler penetration. Paratransit is still a popular mode of travel in most cities, especially for short distances. It is often used as a substitute to public transit in cities where the transit supply is not sufficient.

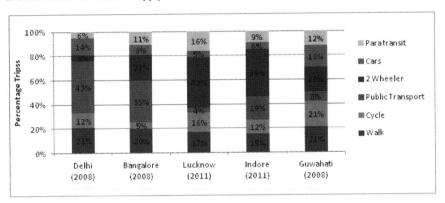

Figure 4.11: Mode Share by Various Modes
Source: Ministry of Urban Development(2008); UMTC (2012); RITES (2012).

Having established the basic mode choice behavior in the five sample cities, we would now go through each of these modes one by one for a detailed understanding.

4.5.3.2 Non-motorized transport

As shown in Figure 4.11, irrespective of city size, Indian cities have a high share of cycle and walk trips ranging from 25% to 42% in the five sample cities. Looking at the cities from the developed countries, these values are much higher compared to the cities in the U.S. (9.5% for Los Angeles, 10.2% for Chicago), and comparable to some of the European cities (32.1% for Berlin, 39% for Paris) and Japanese cities (37.4% for Tokyo) (ifmo, 2013). Despite such a high share of NMT trips, there is a massive lack of infrastructure required to support such trips. Table 4.10 shows the length of cycle paths and the proportion of roads with footpaths for each of the sample cities. These values are much lower compared to the cities around the world, where walk and cycle trips are encouraged by providing safe and clean foot paths and segregated bicycle lanes.

Table 4.10: Demographic and Economic Indicators for Sample Cities

City	Length of Cycle Path (in km)	Share of Roads with Foot Path
Delhi	34.03	60%
Bangalore	45	80%
Lucknow	43.7	40.4%
Indore	40	24%
Guwahati	0	47.9%

Source: *Planning for Non-motorized Transport in Cities - DIMTS-UITP Symposium, 2010; DDA (2007); Central Road Research Institute, Delhi; Bruhat Bengaluru Mahanagara Palike; Mobility Indicators, DULT, 2010-11; UMTC (2012); Indore Municipal Corporation; RITES (2012); Wilbur Smith Associates (2008); Guwahati Metropolitan Development Authority*

Even at the places where these cycle paths and foot paths have been provided, they are often occupied by hawkers and utilized for on-street parking. Also, the pavement surfaces are not up to the mark. The pedestrians and cycle users are hence forced to share the same right of way with bigger vehicles thereby increasing the risk of road accidents. Also with the heavy traffic in most of the cities, crossing the road becomes an issue for NMT users. The NMT mode share hence, is expected to decline in all categories of Indian cities in near future (Ministry of Urban Development, 2008).

A bicycle sharing system is one concept that could be adopted and promoted as a way of sustaining and increasing the bicycle usage in the cities. Currently, the awareness of bicycle sharing systems is very negligible in Indian cities. In the cities of Bangalore and Delhi, it is being promoted as a feeder to metro systems. However, it has not been very successful until now. Smaller cities like Indore and Lucknow have more of a bicycle renting system where one can use and return the cycle to the same station/shop at minimal charges. However, such a system is limited to a closed user group at most locations and is limited to low income areas, some of them around transport terminals like bus stands, railway stations, etc.

Many studies in the past have highlighted the need for developing NMT infrastructure to cater to the needs of high share of the NMT users in India (Reddy and Balachandra, 2012; Pucher et al., 2005; Singh, 2005). Santos et al. suggest a lot of physical measures that could be used to make NMT travel more attractive. Some of them which could be adopted in Indian cities include making the streets safer, cleaner, and well-maintained with attractive street furniture, safe crossings with shorter waiting times, dedicated cycle paths, lower speed limits, etc.

4.5.3.3 Public transit

Along with NMT, public transit is another heavily used mode of travel in India, especially in the bigger cities like Delhi and Bangalore (Figure 4.11). Indian cities have an advantage of having a much higher share of public transit compared to the cities around the world e.g., 4.5% in Chicago, 2.3% in Los Angeles, 15.8% in London, 23.6% in Berlin, and 30.7% for Tokyo (ifmo, 2013). However, for most of the Indian cities, buses are the only means of public transportation. Most of these buses are government operated and are run by the respective state transport undertakings (STUs). The concept of metro rail is relatively new to India. It was first introduced in the city of Kolkata in 1984. Following its success, Delhi started the operation of its metro system in 2002 and is now running successfully for a length of 187 km. Bangalore has also introduced a metro line in 2011, which is yet to be fully developed. Some of the Indian cities like Mumbai and Hyderabad, which are not included in this study, have a successfully running suburban rail system.

Table 4.11: Annual Vehicle km by Urban Public Transport

City	Mode	Annual Vehicle km (2011)	Passenger km Traveled Per Day (2011)	Passenger km Traveled by Public Transport (2011) Per Population Per Day
Delhi	Bus	292.07 million km	24.81 million km	1.52 km
	Metro	47.8 million km	270.12 million km	16.56 km
Bangalore	Bus	465.5 million km	62.73 million km	7.38 km
	Metro *	NA	NA	NA
Lucknow	Bus	16 million km	1.23 million km	0.42 km
Indore**	Bus	9.24 million km	1.27 million km	0.58 km
Guwahati**	Bus	3.907 million km	0.32 million km	0.33 km

*Source: CIRT (2011); Delhi Metro Rail Corporation Limited; Bangalore Metropolitan Transport Corporation; Uttar Pradesh State Road Transport Corporation; RITES (2012); Assam State Road Transport Corporation; RITES (2011b) Note: For buses, this includes data from State Transport Undertakings only and does not take into account the private bus service providers *Metro system for Bangalore was introduced in October 2011; hence it has not been included here.*

The cost per passenger km as a proportion of the per capita GDP is 0.00040% and 0.00055% for Delhi and Bangalore, respectively. Whereas in cities from developed countries, even though the fuel prices are much lower, this ratio is much higher (0.0075% for London, 0.0048% for Berlin, 0.0027% for Tokyo) (ifmo, 2013). But as mentioned earlier, even the low public transportation cost is not affordable to many of the urban poor. Table 4.12 gives a comparative view of the cost of public transport in the five sample cities for a distance of 10 km. Air-conditioned buses are available only in Delhi, Bangalore, and Lucknow.

Table 4.12: Cost of Traveling a 10 km Distance in Public Transport

City	Ordinary Bus	Express Bus/Low Floor Bus	A/C Bus	Metro
Delhi	Rs. 10	Rs.10	Rs. 20	Rs. 16
Bangalore	Rs. 14	-	Rs. 50	-
Lucknow	Rs. 10	-	Rs. 15	NA*
Indore	Rs. 12	-	-	-
Guwahati	Rs. 11	Rs. 15	-	-

*Source: Delhi Transport Corporation; Delhi Metro Rail Corporation; Uttar Pradesh State Road Transport Corporation; Atal Indore City Transport Services, Ltd.; Assam State Transport Corporation *Bangalore metro serves only 7km presently the fare for which is Rs.*

15

It is interesting to note that even though the cost is highest for Bangalore and Delhi, the services are very popular with a mode share of more than 4% (Figure 4.11). The air-conditioned buses in these cities are operated in order to cater to the needs of people in the middle income group. In both Bangalore and Delhi, around 400 out of a fleet size of 6000 buses are air-conditioned. In Bangalore, these buses are especially popular among the IT professionals.

The sudden population growth in the cities (Figure 4.9) has posed high demand on public transit. The growth in public transit in most cities has not been sufficient to cater to the increased demand and is now resulting in the growth in private vehicle ownership (Singh, 2005). The increased congestion due to this and hence the decreased speed and efficiency of buses further make public transit less attractive. The government is making an effort to solve this problem by providing reserved transit routes in the form of bus rapid transit lanes and metro rails in many Indian cities. Currently, very few Indian cities have reserved transit routes. These are summarized in Table 4.13, along with the values for some of the developed cities. For most Indian cities, they are still under construction and are yet to be fully developed. Among the five sample cities only Delhi and Bangalore have reserved transit routes. Some of the other Indian cities like Mumbai, Kolkata, and Ahemdabad have them in place and many cities like Indore, Bhopal, Pune, etc. have plans of introducing them in the near future.

Table 4.13: Length of Rapid Transit (km) per Million Population (2011)

City	Length of Reserved Transit Routes (m) Per 1000 Population
Bangalore (Metro)	0.82
Kolkata (Metro)	1.81
Ahmadabad (BRTS)	7.43
Delhi (Metro +BRTS)	10.07
Mumbai (Suburban Rail)	16.17
Berlin	140.16
Tokyo	92.39

Source: Delhi Metro Rail Corporation Limited; Bangalore Metro Rail Corporation Limited; Central Road Research Institute, Delhi; ifmo (2013).

As the government introduces new transit modes in the cities, it is important to integrate the various public transit modes to provide an optimized network. Currently, both in Delhi and Bangalore, the bus and the metro services are operated by different organizations leading to overlapping of routes and competition. The time tables and routes need to be organized so as to provide seamless intermodal travel. Integrated ticket systems are also important to make intermodal travel more attractive and convenient. Successful examples of such systems can be found in Singapore and London.

4.5.3.4 Road infrastructure

India has an average road length of 3.87 m per person. The road density is much higher for developed countries with U.S., Japan, and Germany having a road network length of

21, 9, and 8 m per person, respectively (Ministry of Road Transport and Highways, India; Institute for Mobility Research, Germany). Because of the higher population density, this ratio is significantly lower for urban areas. Guwahati, closely followed by Delhi have the highest road length to population ratio among the five study cities (Figure 4.11). In terms of absolute length, Delhi has the longest and the densest road network among the five cities whereas it is the least for Indore. Guwahati has the highest road network among the smaller cities.

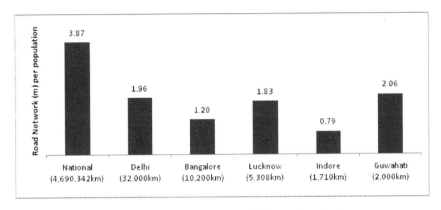

Figure 4.12: Road Length (m) Per Population

4.5.3.5 Fatalities due to road accidents

The number of fatalities due to transport related accidents for India is alarmingly high. In 2011, a total of 142,485 people died due to road transport accidents, which is the highest for any country in the world (Ministry of Road Transport and Highways, 2008-2011). It is observed that the fatalities per million population due to road accidents is much higher in case of second order metropolitan cities like Indore, Guwahati, and Lucknow (Figure 4.13) compared to the bigger cities of Delhi and Bangalore. The lower fatality rate in bigger cities is also explained by the higher public transit mode share, which is less prone to accidents. A majority of these fatalities involve pedestrians, cyclists, and two wheeler users. Compared to the national average (118 per million population), the fatality rate is higher for most of the cities. Again, it is interesting to note that even though the private vehicle ownership in India is much lower, the road fatalities per million population is much higher than what is found in the countries of Germany (45), Japan (45), and Australia (61) (International Transport Forum, 2011). The major factors responsible for such high accident rates include nonabidance of basic rules of road safety in the country due to lack of enforcement. Only 27% of Indian drivers wear seat belts, whereas only 50% wear helmets (WHO, 2011). The road infrastructure also is not up to the mark with very little importance given to road safety.

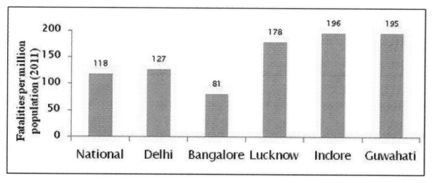

Figure 4.13: Fatalities Per Million Population Due to Road Transport Accidents (2011)

4.5.3.6 Congestion

All the cities, irrespective of size, are facing similar congestion issues. Figure 4.14 shows the peak hour travel speed for the five sample cities. The speeds range from 15 kmph in Lucknow to a maximum of 20 kmph for Guwahati. Although the car ownership rate is much lower compared to many international cities, the congestion levels are almost the same, one of the reasons being insufficient road infrastructure. The increasing congestion encourages people to use personal vehicles over public transit, which in turn is adding to the congestion in cities. Although the road length per population is much higher for Guwahati and Delhi, the congestion levels are similar. Studies have shown that expanding road infrastructure increases the congestion levels rather than decreasing them, by inducing travel demand (Hills, 1996). Hence, the solution lies not in increasing the supply but in managing the demand. Some of the measures have already been taken in this direction by the Indian government which are discussed in earlier sections.

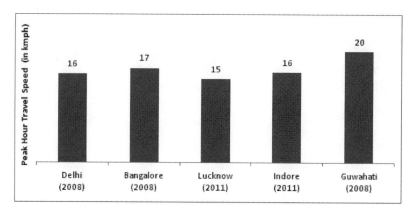

Figure 4.14: Peak Hour Car Travel Speeds

Source: Ministry of Urban Development (2008); UMTC (2012); RITES (2012).

4.5.4 Transport policy and regulations

The rapid urbanization taking place in India has caused the government to take the issue of transportation more seriously and in 2006 the Ministry of Urban Development launched the National Urban Transport Policy with an aim to address mobility needs of the cities. It has given a framework of transportation infrastructure development. The objectives include promotion of integrated land use and transport planning, measures to enable equitable allocation of road space, priority to public transport and non-motorized transport, promotion of intelligent transportation systems, use of technology in public transportation systems and integration of public transportation systems, use of cleaner technologies, reorganization of parking spaces, and increase in parking charges, etc. Jawaharlal Nehru Urban Renewal Mission (JnNURM) scheme launched by the Indian government in 2005 supports the implementation of NUTP by providing financial assistance for transportation infrastructure development projects on a cost sharing basis with the state and local governments. The launch of both of these policies has led to massive improvement in transport infrastructure in India, but they have not been able to completely solve the transportation issues. A lot of measures are planned to curb the rising traffic by deincentivising private vehicle usage and providing alternatives in the form of better public transit. There are plans of introducing metro systems as well as bus rapid transit systems in many of the rapidly growing cities and an investment of 160,329 crore INR is planned for the same by Planning Commission. The 12th five year plan recognizes the Indian urban transport problems of lack of integrated land use and transportation planning, low investment in improvement of public transit and NMT services, and the focus on supply instead of managing transport demand.

Currently, there are a very few schemes to control the use of private vehicles. Among the five cities, only Delhi has regulations for entering the city where commercial vehicles older than 15 years are not allowed to enter the city. Also, only CNG fitted buses/autos/taxis can operate in the National Capital Territory of Delhi (NCTD). There are restrictions on trucks entering the CBD area of a majority of Indian cities during the day time.

Regulations for parking are also not very strong in a majority of Indian cities. On-street parking is a common phenomenon, with as high as 45% of the streets being utilized for parking in Guwahati (Ministry of Urban Development, 2008). Parking is haphazard and a major contributor to congestion in CBD areas of most cities. Some of the cities are constructing multilevel parking spaces to curb this issue. As listed in Table 4.14, the parking charges are very nominal compared to cities from developed countries, where the high parking charges act as a deterrent to the use of personal vehicles. To be used as a demand management tool, it is necessary to increase the charges to a level where they can be used as a disincentive for personal vehicle usage. It has been reported that a 10% increase in parking charges results in an average reduction of 1-3% in vehicle trips (Vaca and Kuzmyak, 2005).

Table 4.14: Average Parking Charges in CBD Area for Sample Cities

City	On-Street/ Off-Street	Shopping Malls
Delhi	Rs.20 for the first two hours (six hours for metro) Rs. 5 for every additional hour	Rs. 40 for weekdays, Rs.50 for weekends, no time limit.
Bangalore	Free of cost for most places. Meters have been installed at 2 streets that charge Rs. 5 for every half hour	4 wheeler Rs. 40 for first 2 hrs and Rs. 10 for every additional hour 2 wheeler Rs. 30 for 2 hrs and Rs 10 for every additional hour.
Lucknow	Rs. 10 for 2 wheeler and Rs. 20 for 4 wheeler for four hours	Rs. 15 for 2 wheeler and Rs. 20 for 4 wheeler for eight hours on weekdays Rs. 20 for 2 wheeler and Rs. 25 for 4 wheeler for eight hours on weekends/holidays
Indore	On street - no charges (free) Off-street - Rs. 10 for 4 hours for cars, Rs 5 for 2 wheelers	Mostly free parking. Have weekend charges at some places - Rs. 20 for 2 wheeler, Rs. 40 for 4 wheeler
Guwahati	Rs.10 for first hour; Rs. 5 for every additional hour	-

Source: Primary Survey

To limit private vehicle usage, the Ministry of Urban Development (2013) has recently released an advisory for the urban local bodies of various Indian cities for the introduction of congestion charging in the central business districts of the cities. It is expected that this will ease out the heavy motor vehicle volume found in the central areas of the cities and at the same time generate funds for transportation infrastructure development.

Summary

This chapter mainly covers the detail concept of the public transport (PT) scenario in a developing country like India. The current perception of India is well explained by taking Bangalore city as an example and implementing the SERVQUAL framework for compilation and analysis. Also the current planning and organization of Bangalore city is covered by taking the performance of BMTC from last several years. The chapter also deals with the level of services and coordination issues by taking Mumbai as the case study. It also shows some light on the different funding patterns adopted and how they are performing. Finally this chapter gives the information about the difference in scenario of India with developed countries, in that the mobility indicators are used such as demography and economy, transport demand and supply, and transport policy and regulations. By comparing the 5 cities of India with these indicators and analyzing the result for further improvements.

Chapter 5

Public Transport Planning in Rural Areas

5.1 Planning strategy

Planning strategy depends upon a number of issues such as the spread of rural areas across the country, the resource base of a rural settlement, the population and growth rate of population, the distance between a settlement and nearby agricultural, industrial, and administrative growth centers, and the current accessibility levels to these growth centers. Thus public transport planning in rural areas is a complex phenomenon. It is quite difficult to consider each and every settlement in planning public transport. In India a district is normally considered as a unit for the purpose of planning and developing transport infrastructure. The same criteria could be followed even while planning a public transport network in rural areas.

5.1.1 Geographical setting of rural areas

In India 70% of the population lives in rural areas. Demographers have estimated that 50-55% of the population will continue to live in rural areas even after the year 2030. This rural population is spread across 543 districts in a geographical area of 3,287,260 sqkm, of India. The noticeable feature is the density of population varies very widely between urban and rural areas. For daily passenger movement the catchment area of an urban area is mostly limited to urban agglomeration, whereas the catchment area of a village stretches for the entire district. For different activities, the village population needs to travel to nearby Mandi (agricultural related trading centers) for agricultural related activity, a taluk or district headquarters for administrative requirements, and nearby business centers for other activities. Thus the village population frequently travels to these 3 activity centers. However, in some cases all 3 activity centers may be located at the same city.

Studies have indicated that if the travel distance is less than 8kms villagers mostly prefer bicycles and if the distance is more than 8kms they prefer a bus or an auto. These decisions are based on the cost of travel as well as affordability. Thus, by considering all these factors rural public transport planning need to be developed.

In India the car ownership rate of the rural population is much less compared to urban areas. However, the recent trend indicates that most of the rich village households are able to own a mechanized 2-wheeler (scooter or motorcycle) for their personal use. The penetration of television networks and mass media into rural India had greatly influenced the thinking and perceptions of rural households regarding education of their children. In recent years the education trips especially for college education has grown substantially. It may be noticed that most of the education trips involve a travel distance between 6-10kms. Surveys reveal that the bulk of these trips are made through public bus transport. The main reason for using a bus is due to concessional (35% of the cost of the trip) travel extended to students in almost all the states of India.

All the states in India are also following bus (public transport) connectivity of all the villages at least twice a day to a nearby urban center. This connectivity is followed in order to accelerate the economic development of the rural areas. However, the service provider of public transport encounters a number of difficulties in the implementation of the above policy guidelines.

5.1.2 Role of public transport in developing countries

A good transport system is vital to a country's development. The development of a country is influenced by accessibility and mobility levels of rural households. This in turn influences how a transport system evolves over a period. Ensuring that the transport system develops in this way is most conducive to the overall development of the country, it can produce far reaching benefits, and conversely, failing to do so will have an adverse effect on development. In rural areas, those who own bicycles tend to use them for journeys up to about 8 kms, beyond which public transport is the preferred mode. Public transport is therefore vital for the vast majority without access to private transport.

Road-based public transport modes include conventional buses, informal paratransit vehicles like autos, taxis, and other human and animal powered vehicles.

The market for public transport services is highly diversified, and can conveniently be divided into three main segments namely short, medium, and long distance travel. Short distance travel includes movement to nearby villages (within the taluk), medium distance travel covers mobility to nearby or adjacent districts and long distance travel includes travel to state headquarters or major towns of importance situated far away from the settlement. Planning of public transport in rural areas are mainly concerned with short and medium distances of travel from a settlement.

5.2 Network planning

Rural public transport network development may be conveniently considered under two headings: purely rural and rural-urban transport. Purely rural transport consists of movement wholly within rural areas, to and from work and transporting goods for domestic use. Rural-urban travel is between rural locations and, usually, the nearest market town, and demand often fluctuates considerably according to the incidence of market days. The main purposes of rural-urban travel are normally business related, principally taking goods to and from market. At this level, many journeys are a combination of passenger travel with freight transport. Thus, much of the traffic could be classified as accompanied freight.

Public transport is widely regarded as a critical infrastructure for villages to integrate with other nearby economic activity centers. Much of the focus in public transport planning is on engineering and operational considerations often linked to scheduling algorithms rather than designing an overall network that is coherent to users. Well planned public transport supported by rigorous design and planning of the network of lines and their interconnections is essential to achieving the task of efficient connectivity between rural settlements with cities in the district. Two broad network strategies which were categorized as radial and dispersed network strategies followed in urban areas could be tried even in public transport network planning in a district.

5.2.1 Transport for school children and college students

Transport demand for schoolchildren and college students are a major issue in the network development. As population increases, the number of children of school age increases both in absolute terms and as a proportion of the total population. Improvements in educational facilities and midday meal programs in India to decrease school dropouts has achieved a substantial number of increases in the number of children attending school. This has resulted in the number of children traveling to and from school increasing at a much faster rate than population growth.

Distances up to ten kilometers are relatively common, while some children travel considerably farther, because of inadequate good colleges. Walking to and from the school becoming practically nil as the distance increases. Many states in India through the provision of subsidized transport are able to reduce school dropouts considerably. The provision of public transport to the requirement of the education sector is creating several difficulties to state owned public transport operators. The demands for exclusive school trips from a settlement are low and the timings mostly defer from other economic activity requirements. This has resulted in huge losses to the operators for running exclusive buses for the requirements of the education sector with subsidized fares.

Sometimes the concession is fully funded by government, but in most cases the transport operators are expected to bear part of the cost themselves. Very often, transport operators, particularly those in the private sector, are unwilling to carry children at peak periods at concessionary fares, since this will mean turning away adult passengers who would pay the full fare. Public bus operators are forced to accept this subsidized travel demand. Thus, there exists a complexity in providing public transport in rural areas in many developing countries.

5.2.2 Dedicated public transport for students

Many states in India operate dedicated passenger transport services for the exclusive use of their students. While these cannot be regarded as public transport services, they are relevant in the sense that the large number of students use public transport and may constitute a significant element of the passengers of transport system. Dedicated school buses may be owned by the government, educational authority, or even by individual schools, or may be chartered from transport operators. The buses which carry students in the early morning could be used to provide other services such that the vehicle utilization and revenue earning could be maximized. However this needs proper planning and scheduling of buses to achieve the satisfaction of many users.

5.2.3 Market segmentation

Public transport users even in villages comprise a large cross-section of the public with different requirements and interested in using buses for different purposes. If only one standard of service is provided, it will meet the requirements of only one section of the population leaving perhaps significant unsatisfied demand. There is scope for more than one standard of service to cater for passengers with different requirements. Substantial requirements of the people can be covered from such segmentation of the market. Different services may have to be planned to cater to the needs of each segment. Many passengers are satisfied with the basic level of service usually provided and are prepared to accept overcrowded, uncomfortable, and unreliable vehicles; since, they could not afford to pay higher fares for a better quality of services. There may be other passengers who are prepared to pay higher fares for a convenient, comfortable, reliable service, with a better quality of service. There may in fact be scope for several levels of services, ranging from those using the most basic type of vehicles, with a high passenger capacity and minimal comfort, to premium quality services offering a high degree of comfort.

5.2.4 Mobility and accessibility

The difference between mobility and accessibility is fundamental to the understanding of rural transport provision. In the past, the thrust of policy formulation has generally been to improve mobility with little consideration given to accessibility issues. The modern approach to transport policy is the reverse.

Hillman et al. (1973) define mobility as the capacity that a person has for getting around. It is clear from this definition that individual circumstances are very important. Thus, mobility depends on personal factors such as age group, purpose of travel, status in the society, and financial parameters of the trip maker and upon the range of transport facilities that are available (Tolley and Turton, 1995). Mobility will change throughout a persons life time (typically being fairly poor during childhood, increasing in adulthood with quite likely the ability to afford a car, and then reducing once again in later stages of life). It is usually measured in terms of the number of trips or journeys made per unit of time (normally in a day or a week).

The demand for mobility and variation in mobility levels over a period of time could be obtained through primary data from different households in a village. Table 5.1 below provides a matrix of mobility measurements for different purposes at different time periods.

Table 5.1: Journey Per Person Per Year and Average Length by Journey Purpose

	Journey Per Person Per Year			Average Journey Length (miles)		
	Year 1	Year 2	Year 3	Year 1	Year 2	Year 3
Commuting for Work	X11	X12	X13	D11	D12	D13
Business	X21	X22	X23	D21	D22	D23
Education	X31	X32	X33	D31	D32	D33
Shopping	X41	X42	X43	D41	D42	D43
Social	X51	X52	X53	D51	D52	D53
Recreation	X61	X62	X63	D61	D62	D63
Total	Xt1	Xt2	Xt3	Dt1	Dt2	Dt3

Source: DETR(1997)

Most of the trips in rural areas could be classified with six different purposes. The changes in the quantum of travel and the average distance for each purpose provide information regarding the economic development of the village and provision of infrastructure at or near the village.

5.2.4.1 Defining accessibility

Accessibility is difficult to define. As Gould (1969) says, accessibility is.. a slippery notion one of those common terms which everyone uses until faced with the problem of defining and measuring it. Daly (1975) defined it as the ease with which people can reach distant but necessary services, whilst Mitchell and Town (1976) define it as the ability of people to reach destinations at which they can carry out a given activity.

Buchan (1992), defines accessibility as being one of the quality-of-life objectives for transport and describes the objective thus:

To encourage and provide a transport system which will give people access to workplaces, to shops and public buildings, to industry and commerce, to facilities of health and other services and to one another.

5.2.4.2 The relationship between mobility and accessibility

Mobility and accessibility have been presented thus far as two completely separate concepts. In reality, however, they are interlinked. Some people in rural areas suffer from both lack of mobility and accessibility. Many people in rural areas have no access to a car and often public transport alternatives are inadequate. There are also many low income people in rural areas who cannot afford to travel far. This is the mobility problem. For these people, however, accessibility is more of a problem because access to many facilities requires the use of a mechanized transport. Thus, as far as rural development is concerned, both aspects need to be addressed if rural areas are to be living and thriving areas with economic activity. Improving mobility and accessibility for those without access to a mechanized mode in rural areas is much more difficult because of the dispersed nature of the centers of population and the fact that the solutions to the problem vary between groups of people living in given rural settlements.

In India the problem of road accessibility is being solved on war footing through the introduction of Prime Minister Gram Sadak Yojana (PMGSY). It is expected that all the settlements in India by 2020, irrespective of population of the settlement, will be provided with an all-weather road.

5.2.4.3 Measuring accessibility

Accessibility is usually measured in terms of journey time or cost, or a composite of the two (sometimes referred to as generalized cost). Thus, accessibility to a hospital can be measured in terms of how long it takes to get there or how much it costs to get there, or a mixture of the two. For some people, the time taken is the most determining factor, for others (pensioners for example), it may be the cost which is most critical in making the journey.

In India since a high proportion of rural areas (65%) reported having a bus stop and a grocery shop within a relatively short walking distance (6 minutes), accessibility could be considered as satisfactory. The quantification of accessibilities to bus services in rural settlements with populations between 500 and 2000 based on the level of service needs to be properly understood and planned. The scoring system is outlined below with evening and Sunday scores added together. The higher the numerical value in the given table indicates higher satisfaction.

Table 5.2: Quantification of Satisfaction for Planning Rural Public Services

Daytime Services		Evening and Sunday Services	
No service	0	None	0
One day a week	1	1 return journey before 6 pm	1
Peak service, 6 days a week	2	As above plus 2 sunday returns	2
Peak service and shopping, 6 day a week	3	Better than 2 hourly evening and	3
4 return journeys per day	4	Sunday services	
Hourly or better service	5		
30 minutes or better	6		
20 minutes or better	7		

Source: TAS(1997)

5.2.4.4 Perspectives on mobility and accessibility in policy

As discussed elsewhere the rural transport policy needs to consider both the people who live in rural areas and those who visit areas for economic activity. The needs of the two groups are likely to be quite different and this needs to be reflected in policy development. The first step is to review the rural transport problem. This is illustrated in Figure 5.1. The policy required could be depicted diagrammatically as shown in Figure 5.2 below.

5.2.4.5 Interrelation between mobility and accessibility

The interrelation between the desired mobility and desired accessibility could be better explained through Figure 5.3.

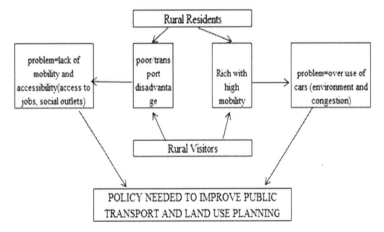

Figure 5.1: The Rural Transport Problem

Source: Stokes et al.1998, Rural Transport Policy

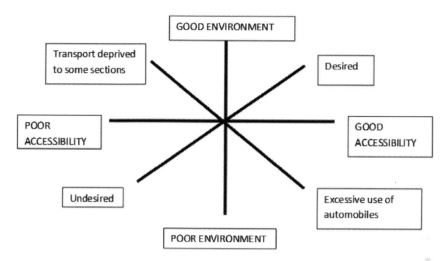

Figure 5.2: The Rural Transport Policy Requirements

Source: Stokes et al.1998, Rural Transport Policy

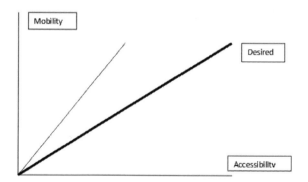

Figure 5.3: The Relation between Mobility and Accessibility

Source: Stokes et al.1998, Rural Transport Policy

It is often assumed that mobility and accessibility refer to the same thing, i.e., that mobility equals accessibility. This is shown by the 45 degree line in Figure 5.3. However, policy should be aimed at reducing the usage of automobile traffic but increasing accessibility to that area.

However, in order to reduce environmental degradation the mobility levels need to be planned properly. Currently the environmental problem does not exists in rural or in cities with less than 0.5 million population. However, if steps are not initiated to promote public transport vigorously, proliferation of mechanized modes for intradistrict and interdistrict travel may create environmental problems in the next two decades even in rural India. The relation between mobility and environment could be diagrammatically presented as shown in Figure 5.4.

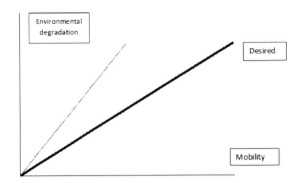

Figure 5.4: The Relationship between Mobility and the Environment

Source: Stokes et al.1998, Rural Transport Policy

With a given technology, environmental problems increase with increasing mobility. Policy should be targeted at reducing the environmental impact of any given level of mobility. This could be done, for instance, by improving technology or by increasing the use of environmentally less damaging vehicles such as buses or trains. The desired policy option is again depicted by the solid line.

There is a relation between income levels of different sections of society and the accessibility levels they enjoy. This relation is diagrammatically represented in Figure 5.5.

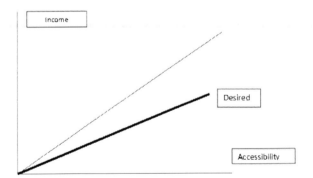

Figure 5.5: Relation between Accessibility and Income

Source: Stokes et al.1998, Rural Transport Policy

Accessibility increases with income as richer people have access to better and improved transport technology, and they can afford to pay for services. Policy should be aimed at increasing accessibility for all levels of income groups. All sections of the public should enjoy a basic level of accessibility and mobility. This could be achieved through increased provision of public transport. The desired policy line is again depicted with a thick solid line in Figure 5.5. This policy helps in the development of inclusive society.

5.2.5 Benefits of public transport network development

The various benefits of implementing an effective rural public transport network is presented in Table 5.3 below.

Table 5.3: Benefits of Rural Public Transport

Item	Benefit
What is the impact of public transport impacts of the proposal?	Public transport will benefit many rural households not owning vehicles.
What will be the impacts on the environment?	The combination of modal switch to public transport will lead to a reduction in pollution. The investment package will target environmental improvements within the district.
What are the impacts in terms of transport economic efficiency?	There is a net economic benifit for all when public transport improvements are added.
What will be the local impacts in terms of employment?	Rural areas likely to develop economically.
What will be the impacts on accessibility?	The investment package will improve accessibility to/from the rural villages.
What will be the impacts in integrating transport modes and services?	Integration of transport modes and services will benifit the investment climate of rural settlements.
What will be the impacts of the proposal against wider government policy?	The proposals integrate with wider government policy on health, education, and the environment.

Thus, in order to bring the rural areas into mainstream of economic activity there is an urgent need that all the rural areas in the country be connected with reliable and sustainable public transport network. In order to achieve this sustainable mobility between rural areas with other nearby towns, a national policy may be more appropriate. The guidelines to develop integrated public transport network to follow certain criteria, norms, etc. This national strategy will provide guidelines for different states in its implementation. The policy should aim at the following aspects:

1. Public transport strategy and an action plan for its implementation during the next 10-15 years.

2. Development of capacity building in village panchayats as well as in municipalities.

3. Identification of the areas of subsidy and quantum of subsidy required to provide sustainable integrated public transport network planning in rural areas.

4. Wherever this is partly in existence the delivery gaps need to be identified and re-addressed.

5. This integrated public transport network may be coordinated with nonmotorized transport (NMT) infrastructure and other transport activities.

6. Piecemeal implementation with a large number of gaps may compromise the effectiveness of the system.

5.2.6 Strategy followed in South Africa in the development of rural public transport network

In South Africa, for the benefit of rural areas an integrated public transport network (IPTN) is put in place under a national guiding framework (NGF). This NGF identifies and focuses on planning and implementation of rural transport network.

1. It will address the implementation gaps and overlaps and consolidate resources and funding.

2. It will address access and mobility through integrated public transport management model.

3. It will document best local practices and provide for appropriate interventions.

4. It integrates transport infrastructure and services through network management.

After its implementation, the improved provision of public transport has achieved the following outcomes

1. KPI (Key Performance Indicators):

Acceptable standard of service

Reduced travel time to work/education and general trips

Acceptable walking time to public transport service

Acceptable waiting time for public transport service

Acceptable cost of transportation.

2. Enhanced social and economy activities:

The improvement of transport systems that will have multiplier effects of increasing accessibility, reducing poverty and enhancing social and economic development.

3. Improved connectivity with good provision of infrastructure:

Safety and reliability of public transport services, differentiated choice of modes, organized and licensed operations, safe roads, and reduced level of accidents

4. Improved status of rural transport planning in the district, responds to new demands

5. Aligned and well-coordinated transportation services/operations, well defined roles for all transport players

6. Reduced level of migration to the metropolitan municipalities, social stability and cohesion

7. Rejuvenating the local economy and tax base and sustaining rural livelihood:

The above example in a developing country has achieved a number of benefits. Thus it is more appropriate to follow a similar strategy in India.

5.2.7 Strategy for rural transport network development in India

Rural settlements are normally spread across the entire nation. India is no exception to this phenomenon. In order to develop a comprehensive rural public transport network, evolving a national policy may be the first step. In India PMGSY policy addresses rural road connectivity which is already in progress. Public transport network development invariably requires good all-weather road networks, it is appropriate to consider rural network as a starting point to plan public transport network covering rural settlements. Most of the states in India are already involved in providing public transport connectivity to many villages. However what is really needed is whether this fits into integrated and sustainable rural development needs to be studied. In India while implementing PMGSY, a core network for a district is prepared connecting all the settlements. This may be considered as a first step in planning public transport network in the district. If required additional bus routes from a particular village may be initiated. A comprehensive rural public transport network development may be initiated at the national level through legislation in the parliament, similar to that of PMGSY. This policy helps in providing resources for implementing the national strategy.

The benefits of this strategy could be summarized with table below:

While developing core public transport network for the entire district covering all settlements, the following criteria may be followed.

1. Simple and direct network structure:

Every village as per their requirements should be connected to nearby economic activity centers.

2. Plan a hierarchy of routes into a network:

Since the demand from rural areas will be meager, a hierarchy of routes may be developed so that from a given settlement to reach far off places, a transport at a nearby economic center will provide opportunities for long distance travel.

3. Plan for consistency and reliability:

This will ensure that rural households can develop upon this network plan with confidence and may increase the patronage in the long run.

4. Coordinate convenient transfers:

This policy will help to minimize long waiting times for multiple journeys.

5. Integrate fare systems with the full journey:

Normally long distance travel by a single bus is less costly than journeys with multiple boardings at two locations. In order to encourage more and more people to use a newly initiated public transport network the fare structure may be integrated. This will help in the long-run to achieve better occupancy ratios and maximize income to public transport operators. This may be attempted initially at least to movements to neighboring districts if not state headquarters.

5.3 Travel demand estimation

There are two terms associated with the measurement of mobility of family or an individual. These two terms are NEED and DEMAND. NEED is a social concept and DEMAND is an economical concept. This distinction could be better understood by considering the food intake of different sections of society. For healthy growth every individual requires to take a minimum quantity of minerals, carbohydrates, and other nutrients, etc. This criterion provides the true estimation of the NEED. However, what a family consumes on an average per day provides the DEMAND for food items of that family. If you compare this DEMAND with NEED for different sections of people there will be wide fluctuations. In some cases the DEMAND is much higher than NEED and in some other sections the DEMAND is much below the NEED. In a society with inclusive growth objectives the difference between DEMAND and NEED should be nil or positive. If you apply the same concept to transport related issues every individual has to undertake some minimum number of trips to achieve social and economic objectives/goals. However, it is very difficult to measure the NEEDS for travel of different sections of society. One simple way to measure this is make public transport free to all individuals. In the long run the demand for travel under such a situation can be taken as NEED for travel. The actual quantum of travel at the current prices provides DEMAND for travel. This process also provides answers to the impact of price on DEMAND.

In addition to this philosophical distinction the actual quantum of travel by public bus depends on routing and scheduling of public bus services from that settlement with that of surrounding villages and towns. Bus transport operators both public and private need to consider this aspect while estimating the fleet strength.

5.3.1 Classification of transport services

The passenger road transport services in general could be broadly divided into four categories on the basis of different characteristics as follows:

a. Interstate

b. Interdistrict

c. Intradistrict and rural and

d. Urban operations

The analysis in this section broadly follows this classification as the characteristics of these segments vary requiring different interventions. The characteristics of each of these services vary widely with respect to vehicle utilization, time of operation, crew requirements, profitability, and major players for the types of services. **This categorization means that these categories would require different types of policy and financial support (in Table 5.4).**

Table 5.4: Classification of Transport Services According to Financial Support and Different Types of Policy

Category	VU (kms/ day)	Service Types	Players	Profitability	Main Competitors to STUs
Interstate	>600	Volvo, luxury deluxe	Public and private	Very high	Private
Interdistrict	300-450	Luxury, express, Volvo	Public and private	Moderate and high	Private
Intradistrict	250-350	Express, ordinary, limited halt	Mostly private, maxi cabs	Low and loss making	Illegal contract buses, maxi cabs
Urban	200-250	Ordinary, limited halt	Mostly private autos	Mostly loss making	Illegal contract buses, maxi cabs

The demand is analyzed for the various sectors of urban operations, intradistrict, rural services, interdistrict services, and interstate operations. The characteristics of each one of these services are quite different with respect to frequency of service, time of service, service quality, willingness to pay, and the expectations of the public, etc.

5.3.2 Demands for intradistrict and rural services

In any road transport undertaking, the maximum number of buses operates as intradistrict and rural services. For example in the case of Andhra Pradesh, APSRTC is roughly operating 50% of their total fleet (10,000 buses out of 20,000) for this service. These rural operations provide two major categories of services. One, by providing accessibility to villages with administrative and economic activity centers at the district level. Two, by providing service within the district between and among the places of importance such as business locations, historical places, linking taluk headquarters and district headquarters, and interlinking other major economic activity locations. Thus, the demand for these services is linked to:

1. Number of settlements in the state
2. Number of economic activity centers in the state

However, it is difficult to estimate the number of activity locations in the state as their number changes and grows with the development of the state. The proxy to this is the size of the rural population undertaking journeys in the state. The number of trips in a rural settlement will be much less compared to urban areas. One bus on an average will be able to cater to four rural settlements. In addition, it is felt that sixty buses may be required per million of population to link various economic activity centers in a state.

These norms are applied to the state of Andhra Pradesh to validate the model in a study done by IIM Banglore. The demand for services as per the model suggested above works out to about 10,250 buses, given the number of settlements at 26,613 and estimated rural population of 60.1 million as of 2006. However, APSRTC is currently running about 10,000 buses to cater to this segment. The recent survey conducted by IIM Bangalore in 9 districts of A.P. clearly brought out that the services are adequate in the sample districts. In addition, a small number of private operators are also providing service in this segment in the state of Andhra Pradesh. This norm is also applied to estimate the fleet strength in three public bus corporations of Karnataka State and the results are in tune with the opinion of policy makers and officials of KSRTC. If this norm is applied at all India levels the demand for bus fleet to cater to this demand during different time periods is presented in the table below. Currently the deficit in this segment is quite high to the extent of 50% of the requirement.

Table 5.5: Bus Fleet for Intra and Rural Operations in India

Item	2006	2011	2016
Number of Settlements	600000	600000	600000
Buses at 1 for 4 Settlements	150000	150000	150000
Rural Population (million)	805	874	950
Buses at 60 per million	48327	52484	56998
Total Bus Fleet Needed	198327	202484	206998
Share of SRTU at 50% Level	99168	101242	103499

5.4 Stakeholder consultation and preferences

Public bus transportation plays a pivotal role in India in bringing about greater mobility both within and between rural and urban areas. Through increased mobility it also contributes immensely to social and economic development of different regions of the country. Realizing the importance of this link, the government of India, in course of time, has invested heavily in the development of a network of bus services to link up towns and villages all over the country.

The 67 public sector transport undertakings (STUs) in India today own 116,028 buses with an investment of more than Rs.120000 millions. These undertakings together operate 12,000 million passenger-kilometers daily, and carry over 300 million passengers daily. The STUs in the country are set up under four forms (i) departmental undertaking directly under the state governments, (ii) municipal undertakings owned and controlled by the municipal corporations, (iii) companies formed under the Indian Companies Act 1956, and (iv) road transport corporations formed under the RTC Act 1950. While the objectives that the STUs set out to achieve are laudable and, indeed, the effort began in right earnest, the support needed from state and central governments to sustain the effort suffered a setback beginning in the seventies. Currently, while the need of STUs to meet its social obligation is retained, the budgetary support to achieve the objective has drastically shrunk over time. There is a necessity to obtain an insight into the needs and expectations of the public in respect of passenger transport service in general and rural areas in particular. In addition the current level of customer satisfaction, with the transport services provided can play a significant role in network planning of public transport services in rural areas. Network planning involves two major components namely identification of route and frequency of operations on the route. Before the development of public transport network connecting various settlements the operators need to gauge the perception of commuters to balance the need/demand for travel and the resources available with the operator. Stakeholders of public transport judge the operators on the basis of quality of service enjoyed by them.

Quality is an abstract entity and subjective in character. It is simply an expression of the extent to which the service provided by an operator fulfills the expectations of the customers/stakeholders concerned. As such, there will be variations in perception of quality of service enjoyed by different customers for the same operation. The term quality may include many components such as:

1. Comfort and convenience
2. Schedule and operations
3. Crew behavior
4. Cost and other factors

Each of these components could include many attributes and the same are included in the following Table 5.6.

In order to gauge the perceptions primary data needs to be collected from the stakeholders on the attributes listed above. Unfortunately there is no evidence that this exercise is undertaken periodically by any public or private operator. IIMB was involved in one such exercise for Karnataka State Road Transport Corporation (KSRTC) along with a number of bus operations provided by private operators in the state of Karnataka. The results indicate that the satisfaction levels on most of the attributes are much above for KSRTC compared to any private operator. IIMB was also involved in obtaining the quality of service provided by Andhra Pradesh State Road Transport Corporation (APSRTC). The results indicate that commuters are quite satisfied with the operations of APSRTC.

Table 5.6: Attributes Considered for Service Quality

Comfort and Convenience	Schedule and Operations	Crew Behavior	Cost and Others Aspects
Overloading	Notification of Schedules	Courteousness with Passengers	Notification of Fares
Boarding and Alighting	Following the Schedule	Helping Children and Old Age People	Returning Small Changes
Seating Arrangement	Prompt Service During Break Down	Rash and Negligent	Adequacy of Fares
Movement within the Bus	Maintenance of Vehicles	Appearence of the Crew	Charges for Luggage
Driving Comfort	Cancellation of Schedules	Neatness and Professionalism	
Travel Time	Arrival/Departure Timings	Attitude of the Crew in General	
Luggage Allowance			
Stopping at the Bus Stops			

5.5 Public transport mode options

It is well understood that the demand for movement from rural settlements is quite low. Transport studies from various researches clearly brought out that the catchment area of rural settlements is mostly limited to within the district. The substantial number of trips are short/medium distance trips to nearby marketing towns, taluk headquarters for a number of administrative reasons. The studies also reveal that most of rural households carry some amount of luggage while making the trip. As such, the rural public transport must be able to accommodate a considerable quantity of luggage along with people. Previous sections have outlined the number of buses to cater to this rural segment. Since this number is so huge it is essential to persuade public transport vehicle manufacturers to develop a new design to suit the requirements of rural travel needs. The conventional bus fleet used in urban areas may not be quite appropriate to operate in rural areas. Since the demand is not very high a twenty seater sitting with enough luggage holding may be desirable to connect rural areas with nearby economic activity centers.

In addition if the travel distance is less than 5 kms, shared auto (three wheelers) are more convenient. In fact, this practice of shared auto is already in practice in many rural and suburbs of many cities in India. Most of the autos are owned by drivers themselves or many individuals involved in the transport business. Thus, in the operation of autos the contribution of the government in the capital costs of vehicles is almost negligible. Market forces will determine the routing and scheduling and number of trips they should make. Even if there are multiple players they amicably solve routes to be followed among themselves. However, technically in India this type of shared auto operations are illegal, and the drivers/ owners are subjected to a number of difficulties from authorities of police departments and transport departments. There is a necessity to legalize this in rural areas for intradistrict movement. A new color scheme or some other physical appearance of these autos with other autos operating in the city could be followed to avoid misuse. Accepting this reality and encouraging this paratransit operation for rural and intradistrict mobility will reduce public bus fleet requirements from private/public operators of bus fleets. This will also help the operators to minimize losses since rural operators are mostly loss making. For efficient intradistrict rural operations each district may have a bus depot. From that depot rural service, intradistrict services, and trips to neighboring districts may have to be planned.

As an example, Mahindra Reva electric vehicle private limited is currently producing 5, 8, and 10 seat vehicles. They have developed complete sustainable solutions for frequent charging using portable solar devices. However, the economic viability of these vehicles as a rural public transport mode needs to be assessed in different states. If this experiment succeeds, there will be many companies to associate in the design and development of small capacity vehicles.

Summary

This chapter highlights information about public transport planning in rural areas, which mainly covers topics like planning strategy in which geographical settings of rural areas are discussed and also the information consists of network planning for school and college students and also it deals with the market segmentation, the relation between mobility and accessibility. This chapter also contains the details of travel demand estimation its types and bus fleet for intra and rural operations in India, and it also shows some light on stakeholder consultation and on public transport mode options which rural people most often adopt according to their convenience.

Chapter 6

Public Transport Planning in Urban Areas

6.1 Urban transport planning

The development of the 3Cs (continuing, cooperative, and comprehensive) is very important in the planning and development of sustainable transportation infrastructure.

a) Continuing specifies that the planning process be ongoing, frequently reevaluating and updating the transit plan to reflect changes in the urban area.

b) Cooperative is defined as the need for coordination not only between the various levels of government (local, state, and central), but also among individual agencies at the same level. It also implies cooperation between disciplines during the planning process and mandates that planning teams be interdisciplinary.

c) Comprehensive implies the set of the following 10 elements for which inventories and analyses are required:

1. Economic factors affecting development

2. Population

3. Land use

4. Travel patterns

5. Existing transportation facilities

6. Terminal and transfer facilities

7. Traffic control features

8. Zoning ordinances, subdivision regulations, building codes, etc.

9. Financial resources

10. Numerous qualitative elements, including social and community value factors, such as preservation of open space, environmental amenities, and aesthetics.

For any metropolitan planning organization (MPO) like the development authorities in Indian cities will typically include the sustainable transport infrastructure planning as shown in Figure 6.1. As can be seen in the figure, any such organization should have a planning works programe, based on both short term and long term planning elements. The short term planning elements, generally known as transportation system management (TSM) elements, are basically meant for efficient use of existing and proposed infrastructure. Together with short and long term elements, the organization will have annual and multiyear transportation improvement programs, which will be frequently updated and monitored from time to time.

Figure 6.2 gives the basic steps in a comprehensive urban transport infrastructure planning process. The same are described as follows:

a. Definition of goals and objectives for the transportation system in the future.

b. Collection of inventories: data about the existing city and its transportation system.

c. Forecasts of changes and conditions in the selected target year for plans.

d. A set of criteria for plan evaluation derived from the goals and objectives.

e. Development of alternative infrastructure plans for the projected future conditions, meeting the defined goals.

f. Technical elaboration and testing of alternative plans, considering their impact on projected demand and urban development.

g. Comparative evaluation of alternative infrastructure plans using the set of goal-based criteria and public hearings, resulting in selection of the preferred plan.

h. Finalization of the selected plan and preparation for its implementation.

This is a conceptual organization of a planning process that includes the entire planning from data collection to the production of the final plan and its implementation. Each of these steps further consists of data handling, modelling, technical analysis, etc. Figure 6.3 shows the planning process with more technical details.

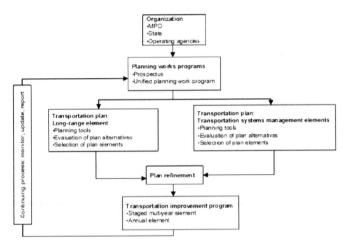

Figure 6.1: Planning Process of an Organization

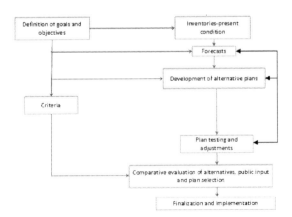

Figure 6.2: Sequence of Basic Steps in Comprehensive Urban Transportation Infrastructure Planning

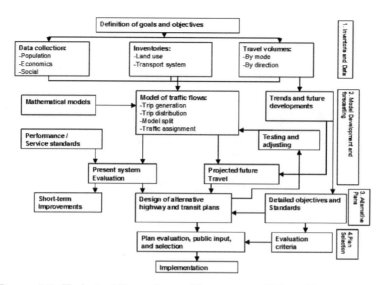

Figure 6.3: Technical Procedure of Long-range Urban Transportation Infrastructure

The data collection usually consists of collecting comprehensive information about the present transportation system and urban area. The following are the main categories of the essential data required for sustainable infrastructure purpose:

a. Land use characteristics

1. Population of localities

2. Residential areas

3. Commercial areas

4. Educational areas

5. Recreational areas

6. Developable areas

7. Other land uses

For example, Figure 6.4 shows the land use map of Bangalore city for 2003

b. Network characteristics

1. Roads by classification

2. Road properties

3. Road geometry

4. Rail way system properties

5. Other network properties

Fig.6.5 shows the network map of Mumbai Metropolitan Region (MMR)

c. Topographical features

1. Contours

2. Soil classification

3. Water bodies

4. Drainage patterns
5. Quarry identification
6. Forest cover
7. Identification of obligatory points

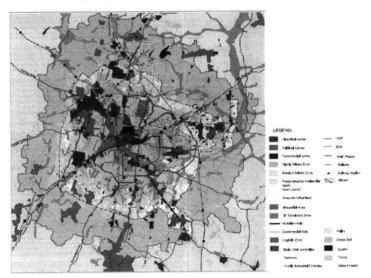

Figure 6.4: Land Use Map of Bangalore City for 2003

d. Socio-economic data

1. Demographic information
2. Income levels
3. Vehicle ownership levels
4. Occupation
5. Education
6. Family structure
7. Employment (Figure 6.6)

e. Activity information

1. Industrial employment
2. Educational employment
3. Administrative employment
4. Wholesale and retail employment
5. Service employment
6. Informal sector employment

f. Transport system characteristics

1. Capacity
2. Speeds
3. Frequency
4. Comfort

5. Reliability
6. Time of travel
7. Modal integration

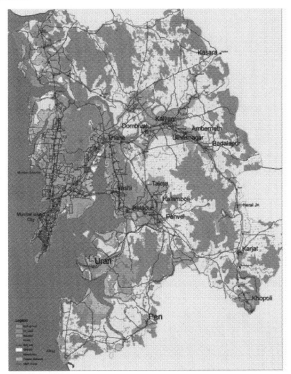

Figure 6.5: Network Map of Mumbai Metropolitan Region (MMR)

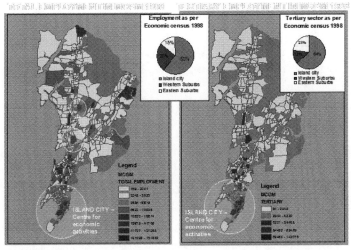

Figure 6.6: Employment Distribution in MCGM for 1998

The purpose of the travel demand modelling phase of the urban transportation infrastructure planning process is to perform a conditional prediction of travel demand in order to estimate the likely transportation consequences of several transportation alternatives that are being considered for implementation. This prediction is also conditional on a predicted target-year land-use pattern. The major components of travel behavior were identified as:

1. The decision to travel for a given purpose (trip generation).
2. The choice of destination (trip distribution).
3. The choice of travel mode (mode choice).
4. The choice of route or path (route assignment).

The four-step modelling process was originally developed in connection with the planning of major highway facilities during the 1950s and 1960s. At first glance the process may appear to have remained unchanged since that time. In reality, however, it has undergone significant modification in response to an improved understanding of travel behavior by modellers, the need to address emerging policy questions, and advances in computational technology. More powerful personal computers allowed the specification of more complex and detailed models. This evolutionary step will undoubtedly continue.

6.1.1 The structure of the classical transport model

Years of experimentation and development have resulted in a general structure which has been called the classic transport model. This structure is, in effect, a result from practice in the 1960s but has remained more or less unaltered despite major improvements in modelling techniques during the 1970s and 1980s.

The classic model is presented as a sequence of four submodels. These are:

a. Trip generation: It determines the frequency of origins or destinations of trips in each zone by trip purpose, as a function of land uses and household demographics, and other socio-economic factors.

b. Trip distribution: It matches origins with destinations and is concerned with the estimation of target year trip volumes that interchange between all pairs of zones i and j, where i is the trip-producing zone, and j is the trip-attracting zone of the pair.

c. Mode choice: This step computes the proportion of trips between each origin and destination that use a particular transportation mode.

d. Route assignment: In this step, trips between an origin and destination are allocated by a particular mode to a route.

6.1.2 Trip generation

Trip generation is the process by which measures of urban activity are converted into number of trips. For example, the number of trips that are generated by a shopping center is quite different from the number of trips generated by an industrial complex that takes up about the same amount of space. In trip generation, the planner attempts to quantify the relationship between urban activity and travel.

The study area is divided into zones for analysis purposes. After trip-generation analysis, the planner knows how many trips are produced by each zone and how many are attracted by each zone. In addition, the planner knows the purposes for the trips—the trips are put into several categories, like trips from home to work, or home to shop, or home to school. This categorization is necessary because each trip purpose reflects the behavior of the trip maker. For example, school trips and work trips are pretty regular; shopping and recreation trips are less so. The three most common mathematical formulations of trip generation are multiple linear regression technique, trip rate-analysis technique, and cross-classification technique. Before going into these models, let us have a look at some of the basic definitions.

a. Journey: This is a one-way movement from a point of origin to a point of destination.

b. Home-based (HB) trip: This is one where the home of the trip maker is either the origin or the destination of the journey.

c. Non-home-based (NHB) trip: This, conversely, is one where neither end of the trip is the home of the traveler.

d. Trip production: This is defined as the home end of an HB trip or as the origin of an NHB trip.

e. Trip attraction: This is defined as the nonhome end of an HB trip or the destination of an NHB trip.

f. Trip generation: This is often defined as the total number of trips generated by households in a zone, be they HB or NHB.

6.1.2.1 Multiple linear regression technique

Transportation studies have shown that residential land use is an important trip generator. Also, nonresidential land use in many cases is a good attractor of trips. A typical equation connecting estimated trips generated by a residential zone could be:

$Y = A + B_1 X_1 + B_2 X_2 + B_3 X_3$

where,

Y = trips/household

X_1 = car ownership

X_2 = family income

X_3 = family size

Model parameters and variables vary from one study area to another and are established by using base-year information. Once the equations are calibrated, they are used to estimate future travel for a target year. In developing regression equations the following is assumed:

1. All the independent variables are independent of each other.

2. All the independent variables are normally distributed.

3. The independent variables are continuous.

It is not possible for the planner to conform to these specifications, and because of this departure, regression analysis has come under considerable criticism. A typical regression equation may appear as follows:

$Y = 0.0649 X_1 - 0.0034 X_2 + 0.0063 X_3 + 0.9486 X_4$

To derive an estimate of a zone for a future year, appropriate estimates of X_1, X_2, X_3, and X_4 are substituted and the equation is solved. The quality of fit of a regression line determined by coefficient of determination (goodness of fit) represented by R^2, the value being between 0 and 1. The closer R is to 1, the better the linear relationship between the variables.

The multiple regression technique is appealing to transportation analysts because it is easy to determine the degree of relationship between the dependent and independent variables. Also, it is possible to determine the ability of the equation to predict accurately. Apart from the coefficient of multiple correlation referred to before, it is the practice to determine the standard error of estimate (S$_Y$), which is a measure of the deviation of, say, observed trips from values predicted by the equation. In addition, the partial correlation coefficients (r$_j$) of each of the independent variables is calculated. It provides the relationship between the dependent variable (y) and the particular independent variable (X$_i$) under investigation. The t-test may be used to determine whether an estimated regression coefficient is significant. In summary, if

$$Y_c = A + B_1X_1 + B_2X_2 + B_3X_3 \ldots \ldots B_n + X_n$$

then,

$$R^2 = \frac{\sum(Y_c - \mu_y)^2}{\sum(Y_i * \mu_y)^2}$$

$$S_e = \frac{\sum(Y_c)^2}{N - (n+1)}$$

$$S_{Bn} = \frac{(S_c)^2}{S_{xi} * N(1 - ((R_{xi})^2))}$$

$$t = \frac{B_n}{S_n}$$

> where
>
> Y_t = estimated magnitude of the dependent variable
>
> μ_T = mean of the dependent variable
>
> R^2 = coefficient of multiple determination
>
> R = multiple correlation coefficient
>
> s_t = standard error of estimate
>
> $s_{\bar{x}}$ = standard deviation of the independent variable X.
>
> $R_{\bar{x}}$ = coefficient of multiple correlation between X_i and all other independent variables

6.1.2.2 Trip-rate analysis technique

Trip-rate analysis refers to several models that are based on the determination of the average trip-production or trip-attraction rates associated with the important trip generators within the region. Table 6.1, for example, displays the trip-generation rates associated with various land-use categories in downtown Pittsburgh, which were obtained by one of the very first major urban transportation studies.

This table includes production rates by residential land uses and attraction rates by several nonresidential land uses. Care must be exercised to apply trip-rate models in the same context that they were calibrated. In this case the rates represent person-trips (rather than vehicle trips) per thousand square feet of each land use.

Table 6.1: Floor-Space Trip-Generation Rates Grouped by Generalized Land-Use Categories

Land-Use Category	Thousands of Square Feet	Person-Trips	Trips per Thousand Square Feet
Residential	2744	6574	2.4
Commercial			
Retail	6732	54,833	8.1
Services	13,506	70,014	5.2
Wholesale	2599	3162	1.2
Manufacturing	1392	1335	1.0
Transportation	1394	5630	4.0
Public Buildings	2977	11,746	3.9
Total Average	31,344	153.294	4.9

6.1.2.3 Cross-classification technique

Cross-classification (or category analysis) models may be thought of as extensions of the simple trip-rate models. Although they can be calibrated as area- or zone-based models, in trip-generation studies they are almost exclusively used as disaggregate models. In the residential-generation context, household types are classified according to a set of categories that are highly correlated with trip making. Three to four explanatory variables, each broken into about three discrete levels, are usually sufficient. Typically household size, automobile ownership, household income, and some measure of land development intensity are used to classify household types.

The trip rates associated with each type of household are estimated by statistical methods, and these rates are assumed to remain stable over time. Table 6.2 presents a cross-classification table that shows the calibrated nonwork home-based trip-production rates for various types of households defined by (1) four levels of household size (i.e., number of persons per household), and (2) three levels of car ownership (i.e., dwelling units per acre), a surrogate for accessibility to nonwork activities (e.g., shopping, entertainment).

Table 6.2: Total Home-Based-Nonwork Trip Rates

Area Type	Vehicles Available per Household	Persons per Household			
		1	2,3	4	5+
1. Urban: High Density	0	0.57	2.07	4.57	6.95
	1	1.45	3.02	5.52	7.90
	2+	1.82	3.39	5.89	8.27
2. Suburban: Medium Density	0	0.97	2.54	5.04	7.42
	1	1.92	3.49	5.99	8.37
	2+	2.29	3.86	6.36	8.74
3. Rural: Low Density	0	0.54	1.94	4.44	6.82
	1	1.32	2.89	5.39	7.77
	2+	1.69	3.26	5.76	8.14

Example 1: An urban zone contains 200 acres of residential land, 50 acres devoted to commercial uses, and 10 acres of park land. The following table presents the zone's expected household composition at some future (target) year. Using the calibrated cross-classification table of Table 6.2, estimate the total nonwork home-based trips that the zone will produce during a typical target-year day. The rates are given as trips per household per day.

Table 6.3: Persons per Household

Vehicles per Household	Persons per Household			
	1	2,3	4	5+
0	100	200	150	20
1	300	500	210	50
2+	150	100	60	0

Solution: The total productions are estimated by summing the contribution of each household type:

$$p_1 = \sum_h N_h R_h$$

where N_h and R_h are the number of households of type h and their corresponding production rate. For example, the 300 single-person one-car households contribute (300) (1.45) =435 nonwork home-based trips per day. Summing over all household types gives $p_1 = 5760$ trips per day.

Source: (Papacostas and Prevedouras, 2002)

6.1.3 Trip distribution

Trip generation models can be used to estimate the total number of trips emanating from a zone and those attracted to each zone. Generations and attractions provide an idea of the level of trip making in a study area, but this is often not enough for modelling and decision making. What is needed is a better idea of the pattern of trip making, from where to where do trips take place, the modes of transport chosen, and the routes taken. Figure 6.7 shows a desire line diagram showing trips made between different places in MMR.

Figure 6.7: Desire Line Diagram of MMR

6.1.3.1 Growth factor methods

Let us consider first a situation where we have a basic trip matrix t, perhaps obtained from a previous study or estimated from recent survey data. We would like to estimate the matrix corresponding to the design year, say 10 years into the future. We may have information about the growth rate to be expected in this 10-year period for the whole study area; alternatively, we may have information on the likely growth in the number of trips originating and/or attracted to each zone. Depending on this information we may be able to use different growth-factor methods in our estimation of future trip patterns.

6.1.3.1.1 Uniform growth factor

If the only information available is about a general growth rate τ for the whole of the study area, then we can only assume that it will apply to each cell in the matrix:

$T_{ij} = \tau t_{ij}$

where $\tau = T/t$, i.e., the ratio of expanded over previous total number of trips.

Example 2: Consider the simple four-by-four base-year trip matrix of Table 6.4. If the growth in traffic in the study area is expected to be 20% in the next three years, it is a simple matter to multiply all cell values by 1.2 to obtain a new matrix as in Table 6.5.

Table 6.4: Base-Year Trip Matrix

	1	2	3	4	$\sum_j$
1	5	50	100	200	355
2	50	5	100	300	455
3	50	100	5	100	255
4	100	200	250	20	570
$\sum_i$	205	355	455	620	1635

Table 6.5: Future Estimated Trip Matrix with $\tau = 1.2$

	1	2	3	4	$\sum_j$
1	6	60	120	240	426
2	60	6	120	360	546
3	60	120	6	120	306
4	120	240	300	24	684
$\sum_i$	246	426	546	744	1962

6.1.3.1.2 Singly constrained growth factor

Consider the situation where information is available on the expected growth in trips originating in each zone, for example shopping trips. In this case it would be possible to apply this origin-specific growth factor (τ_i) to the corresponding rows in the trip matrix. The same approach can be followed if the information is available for trips attracted to each zone; in this case the destination-specific growth factors (τ_i) would be applied to the corresponding columns. This can be written as:

Example 3: Consider the following revised version of Table 6.6 with growth predicted for origins:

Table 6.6: Origin-Constrained Growth Trip Table

	1	2	3	4	$\sum_j$	Target O_i
1	5	50	100	200	355	400
2	50	5	100	300	455	460
3	50	100	5	100	255	400
4	100	200	250	20	570	702
$\sum_i$	205	355	455	620	1635	1962

This problem can be solved immediately by multiplying each row by the ratio of target over the base year total ($\sum_j$), thus giving the results in Table 6.7.

Table 6.7: Expanded Origin-Constrained Growth Trip Table

	1	2	3	4	$\sum_j$	Target O_i
1	5.6	56.3	112.7	225.4	400	400
2	50.5	5.1	101.1	303.3	460	460
3	78.4	156.9	7.8	156.9	400	400
4	123.2	246.3	307.9	24.6	702	702
$\sum_i$	257.7	464.6	529.5	701.2	1962	1962

Source: Ortuzer and Willumsen (1999)

6.1.3.1.3 Doubly constrained growth factors

An interesting problem is generated when information is available on the future number of trips originating and terminating in each zone say τ_i and T_j. This implies different growth rates for trips in and out of each zone and consequently having two sets of growth factors for each zone, say $F_{ij}=0.5(\tau_i - T_j)$. The application of an average growth factor, say is only a poor compromise as none of the two targets or trip-end constraints will be satisfied. Historically a number of iterative methods have been proposed to obtain an estimated trip matrix which satisfies both sets of trip-end constraints, or the two sets of growth factors, which is the same thing.

All these methods involve calculating a set of intermediate correction coefficients which are then applied to cell entries in each row or column as appropriate. After applying these corrections to say, each row, the totals for each column are calculated and compared with the target values. If the differences are significant, new correction coefficients are calculated and applied as necessary. The best known of these methods is due to Furness (1965), who introduced balancing factors A_i anb B_j as follows:

$T_{ij} = t_{ij} \tau_i T_j A_i B_j$

or incorporating the growth rates into new variables a_i and b_j :

$T_{ij} = t_{ij} a_i b_j$

with $a_i = \tau_i A_i$ and $b_j = T_j B_j$.

The Factors a_i and b_j (or A_i and B_j) must be calculated so that the constraints are satisfied. This is achieved in an iterative process which in outline is as follows:
1. Set all $b_j = 1.0$ and solve for a_j.
2. With the latest a_j solve for b_j, e.g., satisfy the trip attraction constraint.
3. Keeping the b_js fixed, solve for a_j and repeat steps 2 and 3 until the changes are sufficiently small.

This method produces solutions within 3 to 5% of the target values in a few iterations. There is not much point in enforcing the constraints to a level greater than the accuracy of the estimated trip end totals. This method is often called a bi-proportional algorithm because of the nature of the corrections involved. This method is a special case of entropy-maximizing models of the gravity type, if the effect of distance or separation between zones is excluded. But in any case, the Furness method tries to produce the minimum corrections to the base-year matrix necessary to satisfy the future year trip-end constraints.

The most important condition required for the convergence of this method is that the growth rates produce target values T_i and $T - j$ such that

$$\sum_i \tau_i \sum_j t_{ij} = \sum_i T_j \sum_i T_{ij} = \text{T}.$$

Table 6.8: Doubly Constrained Matrix Expansion Problem

	1	2	3	4	$\sum_j$	Target O_i
1	5	50	100	200	355	400
2	50	5	100	300	455	460
3	50	100	5	100	255	400
4	100	200	250	20	570	702
$\sum_i$	205	355	455	620	1635	
Target D_j	260	400	500	802		1962

Example 4: Table 6.8 represents a doubly constrained growth factor problem. The solution to this problem, after three iterations on rows and columns (three sets of corrections for all rows and three for all columns), can be shown to be:

Table 6.9: Solution to the Doubly Constrained Matrix Expansion Problem

	1	2	3	4	$\sum_j$	Target O_i
1	5.25	44.12	98.24	254.25	401.85	400
2	45.30	3.81	84.78	329.11	462.99	460
3	77.04	129.50	7.21	186.58	400.34	400
4	132.41	222.57	309.77	32.07	696.82	702
$\sum_i$	260.00	400.00	500.00	802.00	1962	
Target D_j	260	400	500	802		1962

Source: Ortuzer and Wilumsen (1999)

Note that this estimated matrix is within 1% of meeting the target trip ends, more than enough accuracy for this problem.

a. Advantages and Limitations of Growth-Factor Methods

Growth-factor methods are simple to understand and make direct use of observed trip matrices and forecasts of trip-end growth. They preserve the observations as much as is consistent with the information available on growth rates. This advantage is also their limitation as they are probably only reasonable for short-term planning horizons.

Growth-factor methods require the same database as synthetic methods, namely an observed (sampled) trip matrix; this is an expensive data item. The methods are heavily dependent on the accuracy of the base-year trip matrix. This is never very high for individual cell entries and therefore the resulting matrices are no more reliable than the sampled or observed ones. Any error in the base-year may well be amplified by the application of successive correction factors. Moreover, if parts of the base-year matrix are unobserved, they will remain so in the forecasts. Therefore, these methods cannot be used to fill in observed cells of partially observed trip matrices.

Another limitation is that the methods do not take into account changes in transport costs due to improvements (or new congestion) in the network. Therefore they are of limited use in the analysis of policy options involving new modes, new links, pricing policies, and new zones.

123

6.1.3.2 Synthetic or gravity models

6.1.3.2.1 The gravity distribution model

Distribution models of a different kind have been developed to assist in forecasting future trip patterns when important changes in the network take place. They start from assumptions about group trip making behavior and the way this is influenced by external factors such as total trip ends and distance traveled. The best known of these models is the gravity model, originally generated from an analogy with Newton's gravitational law. They estimate trips for each cell in the matrix without directly using the observed trip pattern; therefore, they are sometimes called synthetic as opposed to growth-factor models.

Probably the first rigorous use of a gravity model was by Casey (1955), who suggested such an approach to synthesize shopping trips and catchment areas between towns in a region. In its simplest formulation the model has the following functional form:

$$T_{ij} = \frac{\alpha P_i P_j}{(d_{ij})^2}$$

Where, P_i and P_j are the populations of the towns of origin and destination, d_{ij} is the distance between i and j, and α is a proportionality factor.

This was soon considered to be too simplistic an analogy with the gravitational law and early improvements included the use of total trip ends (O_i and D_j) instead of total populations, and a parameter n for calibration as the power for d_{ij}. This new parameter was not restricted to being an integer and different studies estimated value between 0.6 and 3.5. The model was further generalized by assuming that the effect of distance or separation could be modelled better by a decreasing function, to be specified, of the distance or travel cost between the zones. This can be written as:

$$T_{ij} = \alpha O D_j f(C_{ij})$$

where, $f(C_{ij})$ is a generalized function of the travel costs with one or more parameters for calibration. This function often receives the name of deterrence function because it represents the disincentive to travel as distance (time) or cost increases. Popular versions for this function are:

$f(C_{ij}) = \exp(-\beta C_{ij})$ exponential function

$f(C_{ij}) = C_{ij}^n$ power function

$f(C_{ij}) = C_{ij}^n \exp(-\beta C_{ij})$ combined function

Singly and Doubly Constrained Models

The need to ensure that the restrictions are met requires replacing the single proportionality factor α by two sets of balancing factors A_i and B_j in the furnace model, yielding:

$$T_{ij} = A_i O_i B_j D_j f(C_{ij})$$

In a similar vein one can again subsume O_i and D_j into these factors and rewrite the model as:

$$T_{ij} = a_i b_j f(C_{ij})$$

The above expression is a doubly constrained gravity model. Singly constrained versions, either origin or destination constrained, can be produced by making one set of balancing factors A_i and B_j equal to one. For an origin-constrained model, B_j is equal to 1 and for all j, and

$$A_i = 1/\sum_j D_j f(C_{ij})$$

In this case of the doubly constrained model the values of the balancing factors are:

$A_i = 1/\sum_j B_j D_j f(C_{ij})$

$B_j = 1/\sum_i A_i O_i f(C_{ij})$

The balancing factors are, therefore, interdependent; this means that the calculation of one set requires the values of the other set. This suggests an iterative process analogous to Furnesss which works well in practice: given set of values for the deterrence function $f(C_{ij})$, start with all $B_j=1$, solve for A_i and then use these values to reestimate the B_js; repeat until convergence is achieved.

6.1.3.2.2 Calibrating a gravity model

Calibration of the gravity model is accomplished by developing friction factors and developing socioeconomic adjustment factors. As noted before, friction factors reflect the travel time of impedance on trip making. A trial-and-error adjustment process is generally adopted. One way, of course, is to use the factors from a past study in a similar urban area. Three items are used as input to the gravity model for calibration: 1. Production-attraction trip table for each purpose. 2. Travel times for all zone pairs, including intrazonal times. 3. Initial friction factors for each increment of travel time. Essentially, then, the calibration process involves adjusting the friction factor parameter until the planner is satisfied that the model adequately reproduces the trip distribution as represented by the input trip table—until the models trip table agrees substantially with the table from the survey data, using indications such as the trip-time frequency distribution and the average trip time. The process is as follows: 1. Use the gravity model to distribute trips based on initial inputs. 2. Total trip attractions at all zones j, as calculated by the model, are compared to those obtained from the input observed trip table. 3. If this comparison shows significant differences, the attraction is adjusted for each zone, where a difference is observed. 4. The model is rerun until the calculated and observed attractions are reasonably balanced. 5. The models trip table and the input travel time table can be used for two comparisons: the trip-time frequency distribution and the average trip time. If there are significant differences, the process begins again.

6.1.4 Modal split

The third stage in travel demand modelling is modal split. The trip matrix of O-D matrix obtained from the trip distribution is sliced into a number of matrices representing each mode. The choice of transport mode is probably one of the most important classic models in transport planning. This is because of the key role played by public transport in policy making. Public transport modes make use of road space more efficiently than private transport. Also they have more social benefits like if more people begin to use public transport, there will be less congestion on the roads and the accidents will be less. Again in public transport, we can travel with low cost. In addition, the fuel is used more efficiently. The main characteristics of public transport are that they will have some particular schedule, frequency, etc.

On the other hand, private transport is highly flexible. It provides more comfortable and convenient travel. It has better accessibility also. The issue of mode choice, therefore, is probably the single most important element in transport planning and policy making. It affects the general efficiency with which we can travel in urban areas. It is important then to develop and use models which are sensitive to those travel attributes that influence individual choices of mode.

6.1.4.1 Factors influencing the choice of mode

The factors may be listed under three groups:

1. Characteristics of the trip maker: The following features are found to be important:
(a) car availability and/or ownership
(b) possession of a driving license
(c) household structure (young couple, couples with children, retired people, etc.)
(d) income
(e) decisions made elsewhere, for example the need to use a car at work, take children to school, etc.
(f) residential activity

2. Characteristics of the journey: Mode choice is strongly influenced by:
(a) the trip purpose; for example, the journey to work is normally easier to undertake by public transport than other journeys because of its regularity and the adjustment possible in the long run
(b) time of the day when the journey is undertaken
(c) late trips are more difficult to accommodate by public transport

3. Characteristics of the transport facility: There are two types of factors. One is quantitative and the other is qualitative.
Quantitative factors are:
(a) relative travel time: in-vehicle, waiting, and walking times by each mode
(b) relative monetary costs (fares, fuel, and direct costs)
(c) availability and cost of parking

Qualitative factors which are less easy to measure are:
(a) comfort and convenience
(b) reliability and regularity
(c) protection and security

6.1.4.2 Trip-end modal split models

Traditionally, the objective of transportation planning was to forecast the growth in demand for car trips so that the investment could be planned to meet the demand. When personal characteristics were thought to be the most important determinants of mode choice, attempts were made to apply modal-split models immediately after trip generation. Such a model is called trip-end modal split model. In this way different characteristics of the

126

person could be preserved and used to estimate modal split. The modal split models of this time related the choice of mode only to features like income, residential density, and car ownership.

The advantage is that these models could be very accurate in the short run, if public transport is available and there is little congestion. The limitation is that they are insensitive to policy decisions, e.g., improving public transport, restricting parking, etc. would have no effect on modal split according to these trip-end models.

6.1.4.3 Trip-interchange modal split models

This is the post-distribution model; that is modal split is applied after the distribution stage. This has the advantage that it is possible to include the characteristics of the journey and that of the alternative modes available to undertake them. It is possible to include policy decisions. This is beneficial for long term modelling.

6.1.4.4 Aggregate and disaggregate models

Mode choice could also be aggregate if they are based on zonal and interzonal information. They can be called disaggregate if they are based on household or individual data.

6.1.4.5 Utility and disutility functions

A utility function measures the degree of satisfaction that people derive from their choices. A disutility function represents the generalized cost (akin to the concept of impedance) that is associated with each choice. The magnitude of either depends on the characteristics of each choice and on the characteristics of the individual making that choice. In the case of modal choice the characteristics of the trip also bear a relationship to the utility associated with choosing a particular mode of travel. To specify a utility function, it is necessary to select both the relevant variables from this list and the particular functional form relating the selected variables.

The disutility, in transportation, can be represented as

$$C_{ij} = a_1 t_{ij}^v + a_2 t_{ij}^w + a_3 t_{ij}^t + a_4 t_{nij} + a_5 F_{ij} + a_6 \phi_j + \delta$$

where t_{ij}^v is the in-vehicle travel time between i and j, is the walking time to and from stops, t_{ij}^t is the waiting time at stops, F_{ij} is the fare charged to travel between i and j, ϕ_j is the parking cost, and δ is a parameter representing comfort and convenience. If the travel cost is low, then that mode has more probability of being chosen.

6.1.4.6 Binary logit model

Binary logit model is the simplest form of mode choice, where the travel choice between two modes is made. Let there be two modes (m=1,2) then the proportion of trips by mode 1 from zone i to zone j is p_{ij}^1. Let c_{ij}^1 be the cost of travelling from zone i to zone j using the mode 1, and c_{ij}^2 be the cost of travelling from i to zone j using the mode 2. There are three cases:

1. If $c_{ij}^2 - c_{ij}^1$ is positive, then mode 1 is chosen.
2. If $c_{ij}^2 - c_{ij}^1$ is negative, then mode 2 is chosen.
3. If $c_{ij}^2 - c_{ij}^1$ is 0, then both modes have equal probability.

This relationship is normally expressed by a logit curve. Therefore, the proportion of trips by mode 1 is given by

$$p^1_{ij} = T^1_{ij}/T_{ij} = \frac{e^{-\beta^1_{cij}}}{e^{-\beta^1_{cij}} + e^{-\beta^2_{cij}}}$$

This functional form is called logit, where c_{ij} is called the generalized cost and is the β parameter for calibration.

Example 5: Let the number of trips from zone i to zone j be 5000, and two modes are available which have the characteristics as shown in table below. Compute the trips made by mode bus, and the fare that is collected from the mode bus. If the fare of the bus is reduced to 6, then find the fare collected.

	t^u_{ij}	t^w_{ij}	t^t_{ij}	f_{ij}	δ
Car	20	-	-	18	4
Bus	30	5	3	9	
a_i	0.03	0.04	0.06	0.1	0.1

Solution:

Cost of travel by car = c_{car} = 0.03*20+18*0.1+4*0.1=2.8

Cost of travel by bus = c_{bus} = 0.03*30+0.04*5+0.06*3+0.1*9=2.18

Probability of choosing mode car = p^{car}_{ij} = $\frac{e^{-2.8}}{e^{-2.8}+e^{-2.18}}$=0.35

Probability of choosing mode bus = p^{bus}_{ij} = $\frac{e^{-2.8}}{e^{-2.8}+e^{-2.18}}$=0.65

Proportion of trips by car = T^{car}_{ij} = 5000*0.35 = 1750

Proportion of trips by bus = T^{bus}_{ij}= 5000*0.65 = 3250

Fare collected from bus = $T^{bus}_{ij}*F_{ij}$ = 3250*9 = 29250

When the fare of bus gets reduced to 6,

Cost function for bus = c_{bus} = 0.03*30+0.04*5+0.06*3+0.1*6=1.88

Probability of choosing mode bus = p^{bus}_{ij} = $\frac{e^{-1.88}}{e^{-2.8}+e^{-1.88}}$=0.175

Proportion of trips by bus = T^{bus}_{ij} = 5000*0.715 = 3575

Fare collected from bus = $T^{bus}_{ij}*F_{ij}$ = 3575*6 = 21450

Multinomial logit model

The binary model can be easily extended to multiple modes. The equation for such a model can be written as:

$$p^1_{ij} = \frac{e^{-\beta^1_{cij}}}{\sum e^{-\beta^1_{cij}}}$$

Example 6: Let the number of trips from i to j be 5000, and three modes are available which have the following characteristics. Compute the trips made by the three modes and the fare required to travel by each mode.

	t^u_{ij}	t^w_{ij}	t^t_{ij}	f_{ij}	δ
Car	20	-	-	18	4
Bus	30	5	3	6	-
Train	12	10	2	4	-
a_i	0.03	0.04	0.06	0.1	0.1

Solution

Cost of travel by car = c_{car}= 0.03*20+18*0.1+4*0.1=2.8

Cost of travel by bus = c_{bus} = 0.03*30+0.04*5+0.06*3+0.1*6=1.88

Cost of travel by train = c_{train}= 0.03*12+0.04*10+0.06*2+0.1*4=1.28

Probability of choosing mode car = p^{car}_{ij} = $\frac{e^{-2.8}}{e^{-2.8}+e^{-1.88}+e^{-1.28}}$=0.1237

Probability of choosing mode bus = p^{bus}_{ij} = $\frac{e^{-2.18}}{e^{-2.8}+e^{-1.88}+e^{-1.28}}$=0.3105

Probability of choosing mode train $= p_{ij}^{train} = \dfrac{e^{-1.28}}{e^{-2.8}+e^{-1.88}+e^{-1.28}} = 0.5657$

Proportion of trips by car $= T_{ij}^{car} = 5000*0.1237 = 618.5$

Proportion of trips by bus $= T_{ij}^{bus} = 5000*0.3105 = 1552.5$

Proportion of trips by train $= T_{ij}^{train} = 5000*0.5657 = 2828.5$

Fare collected from bus $= T_{ij}^{bus} * F_{ij} = 1552.5*6 = 9315$

Fare collected from train $= T_{ij}^{train} * F_{ij} = 2828.5*4 = 11314$

6.1.4.7 The nested logit model

Figures 6.8 and 6.9 compare the multinomial logit (MNL) and a nested logit structure involving three mode choices: the automobile, a local bus service, and rail transit. The MNL places these modes on a single level. By contrast, the nested structure groups the bus and rail together as subchoices of the composite transit mode. This structure permits a change in the utility of one of the transit modes to affect the share of the other transit mode to a greater degree than a mode that does not belong to the transit nest. In other words a greater degree of choice substitution is allowed within nests than between nests.

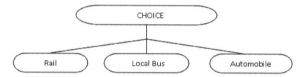

Figure 6.8: Multinomial Logit Structure for a Three-Mode Choice

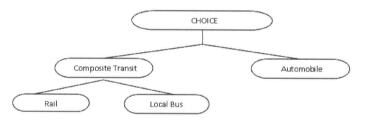

Figure 6.9: Nested Logit Structure

Examining the top-level decision of whether to travel by the automobile (A) or transit (T) gives

P(A)$= \dfrac{Exp(U_A)}{Exp(U_A + Exp(U_T))}$ and P(T)$= \dfrac{Exp(U_T)}{Exp(U_A + Exp(U_T))}$

where the composite transit utility $U_T = f(U_B, U_R)$.

By moving to the lower transit level, the conditional probabilities of choosing the bus (B) or the rail (R), given the decision to travel by transit, become

P(B/T)$= \dfrac{Exp(U_B)}{Exp(U_B + Exp(U_R))}$ and P(R/T)$= \dfrac{Exp(U_R)}{Exp(U_B + Exp(U_R))}$

To calculate the unconditional probabilities of choosing bus or rail, use the following equations:

$P(B) = P(B/T)*P(T)$ and $P(R) = P(R/T)*P(T)$.

The utility of the composite transit mode needs to capture the characteristics of all transit submodes (i.e., bus and rail). This is normally accomplished by including in the transit utility expression the *Logsum* variable multiplied by its calibration coefficient:

$Logsum = \ln \exp(U_B) + \exp(U_R)$.

The numerical value of the *Logsum* coefficient resulting from estimating the model provides information about the appropriateness of the selected nesting structure. If the estimated value of $\theta = 0$, the transit utility is independent of the utilities of the submodes. Consequently the primary choice between transit and auto is not affected by changes in the utilities of the submodes. Any such change redistributes the market shares of the submodes solely between them. In this case the submodes are said to be perfect substitutes of each other.

If the estimated value of turns out to be greater than 0 but less than 1, the selected structure is acceptable. A value of exactly equal to 1 implies that there exists an equivalent MNL model that is equally appropriate, whereas a value greater than 1 indicates that the selected nesting structure is inappropriate and other structures need to be investigated.

Example 7: An estimation procedure for a mode choice model of the nested logit structure shown in Figure 6.8 found that $U_T = a_t + \theta * logsum$ with $a_t = -0.42$ and $\theta = 1.0$. For a particular zonal interchange the following modal utilities were calculated in accordance with the estimated nested logit model:

$U_A = -0.36, U_B = -0.88, U_R = -0.78$

Calculate (a) the corresponding mode shares, and (b) the effect of a policy that is expected to cause a change $\Delta U_R = -0.10$.

Solution:

Part a: Baseline conditions

Nest Level

Mode m	U_m	$exp(U_m)$	$p(m/T)$
B	-0.88	0.415	0.475
R	-0.78	0.458	0.525
		$\sum = 0.873$	$\sum = 1.00$

$U_T = -0.52 + 1.0 - ln(0.839) = -0.56$

Primary choice level

Mode m	U_m	$exp(U_m)$	$p(m/T)$
A	-0.36	0.698	0.550
T	-0.56	0.571	0.450
		$\sum = 1.366$	$\sum = 1.000$

$P(B) = P(B/T) * P(T) = 0.475 * 0.450 = 0.214$

$P(R) = P(R/T) * P(T) = 0.525 * 0.450 = 0.236$

$P(A) = 0.450$

Part b: After change

Nest Level

Mode m	U_m	$exp(U_m)$	$p(m/T)$
B	-0.88	0.415	0.500
R	-0.88	0.415	0.500
		$\sum = 0.830$	$\sum = 1.000$

$U_T = -0.42 + 1.0 * ln(0.830) = -0.61$

Primary choice level

Mode m	U_m	$exp(U_m)$	$p(m/T)$
A	-0.36	0.698	0.462
T	-0.61	0.543	0.438
		$\sum = 1.241$	$\sum = 1.000$

$P(B) = P(B/T) * P(T) = 0.438 * 0.500 = 0.219$

$P(R) = P(R/T) * P(T) = 0.438 * 0.500 = 0.219$

$P(A) = 0.562$

6.1.5 Trip assignment

The last phase of the four-step transportation planning process is concerned with the trip-makers choice of path between pairs of zones by travel mode and with the resulting vehicular flows on the multimodal transportation network. This step may be viewed as the equilibration model between the demand for travel and the supply of transportation in terms of the physical facilities and, in the case of the various possible mass transit modes, the frequency of service provided. Following are the methods employed for the purpose of trip assignment.

6.1.5.1 Free/all-or-nothing traffic assignment

The free/all-or-nothing assignment technique allocates the entire volume interchanging between pairs of zones to the minimum path calculated on the basis of free-flow link impedance. After all interchange volumes are assigned the flow on a particular link is computed by summing all interzonal flows that happen to include that link on their minimum paths.

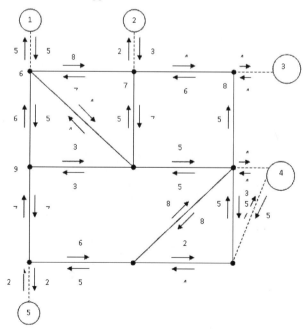

Figure 6.10: Hypothetical Network

131

Example 8: Assign the following interzonal vehicular trips emanating from zone 1 to the network shown.

j	2	3	4	5
Qij	800	500	200	600

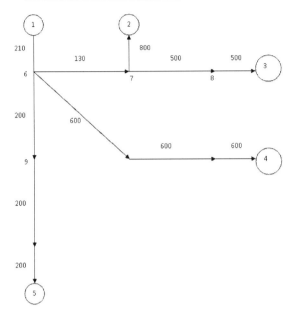

Figure 6.11: Minimum Tree

The minimum tree emanating from zone 1 is reproduced in Figure 6.11. The interzonal flows using each link of the tree are assumed to compute the total contribution of the given flows to these links. Thus link 7-2 takes only the total interchange between zones 1 and 2, and link 7-8 takes the flow from zone 1 to zone 3. Link 6-7 takes the sum of the flows from zone 1 to zone 2 and from zone 1 to zone 3 because it belongs to both minimum paths. These links may also be assigned additional flows if they happen to be part of minimum paths that originate from zones other than zone 1.

6.1.5.2 Free/multipath traffic assignment

In essence, a free/all-or-nothing assignment assumes that all tripmakers travelling between a specific pair of zones actually select the same path. In reality, interchange volumes are divided among a number of paths, and algorithms that are capable of determining several paths between each pair of zones in order of increasing impedance are available. Therefore it is possible to apportion the interchange volume between these paths according to some realistic rule. Irwin and von Cube suggested the following inverse-proportion function to compute the fraction to be assigned to each of a number of interzonal routes:

$$P(r) = \frac{W_{IJr}^{-1}}{\sum_x (W_{IJx}^{-1})}$$

where, W_{IJr} is the impedance of route r from I to J. As the following example illustrates, the use of the multinomial logit (MNL) model with disutilities based on path impedance is another possibility.

6.1.5.3 Capacity-restrained traffic assignment

As the flow increases toward capacity, the average stream speed decreases from the free-flow speed to the speed at maximum flow. Beyond this point the internal friction between vehicles in the stream becomes severe, the traffic conditions worsen, and severe shock waves and slow-moving platoons develop.

The implication of this phenomenon on the results of free-traffic assignment presents the following paradox: The interzonal flows are assigned to the minimum paths computed on the basis of free-flow link impedances. But if the link flows were at the levels dictated by the assignment, the link speeds would be lower and the link travel times would be higher than those corresponding prior to trip assignment may not be the minimum paths after the trips are assigned. Several iterative assignment techniques address the convergence between the link impedances assumed prior to assignment and the link impedances that are implied by the resulting link volumes. These techniques are known as capacity-restrained methods or techniques that employ capacity restraints. The relationship between link flow and link impedance is described as the link-capacity function. Several such functions are found in the technical literature. One of the forms, developed by BPR, is expressed mathematically as

$$w = \overline{w}\,[1 + 0.15(q/qmax)^4]$$

where, w is the impedance of a given link at flow q, $\overline{w}$ is the free flow impedance of the link, qmax is the link's capacity, and q is the link flow.

This function states that at capacity the links impedance is 15% higher than the free-flow impedance. If the demand were to exceed the capacity of the link, the resulting shock waves and their dissipation times would cause a rapid deterioration in the link flow conditions. The outcome of the whole 4-stage travel demand modelling process is the assessment of traffic volume on each and every link of the integrated transport network and the assessment of congestion levels on each link in terms of volume to capacity (v/c) ratio. Figure 6.12 and Figure 6.13 show the traffic assignment output for some case examples.

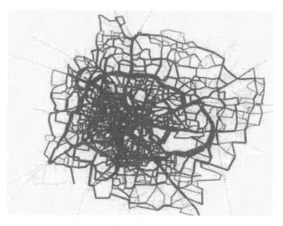

Figure 6.12: Peak Hour Traffic Loading on Transport Network of Bangalore

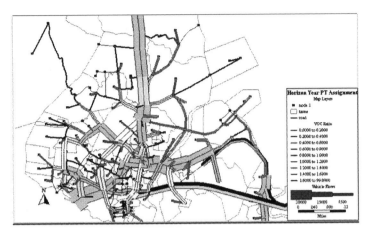

Figure 6.13: Peak Hour Traffic Loading on Transport Network of Thane

6.2 Travel demand estimation

6.2.1 Use of travel demand models

Travel demand modelling is the utilization of a computer software package to replicate the real world transportation system around us (roads, intersections, traffic control devices, congestion delays, use of a transit system, etc.). Once the computer model can accurately replicate the existing conditions of a study area, it can then be used to predict future travel patterns and demands based on changes in the transportation system (e.g., new public transport system, new roads, wider roads with more capacity, closed roads, new bicycle lanes, etc.); changes in the land use (e.g., more residential development, a new industrial site, etc.); and changing demographics (more or less people in a specific area, access to a vehicle, etc.). By simulating the current multi-modal transport network conditions and the travel demand on those networks, deficiencies in the system can be identified. It is also an important tool in planning future network enhancements and analyzing currently proposed projects that may involve a combination of different modes of transport. Travel demand models are developed to simulate actual travel patterns and existing demand conditions.

Networks are constructed using current network inventory files for each mode containing data for each link within the network. Travel demand is generated using socioeconomic data such as household size, population density, income, automobile availability, employment data, etc. Once the existing conditions are evaluated and adjusted to satisfactorily replicate actual travel patterns, the model inputs are then altered to project future-year conditions. Using these inputs, the model is able to derive future capacity limitations relative to the current transportation system that may consist of different modes. Once these deficiencies are identified, potential improvements are evaluated by rerunning the model with an improved or modified transportation system. A range of different mode split levels, transport networks, and even different land use patterns are tested this way. For example, Table 6.14 gives desired modal share for Indian cities based on consideration for sustainability, etc. This can then be taken as a basis to arrive at various combinations of different mode infrastructure mix, which can be tested using developed travel demand models. Future-year traffic projections are based on numerous assumptions about how population, employment, automobile operating costs, public transport cost, and other factors will change over time. As such, future year projections are only as good as the assumptions that are made.

Table 6.10: Desired Modal Share for Indian Cities

City Population(in millions)	Mass Transport	Bicycle	Other Modes
0.1-0.5	30-40	30-40	25-35
0.5-1.0	40-50	25-35	20-30
1.0-2.0	50-60	20-30	15-25
2.0-5.0	60-70	15-25	10-20
5.0+	70-85	15-20	10-15

Figure 6.14: Alternative Corridors Tested for MMR

Travel demand modelling remains a cornerstone of the integrated transportation infrastructure planning process. Travel demand models have achieved sophistication unimaginable by those who laid their foundation in the 1950s. The current generation of travel demand models, however, is unable to analyze many transportation policies under consideration in urban areas, such as pricing, demand management, and air quality strategies. Modern travel demand models can predict highway volumes reasonably well in many circumstances, but they lack precision in several critical areas. These areas include prediction of latent and induced travel demand, intermodal impacts, and land use/transportation relationships. Widening highways and developing new highway corridors in built-up urban areas are often impractical and always expensive. Shortly after suffering the cost and disruption of adding highway capacity, communities see congested conditions return long before the end of the useful life of the facility and well in advance of travel-model horizon years. Although much of this congestion can be attributed to induced demand that is, to travellers shifting from unimproved to improved routes is also the result of realized latent demand that is, to travel resulting from a decline in the cost of travel. We understand this phenomenon only in terms of observed trends but not in terms of the underlying behavioral forces that cause it to occur. Models capable of predicting latent demand are necessary to properly simulate the effect of transportation policies over prolonged periods.

6.2.2 Induced travel demand

While we propose different infrastructure projects, it is important to understand that the benefits projected are sometimes inflated due to lack of consideration of latent and induced demand, which surfaces as a result of change in mode choice and route choice behavior of travellers in light of proposed infrastructure improvements. For example, if a road is widened from say two lane to four lane to improve the travel time of traffic using that road the resultant improvements may not be as anticipated since it is not the same traffic that will continue to use it but more traffic may come on this road either because some people now find it more attractive or some people leave public transport and use private vehicle on this road since they find it more attractive to travel by their own mode using this widened road now. Similar phenomena can occur if say capacity of a metro rail line is doubled. So, induced demand, or latent demand, is the phenomenon that after supply increases more of a good is consumed. This is entirely consistent with the economic theory of supply and demand; however, this idea has become important in the debate over the expansion of transportation systems, and is often used as an argument against widening roads, such as major commuter roads. It is considered by some to be a contributing factor to urban sprawl.

Traffic engineers often compare traffic to a fluid, assuming that a certain volume must flow through the road system. But urban traffic may be more comparable to a gas that expands to fill available space. Road improvements that reduce travel costs attract trips from other routes, times and modes, and encourage longer and more frequent travel. This is called generated traffic, referring to additional vehicle traffic on a particular road. This consists in part of induced travel, which refers to increased total vehicle miles travel (VMT) compared with what would otherwise occur. Generated traffic reflects the economic law of demand, which states that consumption of good increases as its price declines. Roadway improvements that alleviate congestion reduce the generalized cost of driving (i.e., the price), which encourages more vehicle use. Put another way, most urban roads have latent travel demand, additional peak-period vehicle trips that will occur if congestion is relieved. In the short-run generated traffic represents a shift along the demand curve; reduced congestion makes driving cheaper per mile or kilometer in terms of travel time and vehicle operating costs. Over the long run induced travel represents an outward shift in the demand curve as transport systems and land use patterns become more automobile dependent, so people must drive more to maintain a given level of accessibility to goods, services, and activities. Accurate transport planning and project appraisal must consider these three impacts:

1. Generated traffic reduces the predicted congestion reduction benefits of road capacity expansion.

2. Induced travel imposes costs, including downstream congestion, accidents, parking costs, pollution, and other environmental impacts.

3. The additional travel that is generated provides relatively modest user benefits, since it consists of marginal value trips (travel that consumers are most willing to forego).

Ignoring these factors distorts planning decisions. Experts conclude that the economic value of a scheme can be overestimated by the omission of even a small amount of induced traffic. This matter is of profound importance to the value-for-money assessment for the road improvement programs as quite small absolute changes in traffic volumes have a significant impact on the benefit measures. The induced travel effects of changes in land use and trip distribution may be critical to an accurate evaluation of transit and highway alternatives (Litman, 2011).

Having the background of travel demand modelling, as discussed in the previous section, it is easy to take into account the induced demand effect due to the provision of a new facility or any change in the existing infrastructure. This can be done by reflecting the changes in the mode choice and/or network files and rerunning the traffic assignment with revised mode share and network to obtain revised flows on the network, which will eventually reflect the changes in flow due to latent and induced demand effect. Further, we can test various combinations of mode integration and their corresponding infrastructure provisions so as to not only overcome the negative effects of induced demand but to also shift it in favor of more sustainable modes of transport. For example, inducing or generating (latent) more demand in favor of public transport by improving cycling and walking facilities to access public transport and thus provide better door-to-door connectivity compared to travel by private modes.

6.3 Efficient use of existing/proposed infrastructure

The emerging policy on the urban transportation planning issue is the newly promulgated transportation system management (TSM) action program. It is now required that TSM projects be included in the transportation improvement program (TIP) as the short-range element of the overall plan. Generally for all cities exceeding more than two lakhs in population, these TSM plans are compulsory while preparing comprehensive transportation plans. The TSM considers a wide range of actions with low capital investment requirements that can improve the transportation in the short term. It reflects the

a) Steeply rising costs

b) Environmental concerns

c) Intense competition for available resources, and make it imperative that better and more efficient users for existing investments in the transportation infrastructure be found before additional investments are made in costly new facilities. The new concept is therefore to make more efficient use of the highways and transit systems already in place thus reducing the need for new capital investments and for operation assistance.

A. The TSM on implementation provides the following advantages:

a) Fiscal economy

b) Better balance among the various elements of urban transport system.

c) Broader local and national goals of energy conservation

d) Environmental improvement

e) Equity for transit dependents

f) Urban preservation

B. The TSM actions recognize the following features:

a) Characteristics of the existing transportation system

b) Total demand for the transportation purpose in question

c) Geographic distribution

d) Nature of urban environment

e) Locally determined goals

For example a pooled riding system in privately owned vehicles may serve the work trip demand most efficiently in a low demand density sector while the conventional bus transit may serve in another sector. The high occupancy commuter rail may prove efficient in another sector. The TSM plan fosters deliberately the use of the combination of modes that best represents an area's desired balance between the goals of efficient mobility, environmental amenity, and social equity in the operation of a transportation system.

C. The TSM plans are discussed covering the following aspects:

a) Warrants for implementation

b) Prerequisites

c) Advantages and disadvantages

d) Implementation considerations

e) Significant interrelationships among actions

6.4 Routing and scheduling of public transport

Many techniques have been used to solve the basic problem of routing and scheduling in public transportation. Unfortunately, no technique has incorporated all or even most of the practical options or real life restrictions and extensions. Different versions of the vehicle routing and scheduling problems on the transportation network appear in all fields of transportation depending on the specific objective. Well organized vehicle routing or well designed schedules can remarkably contribute towards a decrease in transportation costs and increase the quality of the transportation services. For operation of public buses user and operator are the two agencies involved, both having conflicting objectives to be satisfied. Thus the transit network design problems become complex due to:

a) Difficulty in combining user costs and operator costs in a single objective function.

b) Difficulty in optimizing the objective function.

c) Discrete nature of route design and various other constraints involved with route coverage, route duplication, route length, and directness of service.

Various attempts have been made to solve the routing and scheduling problem with multiple objective functions. Much remains to be done using available computationally efficient algorithms.

Routing and scheduling are planning issues in a transit network, which can be grouped into 3 major categories they are

a. Perform maximum transportation work: This is expressed by the number of passenger-trips or passenger-km. This implies provision of high travel speed, passenger convenience, and other elements that attract passengers. In planning of a given network, if average trip lengths do not vary much among alternative designs, these two objectives may have similar values; however, in comparing an urban transit system with a regional one, both passenger-trips and passenger-km values should be considered because they may be quite different alternative designs.

b. Achieve maximum operating efficiency: This objective can ultimately be expressed as the minimum total system cost for a required performance level.

c. Creative positive impacts: These include a variety of effects, from short-range ones, such as reduction of highway congestion, to the long-range goals, such as achievements of high population mobility, desirable land use patterns, sustainability, and high quality of life.

These three categories of objectives generally correspond, respectively, to the requirements of the three interested parties considered in transit system evaluation: passengers, operators, and community.

6.4.1 Passenger attraction

The greater the number of passenger trips a transit system carries, the better it serves citizen's and a city's needs. The more persons-km a transit network carries, the more economically it operates and the more it reduces less socially desirable automatic travel. Consequently, the dominant goal in designing most transit systems is to attract as many passengers as possible. The main network design features that affect transit service quality and thereby influence passenger attraction are defined here.

a) Area coverage, defined as % of the total urban area that is within 5-min and 10-min walking of transit stations, represents the basic element of transit system availability. For planning purposes, it can be considered that most potential transit users within a 5 min (400m) walking distance will use the system. Between that distance and a 10 min (800m) walking distance the potential ridership gradually decreases practically to zero.

b) Operating speed is mostly a function of ROW category and station spacings. In street operations (ROW category C), the speed depends on street and traffic conditions; in rapid transit (ROW category A), station spacing is usually the determination factor. Station planning is therefore a major element influencing travel speeds.

c) Transit lines should be designed to follow as closely as possible major origin-destination (O-D) patterns of travel in order to attract and serve efficiently the maximum number of passengers.

d) Direction of travel, measured as the ratio of passenger-km traveled on the network to passenger-km along straight O-D lines, express an efficiency of the network design. For a given travel demand, the network configuration that results in the smallest ratio is most efficient.

e) Simplicity, connectivity, and easy transfers must be considered in design because they are important for passenger convenience and attraction. The greatest operational simplicity is achieved by operating lines independently of each other with easy passenger transfer among them.

6.4.2 Network operating efficiency

Operating efficiency, representing performance and cost of transit operations, is a major concern of the second interested party.

There are five major determinants of efficiency.

a) Continuity and balancing of lines, or provisions of direct services among areas with heavy travel demand, is desirable for both passenger convenience and operating efficiency. Continuity should be planned so that each line has reasonably well-balanced capacity requirements on all of its major sections.

b) Operating flexibility is increased through provisions of connections between lines at which TUs can be switched among lines for scheduled or unforeseen change of service. Greater extensiveness of networks and track connections among lines always increase operating flexibility. Turn back tracks, usually center dead-end tracks connected with both through tracks; allow short-turn operations, i.e., use of intermediate stations as terminals.

c) Integration with other modes ensures that a network provides a service in an area greater than immediate sheds of its stations. It allows efficient utilization of joint rail/highway corridors. Most important are intermodal stations, which permit easy interchange of passengers between different modes such as bus feeders to rail trunk lines, P+R facilities, etc.

d) Terminals, depots, and yards should be placed at such locations that deadheading, i.e., travel between depots and the lines, is minimized. Also because these facilities occupy large areas, they should be located where cost of land is not high. Both requirements make outlying sites better suited for depot and yard locations than central city areas. Terminals should be placed near major streets to allow good accessibility by walking and vehicles of different access modes.

e) Cost of the system is, of course, often the most important single factor in network design. Investment cost depends mostly on ROW category and alignment, its type (at grade, elevated, tunnel, or other), and stations (their size, complexity, equipment, storage facilities, etc.).

6.4.3 Network city interactions

To ensure that the transit system will have positive impacts and minimal undesirable effects on the community (the third interested party), the following major factors must be considered in its design.

a) Land use should always be a major factor in planning a transit network, particularly metro and other rail systems. In many cities, the main objectives of building a metro system are to enable and stimulate development of certain land use patterns.

b) Topography and environment usually impose stringent requirements and constraints on a transit system. Hilly terrain restricts the possibilities of the network design. The existence of valleys, rivers, or lakes often gives natural corridors for transit facilities.

c) Major geographical constraints, such as hills, valleys, rivers, or bays requiring major tunnels or bridges for crossing, always make construction of high-capacity transit lines far more efficient than construction of roads because two track transit lines have capacities equivalent to 10 or more highway lines per direction.

d) The existing transportation network must be taken into account since it may be utilized for location of transit facilities (bus lanes, light rail medians, metro tunnels, or railway corridors), or it may sometimes create obstacles, such as difficult at-grade crossings.

As mentioned, the influence of most of these factors on transit network design cannot be defined precisely; however, it is important that the designer be familiar with them and considers them carefully.

6.4.4 Optimum TU capacity

The following example referred from V.R. Vuchic (2005), explains how optimium TU capacity is obtained.

On a transit line with a given p_{max}, the operator is interested in providing a required transporting capacity by a smaller number of large TUs because of their lower cost per unit capacity. However, passengers require shorter headways, i.e, and higher frequency of service, which dictates the use of a greater number of smaller TUs.

To find the optimal balance between the interests of the two parties considering costs only, a model including the operating costs C_o (Rs/h) and passenger costs C_p (Rs/h) should be developed and used to derive the expression for the total cost, C=C_o+Cp. With mathematical expressions for these costs, the TU capacity that results in the minimum total costs C should then result in the minimum total cost C. This is illustrated here by a rather simple model of a transit line with length L (km), headway h (min), cycle time T (min), and load factor α_{max} (prs/sp). The TU (bus or train) capacity is C_{TU} (sps/TU).

Simplifying assumptions for this model are:

a) Total hourly cost of operation of the line C_o is equal to the product of unit vehicle operating cost c_o (Rs/TU-h) and the number of TUs on the line NTU $C_o=c_o*NTU$.

b) Passenger demand (design hour volume p_{max}) is constant and is related to the total number of passengers boarding along the entire line, PL, by a coefficient: $p_{max} = \eta_p$ PL.

c) Cycle speed V_c on the line is independent of TU size and of the number of passengers.

d) Average passenger waiting time is equal to half of the headway, h/2.

e) Average value of passenger time is c_p (Rs/prs-h).

First the number of TUs is expressed by the given line parameters. Using the below equations one obtains the equations for T and h:

$$T = \frac{120L}{V_c} \quad \text{and} \quad h = \frac{60\alpha_{max}*C_{TU}}{P_{max}}$$

$$\left|\frac{T,h}{min}\right|\frac{L}{km}\left|\frac{V}{km/h}\right|\frac{\alpha}{prs/sp}\left|\frac{C_{TU}}{sps/TU}\right|\frac{P}{prs/h}\left|\ldots\ldots\ldots1\right.$$

N_{TU} can be expressed by these operating elements as:

$$N_{TU} = \frac{T}{h} = \frac{2L.P_{max}}{\alpha_{max}.C_{TU}.V_c}$$

$$\left|\frac{N}{TU}\right|\frac{T,h}{min}\left|\frac{L}{km}\right|\frac{V}{km/h}\left|\frac{\alpha}{prs/sp}\right|\frac{C_{TU}}{sps/TU}\left|\frac{P}{prs/h}\right|\ldots\ldots2$$

Operating cost can now be expressed, using the first assumption above as:

$$C_o = N_{TU}.C_o = \frac{2L.P_{max}}{\alpha_{max}.C_{TU}.V_c}.c_o$$

$$\left|\frac{C}{RS/h}\right|\frac{L}{km}\left|\frac{V}{km/h}\right|\frac{\alpha}{prs/sp}\left|\frac{C_{TU}}{sps/TU}\right|\frac{P}{prs/h}\left|\frac{c_o}{Rs/TU_h}\right.\ldots\ldots\ldots3$$

Passenger cost for all passengers on the line, P_L is:

$$C_p = P_L.\frac{h}{120}.c_p = \frac{P_L.\alpha_{max}.C_{TU}}{2P_{max}}.c_p$$

$$\left|\frac{C}{RS/h}\right|\frac{P}{prs/h}\left|\frac{h}{min}\right|\frac{c_p}{Rs/(prs-h)}\left|\frac{\alpha}{prs/sp}\right|\frac{C_{TU}}{sps/TU}\left|\ldots\ldots4\right.$$

Total cost, consisting of the operation and passenger cost, is obtained by summing up Eqs. 3 and 4

$$C = \frac{2L.P_{max}}{\alpha_{max}.C_{TU}.V_c}.c_o + \frac{P_L.\alpha_{max}.C_{TU}}{2P_{max}}.c_p$$

$$\left|\frac{C}{RS/h}\right|\frac{P}{prs/h}\left|\frac{h}{min}\right|\frac{c_p}{Rs/(prs-h)}\left|\frac{\alpha}{prs/sp}\right|\frac{C_{TU}}{sps/TU}\left|\frac{c_o}{Rs/TU_h}\right|\ldots\ldots5$$

To find the optimum value of vehicle capacity that will minimize total cost, the derivative of Eqs 5 with respect to C_{TU} is set equal to 0:

$$\frac{C}{C_{TU}} = -\frac{2L.P_{max}}{\alpha_{max}.C_{TU}^2.V_c}.c_o + \frac{P_L.\alpha_{max}}{2P_{max}}.c_p\ldots\ldots\ldots6$$

from which the optimum vehicle capacity, C_{TU}^*, is:

$$C_{TU}^* = \frac{2P_{max}}{\alpha_{max}}\sqrt{\frac{L.c_o}{P_L.V_c.c_p}}\text{(units as above)}\ldots\ldots7$$

Figure 6.15 shows a diagram of C_o, C_p, and C as a function of C_{TU}, as well as the position of C_{TU}^*

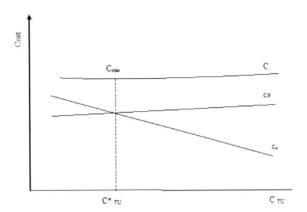

Figure 6.15: Operator and Passenger Costs as Functions of Transit Unit Capacity

6.5 Intermodal coordination

The intermodal coordination is explained through the following example from the author's work. The objective of the approach is to develop an optimum integrated urban mass transit system for any city which has a potential demand for a new rail-based mass transit system besides the street transit system and existing rail-based system (if any). Using the demand pattern for the planning year, the approach tends to develop an integrated mass transit system towards an ideal state. For this, the existing bus transit route network is neglected, as the same may not be optimum in the planning year and may create some bias towards developing an ideal state. After developing the integrated system, the existing buses can be rerouted (without incurring much extra expenditure) to serve as a feeder system to the higher order rail system, and the commuters can then use the integrated system to optimize their daily commuting. Putting this in more specific terms, given the assigned flows (as per user equilibrium approach) of planning year peak hour public transport demand on the city transport network, all the corridors which are demand intensive and are beyond the capacity of street transit system to handle, should be served by a rail transit system, and the rest of the city should be covered by a feeder street transit route network. The user equilibrium approach is used here because in general, during peak hour a regular commuter has nearly perfect information about the travel attributes on a city transport network and a path, which minimizes his travel time or distance will be chosen.

Explaining further, consider a commuter who commutes from his residence, say in zone X_1, to his work place in zone X_2 or vice-versa, on an average working day during peak hour (peak hour is chosen because the integrated mass transit network is designed for catering the critical peak hour flow); if given, perfect information about the city transport network, he will chose a path, from his origin to destination (O-D), which will minimize his travel time (measure of travel impedance). Assuming that all travelers have the same valuations of network attributes then the same will be the case for a person commuting between his home zone, say X_3 and workplace zone X_4 or for a commuter travelling between zone X_5 and X_6. When the optimum paths of all such commuters/O-D pairs in the city are accumulated on the city transport network, i.e., they are assigned on the city transport network as per the user equilibrium approach, one gets the cumulative peak hour ridership on each link of the city transport network. In such a flow pattern, there will be high demand intensity (peak hour flow) on major corridors connecting major residential areas with the work place zones. In order to cater to this demand pattern and also to ensure the effective use of capacities of different mass transit modes, all such demand intensive corridors, which are beyond the capacity of the street transit system to handle, should be covered by a rail transit system, and the rest of the city should be covered by feeder street transit route network (to provide full coverage to the users O-D travel, and also to achieve the forecasted ridership on the rail transit corridor). This set-up will allow every individual user to travel from his origin to final destination by the shortest possible path (along the integrated network, i.e., rail and feeder bus) and also allow the operator to achieve maximum possible ridership, as the demand will be assigned as per the user equilibrium approach, and the rail corridor and feeder routes will be identified giving due consideration to the demand. The proposed rail corridor identification and scheduling models will work best in this set-up of trip demand and distribution pattern. The subsequent section discusses the proposed models.

6.5.1 Proposed rail corridor identification model

The objective of the model is to identify a new rail corridor in a city which is optimum from the users and operators standpoint. Typically, the key concern of the user is to minimize the time spent in arriving and transferring at the stations, waiting for the rail in the station, riding in rail, and reaching their destination from the nearest station by walking or other modes. From the operators view, the corridor should be aligned on a high demand passage-way so as to guarantee maximum possible ridership, and at the same time to minimize his operating cost. The construction cost of the rail corridor is also an important variable which the service provider would like to minimize. The proposed model attempts to incorporate most of these concerns. The objective function can be formulated in mathematical terms as follows:

Objective:

Minimum $Z = C_c + O_c + U_c$ 1

where:

$C_c = (\gamma_1 * L) * \frac{[\rho*(1+\rho)^n]}{[(1+\rho)^n - 1]}/(365 * 24)$................2

$O_c = \sum_j (T_j) * R_0 * \gamma_{operating}$ 3

$U_c = \sum_j (q_{wi} * (t_{wi})^a * \gamma_{walk}) + (q_{oi} * (t_{oi})^a) * \gamma_{other}$
$+ \sum_i (p_{wi}) * (t_{wi})^e * \gamma_{walk} + (p_{oi} * (t_{oi})^e * \gamma_{other}) + \sum_j (T_{sj} * R_j * \gamma_{riding})$
..........................$i, j \epsilon I RN$..........................4

Subjected to:

$g_1 = \frac{[q_{max}^k]}{CAP_t}$ less than $L_{max}^t * k \epsilon I RN$ 5

$g_2 = \frac{[q_{max}^k]}{CAP_t}$ greater than $L_{max}^t * k \epsilon I RN$ 6

$g_3 = Rdp_k$ greater than x_t $K \epsilon T R$...............7

where C_c, O_c, U_c = construction cost, operating cost, and user cost in Rupees (Rs.)/hour, respectively; γ_l = average construction cost in Rs. per unit length of the rail alignment including station cost; γ_{walk} = average walk time cost in Rs. per minute per passenger; $\gamma_{operating}$ = average cost of operating a train in Rs. per minute; γ_{riding} = average riding time cost in Rs. per minute per passenger; γ_{other} = average access/egress time cost in Rs. per minute per passenger, for passengers using feeder modes; L = total alignment length; T_j = train travel time on link j; R_o = total number of round trips during peak hour; n= analysis period; ρ= assumed interest rate; q_{wi} = numbers of passengers walking to the ith station; q_{oi}= numbers of passengers reaching the ith station by feeder modes; p_{oi} = numbers of passengers walking out of the ith station; p_{oi}= numbers of passengers going out of the ith station by feeder modes; t_{wia} = access time by walking to the ith station; t^a_{oi} = access time by feeder mode to reach the ith station; t^e_{wi} = egress time by walk from the ith station; t^e_{oi} = egress time by feeder mode to reach destination from the ith station; q^k_{max} = maximum peak hour flow on route k; Rdp_k= average ridership on corridor k in terms of passengers per hour per direction (pphpd); x_t = minimum ridership value for train desired to be achieved on the identified corridor; T_{sj} = passenger riding time on link j; R_j = peak hourly ridership on link j; L^t_{max} = maximum allowable load factor on any train route; L^t_{min} = minimum allowable load factor on any train route; TR = all train routes; and IRN = integrated route network.

6.5.1.1 Objective function

The function Z in equation 1 is a complex multi-objective problem. C_c is the construction cost of rail alignment (including stations) in Rs. per hour, obtained as the equivalent compounded cost spread equally over the analysis period (n); O_c is the operating cost of the rail transit system in Rs. per hour; and U_c is the user cost in Rs. per hour, which includes the access time cost, egress time cost, and riding time cost. Since, the rail corridor is to be obtained based on the peak hour travel; all costs are obtained in terms of equivalent peak hour. There are conflicting objectives within the function, like increasing the corridor length will increase the construction and operating costs; however, the user cost may decrease owing to less access and egress time to/from stations.

6.5.1.2 Constraints

In the following, the meaning of each constraint is briefly described: Constraint g_1 states that the load factor on any route k of an integrated system should be less than the maximum allowable load factor L_{max} for the mode on that route. This constraint has been introduced to maintain a certain minimum comfort levels for the users at the maximum load section during peak hour.

Constraint g_2 assures that the load factor on any route k of the integrated system should be more than the minimum allowable load factor L_{min} for the mode on that route. This constraint has been introduced to maintain certain minimum level of ridership for the operator at the maximum load section during peak hour.

Constraint g_3 states that the average ridership on the train should be equal to or more than a certain minimum ridership value for the train desired to be achieved on the identified corridor. This constraint has been introduced in order to indirectly ensure at least a certain minimum level of revenue generation for the operator because the same could not be considered directly in the model.

6.5.1.3 Solution approach

The above formulation makes the function Z a complex, multi-objective, and data-intensive problem. Hence, a GIS-based approach is used in the proposed model to optimize the above objective function. Figure 6.16a and Figure 6.16b presents the complete flow chart of the solution approach.

The proposed model consists of three stages: public transport demand forecasting, creation of corridor link set, and optimization of rail corridor using GIS. The public transport demand forecasting is done primarily to get the required input data for the model, i.e., peak hour cumulative public transport O-D matrix for the planning year which is used later on for generation and optimization of the rail corridor. It is performed using standard procedure and practice and no research contribution is claimed on this part of the work. It consists of four substages: base year O-D matrix generation, base year travel demand modeling, estimation of modal share for proposed rail transit mode, and forecasting of O-D person trip matrices.

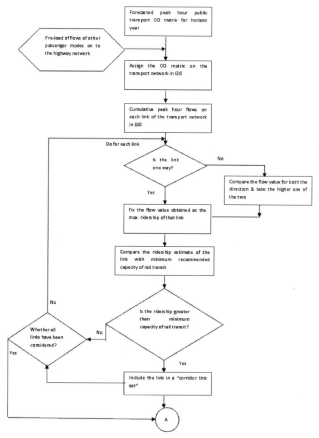

Figure 6.16 a: Solution Approach

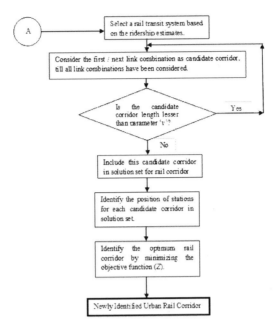

Figure 6.16 b: Solution Approach

a. Public transport demand forecasting

The base year O-D person trips matrices were generated from household interview survey data. In this stage, the model requires home interview survey, screen line, cordon line, and network data. Base year travel demand modelling involves development of trip end and trip distribution models. Trip end models are developed only for intracity trips made by residents of the study area, using a stepwise multiple linear regression technique. All external trips are modelled by the growth factor method. A doubly constrained gravity trip distribution model is calibrated to represent base year travel pattern for intracity trips within the study area.

Now, it is expected that if an efficient and effective rail transit system is planned for any city, which is optimum from both the users and operators point of view, there will be a shift in mode share from all other passenger (OP) modes to proposed rail mode, which will help in maintaining a desired mode share between public transport (bus and rail) and other modes (making the city balanced and sustainable), which is the ultimate goal of integrated mass transit planning. To obtain modal share of proposed rail transit mode, this shift from all OP modes to rail transit mode, is required to be found out. The shift can be estimated by conducting a detailed stated preference (SP) survey, to model the choice of commuters between OP modes and proposed rail mode. Since this survey has to be conducted in absence of the network details of the proposed rail mode (which is essentially to be arrived at through the proposed model), the survey has to be carefully designed based on the target attributes of the integrated public transport system to be developed through the study.

146

Mode wise binary logit models, which give probability of shift from each existing mode to proposed rail mode can be developed using preferences indicated by respondents. Here, it is assumed that all the commuters currently using bus mode will also be a part of mode share of an integrated public transport system (rail and feeder bus system). This assumption holds reasonably well because after rerouting of the bus system as a feeder service to the rail system, the commuter will perform the journey partly on feeder buses and partly on the rail system. To check the reasonableness of the obtained mode share for integrated PT system, the same can be compared with the desired modal share of public transport (if available) based on city population, size, and other attributes.

Finally, the daily O-D person trips matrix for the planning year is forecasted using trip end and trip distribution models developed for the base year and also the mode share obtained from SP survey data. While forecasting the planning variables for trip end models, the expected land use changes for the horizon year are taken into consideration. The daily matrix obtained is factored by average daily to peak hour ratio, in order to obtain a peak hour O-D person trip matrix. This peak hour matrix is then factored by derived mode share of public transport to obtain the peak hour public transport matrix for the horizon year. This matrix is used as an initial input in the next stage for optimization of the rail corridor using GIS.

b. Creation of corridor link set

By and large, the form and structure of Indian cities are not ideal (circular, semicircular or linear/grid), where the rail corridor could be simply aligned on corridors of heavy flow between residential zones and the central business district. There is always some haphazard development of residential and work zones. This haphazard development leads to some level of discontinuity and randomness in the demand intensity on the city transport network which is observed in the form of a set of transport links having very heavy flow which may be beyond the capacity of the street transit system to handle. Often these links indicate many continuous bands on the city transport network for small distances. These bands can be a part of the larger rail corridor which optimally connects many such bands. The set of these transport links having very heavy flow which may be beyond the capacity of the street transit system to handle, is referred to here as the corridor link set.

To identify this corridor link set, the forecasted peak hour public transport O-D matrix for the horizon year is assigned to the base year transport network in GIS, using the user equilibrium approach. This will give a future public transport ridership pattern in terms of pphpd on every link of the transport network. Here, the base year bus transport network is not considered as it may not be optimum for the planning year and may create some bias towards finding an optimal solution. If a link is two-way then the flow value for both directions are compared to the higher one, which is fixed as the maximum peak hour ridership of that link. Flow value for a one-way link is used as it is. Further, if the maximum ridership estimate of a link is beyond the capacity of street transit to handle then it is included in the corridor link set. Similar analysis is done for all the links, to arrive at the complete corridor link set.

c. Identification of rail corridor using GIS based iterative algorithm

The corridor link set can provide many link combinations for the formation of rail corridor. For instance, consider an example city network in Figure 6.17. It shows part of a city network joining a central business district (CBD) and a residential belt. The corridor link set contains the following grouped links:

1. C-1-2-3
2. 10-9-8-5-21-22
3. 18-19-20
4. 5-6-7

The proposed rail corridor can be aligned along various combinations of links. Some of these link combinations for the example city are:

1. C-1-2-3——-5-6-7
2. C-1-2-3——-10-9-5-21-22
3. C-1-2-3——-18-19-20
4. C-1-2-3——-21-5-8-9-10
5. 20-19-18——-10-9-5-21-22 etc.

For an actual city, there may be several such link combinations as potential candidates for the rail corridor. Considering the complexity of the model, lengthy procedure, and substantial data requirements, it will be computationally and time wise prohibitive to test the fitness of each candidate, some of which may be clearly impractical. One of the important aspects to be examined here is the minimum length of a rail corridor. The total length of a candidate rail corridor should be more than a prespecified value of parameter y. This rule ensures that the proposed corridor should not be too small so as to be of no practical value for the user and also justifies the investments made by the operator (particularly for rolling stock, crew, administrative staff, etc., which have not been taken into account explicitly in the model). The value of parameter y should be set such that the corridor covers the study area effectively and the access and egress time forms a smaller percentage of total O-D travel time of the user; otherwise, the system will become unattractive to the user and will therefore affect the actual mode share and correspondingly the ridership and revenue generated from the new system after implementation. The value of y should be in correspondence with the values of various related parameters used earlier in the stated preference (SP) survey design for estimating the mode share of the new rail system.

After arriving at the final set of candidate rail corridors, stations are identified using GIS for each candidate corridor based on the minimum and maximum interstation spacing criteria and land use characteristics, Verma (2010). The minimum and maximum interstation spacing criteria is decided in such a way that the travel time of a commuter from his origin to final destination via the integrated network is as close as possible to its actual shortest path along the city transport network. In other words, the station spacing is decided so as to keep the ratio of travel time of commuter (between his origin and final destination) by transit to that by auto as close to one another as possible. The other factors considered are the system characteristics of the recommended rail technology, different travel regimes of station-to-station train movement, and train stopping time at stations. This finally gives candidate rail corridors consisting of combinations of closely spaced links having high demand, which cannot be handled by street transit and station locations corresponding to each candidate corridor. The most suitable candidate amongst these is the one which minimizes the objective function Z. The same is chosen as the optimum rail corridor for the city.

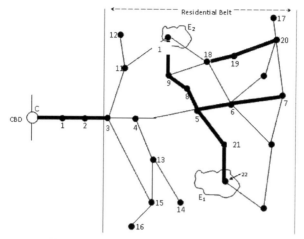

Figure 6.17: Example City Network

6.5.2 Proposed train scheduling model

Given the O-D matrix for the transit trips (for the design period) and the underlying train network (with the required attributes), the problem of train scheduling is to optimally allocate transit units among various available routes and obtain the optimal train fleet size. Considering the O-D flows to be given and fixed, the number of passengers using each path will still be a function of the transit allocation because of the proportionate frequency criterion being applied while assigning the demand to each route. Thus scheduling can be considered as an optimization problem. For the operation of rail transit, the user and the operator which are the two agencies involved have conflicting objectives to be satisfied in a single objective function. The user will be concerned with waiting time, level of service, least in-vehicle time, etc. The operator will be concerned with minimizing fleet size, vehicle operation cost, maximizing profit, etc.

According to the previous study by Verma and Dhingra (2006), the objective function was taken as minimization of the operating cost of trains (operator cost) and waiting time of passengers (user cost) subject to load factor constraint and waiting time constraint. The in-vehicle time of the passenger (user cost) was not included in the objective function, and the dwell time (which influences both the operator and user cost) was considered as a constant. The current study attempts to improve upon these limitations. Also, proportionate frequency criterion has been applied for assigning demand on the overlapping stations. The objective function can be mathematically represented as follows:

Minimize:

Waiting time cost

$$C_1 \left\{ \sum_{all\ k \in SR} \sum_{i=1}^{n} \sum_{j=1}^{n} \left[0.5 \left(d_{ij} \frac{f_k}{\Sigma f_k} \right) \right] \cdot t_{wt\ ij}^{k} \right\}$$

$$+$$

In vehicle travel cost

$$C_2 \left\{ \sum_{all\ k \in SR} \sum_{i=1}^{n} \sum_{j=1}^{n} \left[0.5 \left(d_{ij} \frac{f_k}{\Sigma f_k} \right) \right] \cdot t_{v\,ij} \right\}$$

$+$

Vehicle operating cost

$$C_3 \left\{ \sum_{all\ k \in SR} f_k T_k \right\} \qquad \dots\dots\dots\dots\dots\dots\dots 8$$

Subjected to:

$$g_{1-} \left[\left| q_{max}^k / CAP_t \right| \leq L_{max} \; \forall \; k \in TR \right]$$

$$g_2 = \left[\left| q_{min}^k / CAP_t \right| \geq L_{min} \; \forall \; kc\ TR \right]$$

$$g_3 = \left[\left[t_{wt,ij}^k \leq t_{wt,max} \right] \forall \; k \in TR \right]$$

$$g_4 = \left[\left[t_{wt,ij}^k \geq t_{wt,min} \right] \forall \; k \in TR \right]$$

$t_{v\,ij}^k = t_{avg,ij}^k + t_{dw}^l \quad \forall$ station l between i and j.

C_1 = Waiting time cost in Rupees per min.

C_2 = In- vehicle time cost in Rupees per min.

C_3 = Vehicle operating cost in Rupees per min

d_{ij}^k = Demand from station i to station j along train route k.

$t_{wt,ij}^k$ = Waiting time of passengers traveling from station i to station j along route k

which is estimated as half the headway value.

f_k = Frequency of trains along route k, it will be reciprocal of headway on route k.

L_{min} = Minimum allowable load factor.

L_{max} = Maximum allowable load factor.

$t_{wt,min}$ = Minimum allowable waiting time.

$t_{wt,max}$ = Maximum allowable waiting time.

q_{max}^k = Maximum link flow on train route k

CAP_t = Capacity of the rail transit system, operating on the routes.

TR = Set of all train routes.

$t_{v,ij}^k$ = In vehicle time of passengers traveling from station i to station j along route k

$t_{avg,ij}^k$ = Average running time between station i and j

T_k = Round trip time for trains along route K, including layover time, random delay factor and dwell time

t_{dw}^l = Dwell time at every stations l between i and j. [Ref: People For Modern Transit (2001)]

$\qquad = (P_a t_a + P_b t_b + t_{oc})/n$

t_a = time for each passenger to alight the train taken as 2 second

t_b = time for each passenger to board the train taken as 2 second

t_{oc} = time taken to open and close the doors

P_b = number of persons boarding at the station

P_a = number of persons alighting at the station

n = number of people getting into the train at a time (no. of doors X capacity of each door)

6.5.2.1 Objective function

The formulation in equation 8 is a combinatorial type optimization problem. The user cost component consists of minimizing the total waiting time and in-vehicle time of the commuters. The operator cost component consists of minimizing the total vehicle operating cost. Here, the users and operators objective are conflicting in nature, for example, decrease in waiting time will result in increase in vehicle operating cost for the operator. Also, the in-vehicle travel time is a variable and is a function of dwell time. The dwell time is again a function of total boarding and alighting at any station, which in turn will depend on the frequency/headway chosen during each iteration.

6.5.2.2 Constraints

The meaning of each constraint is briefly described as follows: Constraint g_1 states that the load factor on any train route k should be less than the maximum allowable load factor L_{max} for the train on that route.

Constraint g_2 assures that the load factor on any train route k should be more than the minimum allowable load factor L_{min} for the train on that route.

Constraint g_3 assures that the waiting time $t^k_{wt,ij}$ incurred while traveling between station pair i, j along train route k should be less than the maximum allowable waiting time $t_{wt,max}$ for the commuter on that route.

Constraint g_4 states that the waiting time $t^k_{wt,ij}$ incurred while travelling between station pair i, j along train route k should be more than the minimum allowable waiting time $t_{wt,min}$ for the commuter on that route.

6.5.3 Solution approach

Since, the expected search space and train network is not very large, it is possible to work with total solution space and hence an exhaustive search algorithm (ESA), developed in MATLAB is used to minimize the objective function and obtain the optimum results. The number of trains to be run on each route and the total fleet size of trains can be obtained after getting the optimal frequency for each route from ESA. The following are the steps involved in the algorithm:

Step 1: Input data required comprised of number of passengers boarding and alighting at each station within a fixed period, the train route details, the ridership estimate on each link of the train route, round trip time for each route, value of waiting time, travel time cost of passengers, and train operating cost.

Step 2: Set the upper limit and lower limit of the variable headway.

Step 3: Start the loop and generate different sets of headway for train routes, give the variable for minimum fitness function value a very high initial value.

Step 4: Calculate the dwell time at each station.

Step 5: Calculate the objective function value for the given set of headway for the train routes.

Step 6: In case of violation, calculate the penalty for load factor and waiting time constraint and add it to the objective function to obtain the unconstrained objective function value for the set of headway for train routes.

Step 7: Compare the fitness value with minimum fitness value obtained in previous iteration if it is less then assign the current fitness value to the minimum fitness value variable.

Step 8: Generate the next set of headway and go to Step 3.

Step 9: Iterate until all possible sets of route headways are processed for fitness value. Finally, report the global minimum fitness value and the corresponding solution details.

6.5.4 Case study

6.5.4.1 Study area details

The model is applied on the Thane municipal corporation (TMC) area, a major urban center of the Mumbai metropolitan region (MMR), India (Figure 6.18). In the past, development of various industrial estates and also supporting residential and service employment has created the city more dynamic in nature. The city has developed in a circular fashion, expanding outwards from the initial CBD adjacent to the main railway station, which is served by Central Railways north-south line providing commuter services to MMR as well as longer distance ones. Buses run by various transport undertakings are present modes of public transport in Thane. The closeness of Thane to greater Mumbai, the commercial capital of India, has resulted in rapid growth of both population and employment. This has resulted in an exponential growth in intracity travel demand, which is beyond the capacity of the bus transit system to handle. Hence, the study area requires an intracity rail based mass transit system properly integrated with a street transit system, in a future planning period, to cater to this demand. The population of Thane in base year 2001 is 1.26 million, it is expected to reach 3.04 million by the planning year 2031.

The study area extends over 128.23 sq.km and is divided into 11 sectors and 95 wards. The planning data is currently available at ward level. However, some wards in the periphery of TMC are quite large and have a sparse population. Over the next 30 years, these areas are expected to accommodate most of the new developments within the TMC area. To capture these effects, larger wards are subdivided into two or three smaller zones for analysis. Consequently, travel demand in the study area is analyzed on the basis of 115 traffic analysis zones (TAZs) within the TMC area. Now, the regions beyond the study area are delineated into external zones based on catchments of existing transport links feeding into the study area. The outside world is represented by 30 zones. However, they are aggregated to seven external zones for analysis along seven transport links feeding into the study area, making a total of 122 TAZs for the whole study area, Verma and Dhingra (2005).

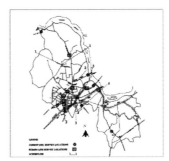

Figure 6.18: Map of the Study Area Thane

6.5.4.2 Data collection

Relevant data was collected for base year 2001 (CES, 2001) from primary and secondary sources. The primary sources are classified volume count and occupancy survey, origin destination survey, household (home interview) survey, stated preference survey, road network inventory survey, speed and delay survey, and rail and bus terminals survey. The data from secondary sources include population and demographic details, employment details, vehicle ownership data, suburban rail passenger data, environmental and land use data, and other data like maps showing ward boundaries, land use distribution, existing transport network, proposed land use, and transport network, etc.

From the data collected, it was found that a total of 1,778,178 trips are generated in the study area, by residents of TMC, on an average working day. The per capita and per household trip rate was worked out to be 1.44 and 5.2, respectively. Out of the total trips generated, 23.66% were found to be intrazonal and 76.34% as interzonal. While classifying the trips by purpose, work trips accounted for the highest share (46.04%) followed by educational trips (38.06%). The present share of public transport was found to be 34%. The average journey speed during peak period on some of the major arterials of Thane was found to vary from a low of 8.2 km/h to a high of 45.3 km/h. Also, the average household size in the TMC area was found to be 3.81, which actually ranges between one to 12 person, CES (2001). All these figures form important input information in developing proposed models, and subsequently identifying new rail corridors.

6.5.4.3 Forecasting of public transport travel demand for study area

The base year O-D person trips matrices were generated from base year data. Also, trip end and trip distribution models were calibrated in TransCAD using the required base year data. The details and results of these stages can be referred to in Verma and Dhingra (2003). The binary logit mode choice model was used to obtain percentage shift from existing modes to proposed rail mode in the horizon year, Verma (2010). After obtaining the percentage shift, actual mode share of public transport in the horizon year was calculated by adding actual shift from each existing mode to proposed rail mode and was obtained as 65%. This value of public transport share is reasonable if compared with desired PT share for Indian cities, as given in Table 6.11. The actual public transport share is used along with the daily to peak hour ratio of 8 to forecast horizon year peak hour public transport matrix using the models developed for base year, Verma and Dhingra (2005). The matrix obtained thus forms a basic input for the identification of rail corridor.

Table 6.11: Desirable Modal Split for Indian Cities (as a % of Total Trips)

City Population(in millions)	Mass Transport	Bicycle	Other Modes
0.10.5	3040	3040	2535
0.51.0	4050	2535	2030
1.02.0	5060	2030	1525
2.05.0	6070	1525	1020
5.0+	7085	1520	1015

6.5.4.4 Creation of corridor link set

To obtain the travel demand pattern for public transport (PT) modes, existing suburban rail links of the study area were converted into equivalent road links in the road layer. To do so, suburban rail links were digitized into equivalent road links in road geographic layer and suitable capacity was assigned to them, Verma and Dhingra (2005).

After converting the existing suburban rail links to equivalent road links, the forecasted peak hour public transport O-D matrix (obtained earlier) is assigned on base year transport network as per the user equilibrium approach, to obtain ridership patterns in terms of pphpd on each link of network. Figure 6.19 shows forecasted ridership patterns on a study area map, as generated in TransCAD.

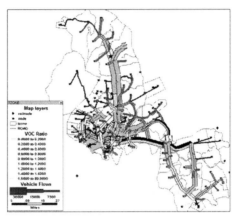

Figure 6.19: Forecasted Ridership Pattern on the Transport Network

To obtain rail transit demand pattern and the corridor link set, the peak hour ridership obtaned for each link (higher one out of the two directions in case of a two-way link to account for critical link flow) is compared with the minimum recommended capacity of the rail transit system, i.e., 12,000 pphpd [value referred from Verma and Dhingra (2001)]. All such links on the city transport network, which have peak hour ridership more than the minimum recommended capacity for rail transit were sorted and grouped together to form a corridor link set in GIS, the number of links included in this set were 37 in number, Figure 6.20. These links emerge in an almost continuous band except at few locations. This discontinuity is due to high diversion of ridership at some of the nodes. The maximum peak hour ridership in the network was found to be on link no. 85 as 34,369 pphpd. Hence, the most suitable system recommended for the operation on the newly identified corridor is light rail transit (LRT) 1 running on right-of-way category B or C. Here, the following capacity ranges were taken for different mass transit systems:

Street transit system = Up to 12,000 pphpd

(Mini-bus, single decker standard bus, double-decker, and articulated)

LRT1(R/w category B or C) = 12,000 to 36,000 pphpd

LRT2(R/w category A) = 36,000 to 50,000 pphpd

RRT (Metro) = 50,000 to 69,000 pphpd
RGR (Regional Rail) = 59,000 to 89,000 pphpd
More detailed calculations of the above values can be found in Verma and Dhingra (2001).

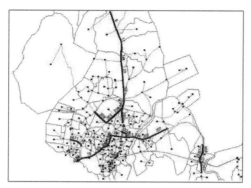

Figure 6.20: Corridor Link Set

To carry out the initial screening of all possible link combinations, the value of parameter y has to be carefully chosen such that the access time forms a smaller percentage of total O-D travel time of the user. For this, a sensitivity analysis was done to understand the change in weighted average accessibility distance with change in corridor length, as shown in Figure 6.21. It can be seen from the figure that the accessibility distance becomes very high and increases sharply with a decrease in corridor length beyond 7 km, accordingly, for the present study the value of parameters y has been taken as 7 km. Further, after applying the parameter y, a total of 6 candidate rail corridors were identified, and the objective function value (Z) was obtained for each one of them as per equation 1.

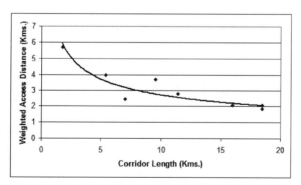

Figure 6.21: Variation in Weighted Average Accessibility Distance with Corridor Length

6.5.4.5 Optimization of rail corridor using GIS

First, the stations were identified on each of the candidate corridors based on the minimum and maximum interstation spacing criteria, Verma (2010). The minimum interstation spacing is taken as 0.64 km based on the system characteristics of the recommended rail technology, different travel regimes of station-to-station movement, and train stopping time at stations. Also, the nearest node after minimum interstation spacing limit from the previous identified station was selected as a station location. This is done so as to allow frequent transfer points along the rail corridor so that the travel time of a commuter from his origin to final destination via the integrated network is as close as possible to its actual shortest path along the city transportation network. The first and the last node on the candidate corridor were taken as the terminal stations. The nodes identified as possible locations of stations are: 8, 10, 12, 16, 25, 36, 43, 153, 157, 148, 70, 164, 165, 169, 170, 182, 184, 186, 210, and 143. The six major corridors and their stations are shown in Figure 6.22 to Figure 6.27. The following subsections describe the cost calculations for deriving the objective function value.

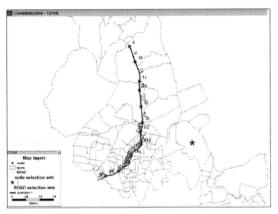

Figure 6.22: Corridor Number 1h

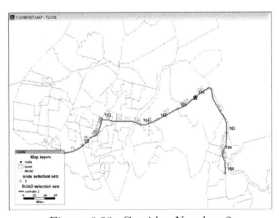

Figure 6.23: Corridor Number 2

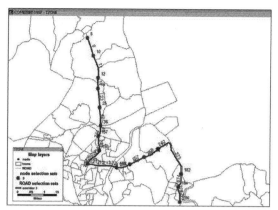

Figure 6.24: Corridor Number 3

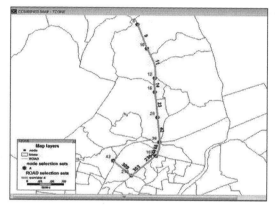

Figure 6.25: Corridor Number 4

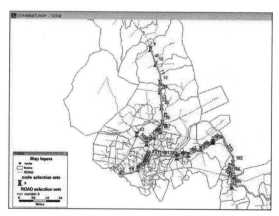

Figure 6.26: Corridor Number 5

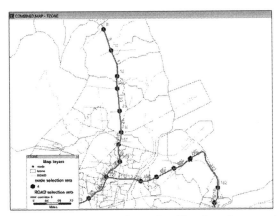

Figure 6.27: Corridor Number 6

a. Construction cost

Using equation (2), the construction cost is calculated for all six corridors separately. The values of the required external parameters are as given below;

γ_t = Rs 53,00,00,000/- per km of alignment obtained from CES (2001)

ρ = Rs. 9.93% obtained from CES (2001)

n = 30 years

The length of each candidate rail corridor along with the total construction cost is summarized in Table 6.12. Apparently, the construction cost increases with the corridor length and hence, corridor no. 5 and 6 with maximum length of 18.45 km have the highest construction cost of Rs.1,18,413/- per hour.

Table 6.12: Cost Calculations for Each Candidate Corridor

Corridor No.	Corridor Length (km)	Weighted Average Distance of Zone Centroids from the Stations (km)	Construction Cost (Cc) in Rs. per Hour	Operating Cost (Oc) in Rs. per Hour	User Cost (Uc) in Rs. per Hour	Total Cost (Z) in Rs. per Hour
1	9.54	3.7	61228	20623	3098680	3180531
2	11.41	2.8	73230	25693	2407285	2506208
3	15.95	2.1	102368	54326	1924691	2081385
4	7.04	2.45	45183	11869	2061425	2118478
5	18.45	1.86	118413	63351	1766852	1948616
6	18.45	2.08	118413	63353	1978209	2159975

b. Operating cost

Using equation (3), the operating cost is calculated for all six corridors separately. The values of the required external parameters are as given below;

$\gamma_{operating}$ = Rs 480/- per minute obtained from MMRDA (2000)

R_o = 2 (in the absence of the availability of schedules, it is assumed constant for all candidate corridors)

T_{sj} and T_j values are obtained from GIS data

The total Operating cost for each corridor is summarized in Table 6.12. It can be seen that corridor no. 5, although having higher construction cost, has the least operating cost of Rs.63,351/- per hour.

c. User cost

Using equation (4), the user cost is calculated for all six corridors separately. The important input for calculating the user cost is the estimate of the number of public transport passengers that are accessing/moving out from the individual stations by walking and by feeder mode. Here it is assumed that, within the feeder area of the station, all the public transport passengers whose origin is within a 500 meter radius from the station will access or egress by walking and the rest will access or egress by feeder mode. Accordingly, simple overlay analysis in TransCAD was used to obtain these figures for each station of each candidate corridor. It is to be noted that these figures may be different between candidate corridors for the same station, as the feeder area of the station may change based on the layout of the candidate corridors.

The values of the required external parameters are as given below:

γ_{walk} = Rs. 0.15/- per minute per person, obtained from Verma (2010)

γ_{riding} , γ_{other} = Rs 0.5/- per person per minute, obtained from Verma (2010)

Figure 6.28 (a) and (b) shows the sensitivity of average riding time and walking time cost on the total objective function value. The figure shows that although the objective function value varies along with the average cost values, the optimum solution remains the same. The total user cost for each corridor is summarized in Table 6.12. Further, the weighted average distance of zone centroids from the railway station is also calculated for each corridor (Table 6.12), which depicts the average accessibility of each candidate rail corridor. Implicitly, the corridor which is relatively away from the zones with larger production or attraction has higher average distance traveled by the user to the station, which eventually leads to higher user cost. Accordingly, corridor no. 1, which has the highest average distance of 3.7 km has the highest user cost; whereas corridor no. 5, which has the least average distance also has the least user cost. After calculating all the costs for each of the six candidate corridors, the objective function value (Z) in terms of total cost is obtained for each corridor, as given in Table 6.12. From the table it can be seen that corridor number 5 is optimum as it has the least cost amongst all the candidate corridors. Also, Table 6.13 presents flow characteristics of each corridor, which basically depicts the demand intensiveness of each corridor. It can be seen that the average flow on each of the corridors is above the minimum recommended capacity of the rail transit system, i.e., 12,000 pphpd (x_t). Further, coefficient of variation of link flows is 2nd least for corridor number 5, indicating the demand intensiveness of the corridor. Therefore, within the integrated framework, corridor number 5 is recommended as the optimum rail corridor for Thane city.

Table 6.13: Link Flow Characteristics for each Candidate Corridor

Corridor No.	Average Link Flow	Standard Deviation	Coefficient of Variation	Minimum	Maximum
1	17969	8050	45	4279	34369
2	15942	7823	49	1170	34369
3	14241	7227	51	1170	24216
4	17450	4585	26	12896	27260
5	16428	6901	42	1169	34369
6	16330	7950	49	1169	34369

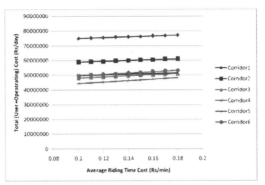

Figure 6.28 (a): Average Riding Time Cost vs. Total Objective Function Value

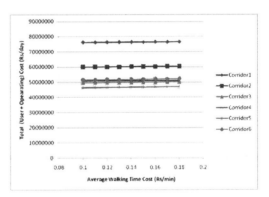

Figure 6.28 (b): Average Walking Time Cost vs. Total Objective Function Value

6.5.4.6 Development of the train scheduling model

To avoid an additional transfer point and therefore to eliminate the discontinuity in the optimal corridor obtained, it was decided that station number 43 and corridor link 309 be omitted (as the link length is small and link flow is just above the 12,000 pphpd level, which can be handled by a feeder street transit system), and also, the disjointed links between stations 210 and 143 were connected and a continuous network was arrived at. Hence, the optimal corridor had the following 17 stations: 8, 10, 12, 16, 25, 36, 157, 210, 65, 70, 164, 165, 169, 170, 182, 184, and 186 (Figure 6.29). Stations 8, 65, and 186 were taken as the terminal nodes and consequently schedules were obtained on the route between stations 8 and 186 (Route 1) and 65 and 186 (Route 2). Table 6.14 shows the links between different station pairs and the distance between them and also the train ridership. The program for train scheduling model was coded and run in MATLAB.

160

Figure 6.29: Modified Optimal Rail Corridor in Thane City

The train scheduling model is developed to obtain the optimal frequencies for rail operation on the newly identified rail routes (Figure 6.29) and also to find the total number of trains required for each route and thus the total train fleet size required for the study area. The external parameters, which are required before running the ESA, are enumerated below.

a. Cost of waiting time = Rs.0.15/minute [adopted from MMPG (1997)]; cost of in-vehicle time = Rs.0.12/minute [adopted from MMPG (1997)]; train operating cost = Rs.480/minute [adopted from MMRDA (2000)]; lay over time = 5 minutes; average train speed = 50 kmph; minimum allowable headway for LRT1 = 1 minute [Verma and Dhingra (2001)]; seating capacity for LRT1 (for 2-vehicle train) = 130 [Verma and Dhingra (2001)]; minimum allowable load factor = 0.3; maximum allowable load factor = 1.0.

b. The penalty for load factor constraint g1 was taken as directly proportional to the load factor (penalty = obj*lf) when the pphpd > 36,000 or lf > 1 and inversely proportional (penalty = obj/lf) when the pphpd < 12,000 or lf < 0.3. This helps in appropriately accounting the penalty of load factor which is greater than 1 or less than a minimum value.

c. The minimum allowable waiting time for constraint g4 was taken as 0.5 minutes while g3 was suitably taken as 4 minutes. The penalty for waiting time constraint, i.e., g3, g4 was decided after a number of trials and was taken as 0.5 times the objective function for both. The purpose of trials was to find the penalty value such that the objective function component and various constraints get equal weightage.

d. The range of decision variable (headway) was taken as 1-10 minutes.

Here, the minimum and maximum allowable load factor for the case study application is taken corresponding to the lower limit (12,000) and upper limit (36,000) in passengers per hour per direction (pphpd) respectively of suitability range of light rail system obtained from Verma and Dhingra (2001). This is done to maintain a minimum acceptable level of ridership in trains from an operator's point of view and also to maintain the load factor in the train to be within the acceptable comfort level of the users in the case study area. With the input of these external parameters, the exhaustive search algorithm (ESA) was run for obtaining the optimal train frequencies for peak period and the fleet size. The output of the algorithm is as given below:

Table 6.14: Route Information for the Modified Rail Corridor in Thane City

Route 1				Route 2			
Station Pair	Link ID	Length (Kms.)	Ridership (pphpd)	Station Pair	Link ID	Length (Kms.)	Ridership (pphpd)
186-184	277	0.57	12155	186-184	277	0.57	12155
	276	0.22	12940		276	0.22	12940
184-182	275	0.27	13771	184-182	275	0.27	13771
	274	0.69	14580		274	0.69	14580
182-170	273	2.77	3522	182-170	273	2.77	3522
	262	0.68	1169		262	0.68	1169
170-169	258	1.02	3621	170-169	258	1.02	3621
169-165	257	0.77	15774	169-165	257	0.77	15774
165-164	252	0.72	18769	165-164	252	0.72	18769
164-210	324	0.3	26959	164-70	324	0.3	26959
	213	0.3	24217		213	0.3	24217
	212	0.25	13227		212	0.25	13227
	221	0.35	15071		224	0.35	15071
	225	0.4	8002		209	0.1	20074
	228	0.4	7450		121	0.2	16105
	318	0.1	7587		117	0.3	16176
	304	0.2	8930		110	0.15	15646
210-157	303	0.69	13716		109	0.15	15984
	239	0.51	13115		83	0.6	14204
157-36	244	0.1	27261	70-65	78	1	26129
	48	0.53	21314	Total Length 11.4 Kms.			
36-25	42	0.83	17378				
25-16	23	0.9	18386				
16-12	14	0.7	18302				
12-10	11	1.03	19159				
10-8	9	0.9	12974				
Total Length 16.2 Kms							

Headway for route 1 is 4.4 minutes and for route 2 is 10 minutes; load factor on route 1 and route 2 = 0.34 and 0.26, respectively; round trip time for route 1 and route 2 = 69.6 and 55.1 minutes, respectively; fleet size for route 1 and route 2 = 16 and 6, respectively; total train fleet size = 22.

The sensitivity analysis of the minimum allowable load factor value reveals that with a decrease in its value, the optimum headway value also decreases. This is reasonable since a lower headway (or higher frequency) of trains leads to less passenger per trains and therefore lower load factors. Also, Figure 6.30 shows the sensitivity of the total objective function value with respect to variation in average waiting time cost. It was observed that although the objective function value increases with an increase in the waiting time cost value, the optimum solution does not change. A similar conclusion was made from the sensitivity of other cost parameters also.

It can be seen from the results that the optimal headway required for the two routes in peak period came out to be 4.4 and 10 minutes, respectively. The frequency of route 1 as compared to route 2 is higher because of the higher demand intensity in the former. The first route passes through the denser region of Thane. To maintain this headway, the fleet size required for peak period is 22 trains. This is for the round trip time of 69.6 and 55.1 minutes for route 1 and route 2, respectively. Also, the load factor achieved for both the routes is close to the minimum allowable load factor, this ensures that there is adequate ridership in the train from an operator's point of view and at the same time the load factor doesn't reach the maximum allowable load factor corresponding to the crush capacity of the train, to increase the discomfort level of users.

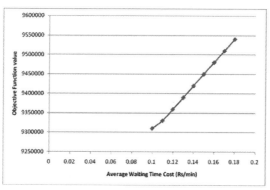

Figure 6.30: Average Waiting Time Cost vs. Total Objective Function Value

6.6 Stakeholder consultation and preferences

Many public authorities seek to incorporate public participation in their decision-making processes, including those processes involving transportation policy and planning. This is done for a number of reasons. At its best, the public participation process is designed to help assure that the people's will is done (Innes and Booher, 2000, p6) in an attempt to design things to meet the aspirations of its citizens. In some cases, transportation planners seek to involve the community while the planning and decision-making is still readily influenced, and attempt to take the opinions and values of the community into account when developing the plan (Shepherd and Bowler, 1997).

Presumably, along with the desire to do the people's will, there are two general assumptions that underlie the decision to include some public participation in decision-making (Mumpower, 2001):

a) the decision-making process can be improved by the inclusion of knowledge and perspectives that would otherwise be absent; and

b) if the public has better access to knowledge and is more able to influence the process, then it may develop a sense of project ownership and thus increase its support.

Open houses, or town hall meetings, are a time-honored method of gauging public opinion regarding proposed transportation projects. But such processes are highly self-selective because those people who are motivated in some way show up, whereas most others do not. So the question arises: to what extent are the opinions expressed in an open house valid indications of actual public opinion? This section considers the issue of measuring public opinions by discussing a study of public opinions regarding a proposed transportation master plan for the City of Edmonton. The same survey instrument was applied to both open house attendees and a randomly selected sample of the population. The instrument asked the respondent in each case to indicate preferences regarding the potential directions that the master plan could take by allocating points to alternative directions considered in sets of two or three possibilities. For example, the respondent was to allocate 12 points between improving accessibility for the mobility disadvantaged vs. saving money (by reducing municipal expenditures on transportation). A given respondent would indicate a preference for a complete emphasis on improving accessibility at the expense of saving money by allocating all 12 points to the first of the two possibilities or indicate a preference for a balance between the two possibilities by allocating 6 points to each. Each respondent was asked to perform a total of 11 of these allocations involving other such potential directions as improving personal mobility by automobile, improving mobility for commerce, preserving and enhancing community integrity, improving personal mobility by bicycle, protecting the city's environment, protecting the global environment, using debt to finance transportation expenditure, and using municipal taxes to finance transportation expenditure. A total of 472 (self-selected) open house attendees and 868 randomly selected individuals responded. Analysis of the results indicates that the two groups displayed significantly different patterns in their responses, with the open house group displaying a greater degree of extremism where the allocations of points tended more to 0 and 12. Notwithstanding these differences, it was also the case that the two groups tended to indicate the same sorts of preference in general but with the open house group showing stronger tendencies. This suggests that such indications of preference from open houses can be taken to be indicative of the directions but not necessarily the magnitudes of the corresponding preferences for the population more generally. Different methods used in this system are discussed in the following section.

6.6.1 The Edmonton opportunity

In 1997, the City of Edmonton sought public opinions using both of these aforementioned methods as part of a larger survey. With both methods, participants were asked to complete the same questionnaire. The collection of data from these two groups of individuals using the same instrument provided an opportunity for comparing the two methods in order to gauge the similarities and differences between these two samples and their corresponding populations.

The intent of the research reported here was to identify and examine any differences in the indications provided by the resulting two samples and, more formally, to establish if there is a significant bias in the self-selected sample obtained in the open ouse process in particular.

6.6.2 Key choices survey

The Edmonton Key Choices Survey was conducted between 25 April and 24 May 1997 as part of the development of the Edmonton Transportation Master Plan.

The Transportation Master Plan was to become the general outline according to which the city would develop its transportation infrastructure and related transportation policy. As such, the Transportation Master Plan had the potential to influence significantly the future of the city and its citizens impacting everything from the mobility of goods and people to the nature of the urban form and the resulting quality of life provided.

The Key Choices Survey questionnaires were distributed in two ways. The city conducted a series of open house meetings concerning the Transportation Master Plan, and all attendees were asked to complete the questionnaire as part of the meeting. Questionnaires were also mailed out to a randomly selected set of households in the City of Edmonton, together with materials describing the Transportation Master Plan process. These households were also subsequently contacted by telephone and encouraged to respond.

6.6.3 The questionnaire

The questionnaire included a series of eleven worksheets designed to elicit the respondents attitudes to elements of policy relevant to the Transportation Master Plan, along with some standard questions seeking personal information about the respondent. In each of these worksheets, the respondent was asked to allocate a set of 12 points among 2 or 3 different possible planning objectives in order to indicate the relative degrees of emphasis the respondent felt was appropriate among the objectives. For example, with two competing objectives, A and B, if the respondent felt A was all important relative to B, then A would get 12 points and B would get 0 points; whereas, if the respondent felt A and B were equally important then both A and B would get 6 points.

The first six worksheets asked the respondent to allocate 12 points among two alternatives each time, as follows:

1. improving mobility versus saving money;
2. improving accessibility for the mobility disadvantaged versus saving money;
3. improving mobility for commerce versus preserving and enhancing neighborhood integrity;
4. improving personal mobility by automobile versus preserving and enhancing neighborhood integrity;
5. improving personal mobility by automobile versus protecting the city's environment; and
6. personal mobility by automobile versus the protecting the global environment.

The last five worksheets asked the respondent to allocate 12 points among three alternatives each time, as follows:

7. improving personal mobility versus protecting the environment versus saving money
8. improving personal mobility by automobile versus improving personal mobility by transit versus improving personal mobility by bicycle;
9. improving accessibility for the mobility disadvantaged, versus improving alternatives to auto use versus saving money;
10. protecting the global environment versus protecting the city's environment versus preserving and enhancing neighborhood integrity; and
11. using debt to finance transportation expenditure versus using user charges to finance transportation expenditure versus using municipal taxes to finance transportation expenditure.

In total, 472 completed questionnaires were obtained at the eight public open houses hosted by the city; and 868 completed questionnaires were returned by the mail-out sample group (representing a response rate of 29%).

The observations in the mail-out sample were then weighted so that the joint distribution for the sample matched that for the population (according to Statistics Canada tables) in terms of age, gender, household size, and dwelling type. All of the results for the mail-out sample presented here use this weighted version of the sample.

6.6.4 Results of the above mentioned methods

6.6.4.1 Distributions of points

Figure 6.31 compares the distributions of points obtained for worksheet 1 for the two samples. Similar sorts of 2-dimensional and 3-dimensional distributions were obtained for the other two-alternative and three-alternative worksheets, and these are presented elsewhere (Mackay, 2004).

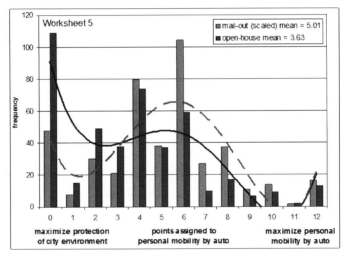

Figure 6.31: Distributions of Points Allocated in Worksheet 1

6.7 Feasibility for higher-order modes like BRT and Metro rail

6.7.1 BRT (bus rapid transit)

The term BRT used for any bus line that has partial separation of lanes, new buses, or distinctive line designation. BRT must also have some or most of the following features.

a) Stations and stops that allow simultaneous stopping of two or more buses, their overtaking or platooning to provide operations with short headways, and a line capacity greater than 3000-5000 spaces per hour.

b) Engines with low level pollution and noise.

c) Convenient transferring to other buses and rail lines.

d) Prepaid or contactless fare collection, which minimize delays during boarding and alighting.

6.7.2 High performance transit modes

The basic features for provision of high-performance transit service are operation on ROW category A only. With exclusive use of protected ROW, guided modes represent the logical technology because guidance allows use of high capacity electric trains with signal control. One of these modes is rail rapid transit (Metro).

6.7.3 Rail rapid transit (metro or RRT)

RRT popularly better known as the metro utilizes high-capacity electric trains with high acceleration and braking rates. It represents the high performance transit modes with the lowest operating cost per space-km. Its implementation requires very high investment and extensive construction, including disruption of areas along future lines. However, RRT systems have virtually unlimited life and exert a strong, permanent impact on mobility of population, urban form, and character.

6.7.4 Interdependence of ROW and system technology

The basic relationship between investment costs of the three ROW categories and mode performance is shown graphically in the below Figure 6.32. The box for each row category shows generally the area where the PCP for the systems in that category belongs. ROW category C, street transit, requires a distinctly lower investment than medium and high-performance modes using ROW categories B and A, respectively. The diagram shows the problem that occurs when a city uses only buses on streets and rapid transit: the former has a relatively low performance, while the latter requires a large investment. A large area of medium-performance modes at medium investment cost levels is provided mainly by LRT, BRT, and AGT modes with their relative PCP positions as shown.

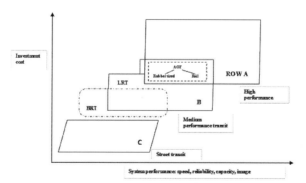

Figure 6.32: Performance-Cost Packages (PCPs) of Different Generic Classes of Transit Modes

6.7.5 Comparison of RRT and LRT

A comparison of RRT with its closest widely used neighbor in the family of modes, standard LRT, is given below

The advantages of metro compared to LRT are:

a) With ROW A only and full signal control, RRT has higher speed, reliability, and safety.

b) Due to long trains and rapid passenger exchange at stations, RRT has a much higher line capacity.

c) With its high performance and strong image, RRT has stronger passenger attraction.

d) Distinct image of its stations and system performance give RRT greater potential for positive impacts on urban development than any other transit mode.

The disadvantages are:

a) RRT requires substantially higher investment cost, causes more disruption due to construction, and requires longer implementation time than LRT.

b) RRT requires more rigid alignment than LRT and cannot penetrate pedestrian areas.

c) LRT is more conducive to construction in stages, utilizing different ROW categories, while RRT is limited to ROW A only.

6.7.6 Light rail compared to buses

Comparison of all major medium performance modes are presented here. The first comparison, given in Table 6.15 to Table 6.17 includes three modes: regular bus, BRT, and LRT. Their characteristics are grouped in three categories: system components, lines and operational components, and system characteristics.

Table 6.15: Comparison of Regular Bus, Bus Rapid Transit, and Light Rail Transit (System Components)

Characteristics/Mode	Regular Bus	Bus Rapid Transit	Light Rail transit
ROW	C	B (C,A)	B (C,A)
Support	Road	Road	Rail
Guidance	Steered	Steered	Guided
Propulsion	ICE	ICE	Electric
TU control	Driver/visual	Driver/visual	Driver/visual
Vehicle capacity	80-120	80-180	100-250
Max TU size	Single vehicle	Single vehicle	1-4 car trains
Max TU capacity	120	180	4*180=720

Table 6.16: Comparison of Regular Bus, Bus Rapid Transit, and Light Rail Transit (Lines/Operational Elements)

Characteristics /Mode	Regular Bus	Bus Rapid Transit	Light Rail Transit
Lines	Many		
Headways on each lines	Long /medium/short	Long /medium/short	Medium /short
Stop spacings (m)	80-250	200-400	250-600
Transfers	Few	Some/many	Many

Table 6.17: Comparison of Regular Bus, Bus Rapid Transit, and Light Rail Transit (System Characteristics)

Characteristics /Mode	Regular Bus	Bus Rapid Transit	Light Rail Transit
Investment cost/km	Low	High	Very high
Operating cost/space	Medium	Medium	Low
System image	Variable	Good	Excellent
Passenger attraction	Limited	Good	Strong
Impacts on land use and city livability	Least	Moderate	Strongest

6.7.7 Comparison of main BRT and LRT features

The evaluation and comparison of BRT and LRT are different in many aspects. Generally, BRT requires lower investment and shorter implementation time than LRT, but LRT provides higher service quality, attracts more passengers, and has stronger and more permanent positive impacts on its served area and often on an entire city. BRT has physical limitations: in cities with high density where exclusive bus ways or lanes cannot be provided, it cannot enter the urban core. LRT can do that either by using short tunnels or by operating on various types of ROW B, including running through pedestrian areas.

The major characteristics are listed and verbally described in below Table 6.18.

Table 6.18: Characteristics of BRT and LRT

Characteristics/ Mode	Bus Rapid Transit	Light Rail Transit	Superior Mode
Vehicle performance and passenger comfort	Good	Excellent	LRT
Investment cost	High	Very high	BRT
Implementation time	Short	Medium	BRT
Operating cost	Lower for low passenger volume	Lower for high passenger volume	-
System image and passenger attraction	Good	Excellent	LRT
Air pollution and noise	considerable	No direct pollution, very low noise level	LRT
Interaction with land development	Limited	Very good	LRT

Summary

This chapter mainly based on the planning of public transport in urban areas. The first part deals with the urban transport planning based on the sustainable transport infrastructure of some cities. It also covers the classical transport models with different types and examples. This chapter also consists of the information about travel demand estimation and its use.

Another part shows some highlights on routing and scheduling of public transport and explaining optimum TU capacity with examples, and it also covers the intermodal coordination of a city having demand for a new rail-based mass transit system besides the street transit system and existing rail-based system (if any). Also it shows some light on stakeholder consultation and its different methods. It also covers the high order modes like BRT and metro rails and how they compare in 3 ROW categories.

Chapter 7

Management of Public Transport

7.1 Urban transport management

Urban areas in India suffer from inadequate road capacity leading to congestion and delays both in the morning peak hour and evening peak hour. This peak period is getting extended for more than two to three hours in the morning and another two to three hours in the evening. This problem is much more critical in all metropolitan cities of India. The congestion is due to demand being much higher than the capacity of the road network that is available to cater to the demand.

Urban transport is an important infrastructure essential for urban growth and sustainability. In India, transportation demand in urban areas continues to increase rapidly as a result of both population growth and changes in travel patterns. Globalization has its impact on urban growth and its planning. The competition between Bangalore, Chennai, Hyderabad, etc. to attract capital and the software industry is well known. At a global level also, this trend is evidenced and city governments (e.g., Sydney, Singapore, and London) have been adapting to their new global environments. It has been assumed that to gain a comparative advantage, it is necessary to beat competitors in the game of attracting investment from the leading sectors of the new globalized economy. Transport with its direct and indirect impact on environment, safety, and energy considerations, has a vital role in the globalized city. To make a city competitive, livable, and attractive, a well functioning urban transport system is very essential. The contribution of a well functioning urban transport system to the City Development Index (CDI) is around 30%. An efficient urban transportation system can increase society's productivity and welfare by improving people's access to jobs, recreational activities, and educational institutes.

7.1.1 Problems of urban transport and consequences

Due to rapid urbanization, there is exponential growth of travel demand and doubling of trip lengths but only a marginal increase in mobility levels. There is no integration of land use planning and transport. The increased urbanization and concentration of population in large cities is putting heavy pressure on the already over saturated urban transport network, adversely affecting the productivity in urban areas. The mass transport systems are inadequate and are unable to cater to the demand imposed on them. As a result, there is a tremendous increase in the use of personalized vehicles, but the carrying capacity of roads has not kept pace.

This is leading to congestion, continuous slowing down of average vehicular speeds, increasing air and noise pollution, increasing accident rates, and excessive use of nonrenewable energy. Mass transit requirements of the metro cities and other large cities need to be addressed on a priority basis. With growing traffic congestion, rush hour traffic is slowing to a crawl. This in turn leads to higher oil consumption and emissions, which are polluting urban areas beyond acceptable limits. There is an urgent need in reducing the total number of vehicles, reducing the total number of kilometers travelled, and reducing congestion, in order to give smooth flow of traffic to achieve better vehicular speeds, reduce the pollution, and travel time. The problem of the pollution faced in Delhi and the measures initiated at the insistance of the Hon. Supreme Court in switching over to CNG as a fuel for buses are well known. A consequence of congestion is long travel times, which adversely affect the productivity of the vehicles and the productivity of the commuters. The road accidents have also been increasing causing loss of human lives.

The urban areas in the country confront a historic transportation crisis that has become a perennial war against increasing mobility, road blocks, and air pollution. Given the financial constraints and environmental concerns, there is a need to adopt a comprehensive strategy for achieving sustainable urban transport. There is need for a strategic land use development policy in all large cities with an aim to integrate land use with mass passenger transport planning models to guide the future growth process of cities. Mass transport systems, both rail and road based need to be developed. Taking into account the growing urbanization and its impact on overall conditions intraurban and sub-urban rail transport, MRTS and suburban rail systems are required to be integrated.

7.1.2 Efficient use of existing/proposed infrastructure

The emerging policy on urban transportation planning issues is the newly promulgated transportation system management (TSM) action program. It is now required that TSM projects be included in the transportation improvement programme (TIP) as the short-range element of the overall plan. Generally in all cities exceeding more than two lakhs in population, these TSM plans are compulsory while preparing comprehensive transportation plans.

The TSM considers a wide range of actions with low capital investment requirements that can improve the transportation in the short term. It reflects the
a) Steeply rising costs.
b) Environmental concerns.
c) Intense competition for available resources,
and make it imperative that better and more efficient users for existing investments in the transportation infrastructure be found before additional investments are made in costly new facilities. The new concept is therefore to make more efficient use of the highways and transit systems already in place thus reducing the need for new capital investments and for operation assistance.

The TSM on implementation provides the following advantages:
a) Fiscal economy
b) Better balance among the various elements of the urban transport system.
c) Broader local and national goals of energy conservation.
d) Environmental improvement.
e) Equity for transit dependents.
f) Urban preservation.
The TSM actions recognize the following features:

a) Characteristics of the existing transportation system.

b) Total demand for the transportation purpose in question.

c) Geographic distribution.

d) Nature of urban environment.

e) Locally determined goals.

For example a pooled riding system in privately owned vehicles may serve the work trip demand most efficiently in a low demand density sector while the conventional bus transit may serve in another sector. The high occupancy commuter rail may prove efficient in another sector. The TSM plan fosters deliberately the use of a combination of modes that best represents an area's desired balance between the goals of efficient mobility, environmental quality, and social equity in the operation of a transportation system. The TSM plans are discussed covering the following aspects:

a) Warrants for implementation.

b) Prerequisites.

c) Advantages and disadvantages.

d) Implementation considerations.

e) Significant interrelationships among actions.

7.1.2.1 Broad classification of methods

All the TSM actions can be broadly classified into three groups:

I) Making more efficient use of existing infrastructure.

II) Reducing automobile usage in congested areas or time periods.

III) Improving transit service and transit management efficiency.

These three groups are generally dealt with in the following action program.

1) Improved vehicular flow

a) Improvements in signalized intersections.

b) Freeway ramp metering.

c) One way streets.

d) Removal of on-street parking.

e) Reversible lanes.

f) Traffic channelization.

g) Off-street loading.

h) Transit stop relocation.

2) Preferential treatment of high-occupancy vehicles

a) Expressway bus and carpool lanes and access ramps.

b) Bus and carpool lanes on city streets and urban arterials.

c) Bus preemption of traffic signals.

d) Toll policies.

3) Reduced peak-period travel

a) Work rescheduling.

b) Congestion pricing.

c) Peak period truck restrictions.

4) Parking management

a) Parking regulations.

b) Park and ride facility.

5) Promotion of nonauto or high occupancy auto use

a) Ridesharing.

b) Human powered travel modes.

c) Auto restricted zones.

6) Transit and paratransit service improvements

a) Transit marketing.

b) Security measures.

c) Transit shelters.

d) Transit terminals.

e) Transit fare policies and fare collection techniques.

f) Extension of transit with paratransit services.

g) Integration of transportation services.

7) Transit management efficiency measures

a) Route evaluation.

b) Vehicle communication and monitoring techniques.

c) Maintenance policies.

d) Evaluation of system performance.

In this article it is proposed to discuss only those actions which relate actions that improve vehicular flow and those that encourage high occupancy vehicles.

7.1.2.2 Improved vehicular flow

The major goal of all TSM actions is to improve vehicular flow by implementing low-cost measures that increase the efficiency of existing road space and thereby avoid the need for roadway expansion. The following actions approach this goal by modifying and/or altering the designated use of road space.

a) Improvements in signalized intersections.

b) Freeway ramp metering.

c) One-way streets.

d) Removal of on-street parking.

e) Reversible lanes.

f) Traffic channelization.

g) Off-street loading.

h) Transit stop relocation.

If these serve to encourage increased use of low occupancy autos, then the purpose is negated. Thus only if these actions are integrated into a comprehensive TSM plan, will lasting benefits accrue.

a) Improvements in signalized intersections

Factors influencing the discharge of traffic at signalized intersections are signal cycle length and network control. Hence, by determining the most efficient use of signal time for each intersection, the amount of time available for individual movements at a group of intersections can be optimized and vehicular throughput can be increased. When for example, 15 different cycle times were analyzed by SIGOP (Signal Optimization Program) a reduction in cycle was proved to improve significantly the average speed throughout. But if cycle is shortened below 40 seconds the pedestrian crossing time became unacceptable and hence was not desirable. In the case of pretimed and traffic actuated signals, research has shown the following facts:

i) Signal time phasing is not a controlling factor when narrow lanes, car parking, and right turns conflict each other.

ii) On major commuter routes through or adjacent to CBD, coordinating timing of demand actuated signals can improve operational efficiency.

iii) When signal time phasing is instituted in favor of a preferred route, the flow of commuter traffic is improved.

iv) In small cities signal maintenance is found to be inadequate. For effective performance either a city staff technician must be adequately trained or the task assigned to an appropriate agency or the task contracted to a fully qualified outside firm.

While going for traffic adjusted computer control signals, the following stage wise improvements are recommended:

Stage 1: Progressive connection of signals.

Stage 2: Manually changing the fixed time rate of pretimed signals.

Stage 3: Altering the demand responsive cycle of traffic actuated systems.

The most efficient control can generally be achieved through a computerized traffic responsive control system. In these processes electrical impulses from traffic sensors that record traffic conditions at intersections in the network are fed into the decision program of a computer, which then selects and initiates the most efficient set of signal times and patterns for the network.

b) Expressway ramp metering

Signalizing expressway ramp intersections to control or meter the entry of vehicles into the expressway system is an increasingly popular and successful way of improving the use of existing facilities and to improve the overall capacity. The following are the two different techniques adopted in practice.

1. Control volume of vehicles entering expressway so that expressway capacity is not exceeded and divert excess capacity to alternate parallel routes or less congested routes.

2. Smoothing of traffic flow since vehicles are allowed to enter only when they can be merged between platoons in the traffic streams.

The following equipment is usually employed for this purpose

1. Gap detector.

2. Merge detector.

3. Input detector.

4. Queue detector.

The expressway ramp metering is applicable up to a lane capacity of 40-50 vehicles per km.

c) One way streets

A one way street system is one of the powerful techniques for increasing the capacity of streets as well as safety. The advantages of one-way streets are:

1. Decreases the number of conflicts at intersections and, hence, improves safety and capacity.

2. More efficient use of capacity than two-way operations.

3. For narrow roads less than 15 mts width without markings and with parking on both sides maximum capacity can be achieved via one way operation.

It is recommended that the following is the order in which this technique can be introduced. First remove on-street parking followed by the introduction of one way streets and then proceed to signal preemption. Experience in other countries have shown that by introducing one way streets:

1. 20% reduction in pedestrian accidents.

2. 22% reduction in travel time.

3. 65% reduction in vehicular stops.

4. 40% cross town delay can be reduced.

5. Signal time can be decreased from 50-90 seconds to 35-60 secs.

6. Can be integrated with contraflow and bus lanes.

The following disadvantages are however observed:

1. Increased walking to bus lanes

2. Increased vehicle kilometers of travel.

3. Business reaction but actually improves the business in due course.

4. Pedestrian safety impeded due to increased speeds.

The following are the implementation considerations:

1. Signalized intersection performance can be improved by one way streets.

2. Reversible lanes and contraflow lanes can be effectively employed by one way streets.

3. One way streets make effective utilization of traffic channelization.

4. Bus preemption at traffic signals can become easy.

5. Bus/car pool lanes can be introduced.

Figure 7.1 to Figure 7.3 shows how the number of conflict points at an intersection decreases by making streets one-way.

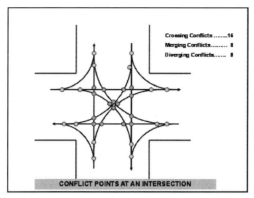

Figure 7.1: Conflict points at an intersection with two-way movement

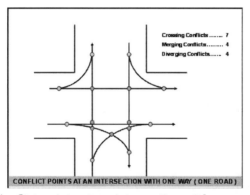

Figure 7.2: Conflict points at an intersection with one-way (one road)

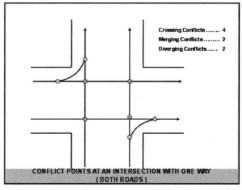

Figure 7.3: Conflict points at an intersection with one-way (both roads)

d) Removal of on street parking

Removal of on-street parking helps to improve vehicular flow by increasing street capacity. By discouraging the use of automobiles in crowded CBDs to permit transit/paratransit usage, the institution of on-street parking regulation constitutes an important element of an area's overall parking policy. However peak period parking restriction is more difficult than enforcement of 24-hour restrictions and violations and interferes severely with peak period traffic.

The following are the advantages:

1. Substantial increase in roadway capacity is observed. Only 55-65% of roadway capacity is utilized on two way streets where on-street parking is permitted. When parking is eliminated, roadway capacity is approximately twice greater than if parking were permitted.

2. Improved traffic speeds of the order of 8 kmph are observed. Reduction in peak period travel to the time of 25% for auto, 10% for local bus, and 50% reduction in traffic delays are observed.

3. Removal of on-street parking also tends to greatly improve safety conditions, as it is a causal factor in 18-19% of all urban accidents.

4. Additional space created by parking banks improves efficiency of TSM actions. For example the left/right turn lanes to relocate transit stops to midblock reduce hazards to cyclists. Bike lanes can also be introduced.

Strict enforcement is generally required to achieve maximum benefit from parking controls. Penalties for violating are to be severe for successful implementation. 40-85% of all parking is on-street in most of the cities. In big cities particularly in CBDs only 15% is for parking. Hence parking restrictions in small cities can improve efficiency substantially. Parking bans in CBDs have an adverse effect in CBD business in smaller cities.

e) Reversible lanes

When directional flow is unbalanced by 65:35 split reversible lanes can be used during peak periods to increase the capacity of the roadway in the directions of flow. They are applicable to roads not separated by a median strip. They are inexpensive and permit additional peak period directional capacity without adding roadways.

The experience says that peak period travel is reduced by 25%, violation of reversible lanes is a common problem compounded by lack of policing capability along the routes. Signing and lane use control devices, overhead signal, lane signals represent the basic costs for reversible lanes. Maintenance/enforcement costs are to be included as permanent costs in the estimates.

The advantages of reversible lanes are in improving the safety, reduce peak period congestion, and reduced travel time by 20%. The disadvantages are when only one lane is available for off peak direction flow long queues can form behind turning or disabled vehicles. On undivided roads the following warrants may be useful for applying reversible lanes:

1. 65% in one direction during peak flows.

2. The roadway capacity in the peak direction is adequate.

3. There is a continuity in the route and in the width of the street.

4. There is no median, or left turns, and parking is restricted.

Progressive signal timing can improve the system with an interconnected signal controller for peak hour and for off peak hour. Figure 7.4 and Figure 7.5 depicts the concept of reversible lanes.

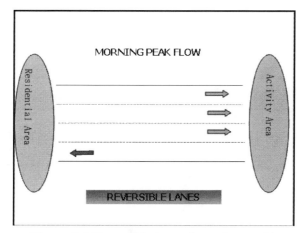

Figure 7.4 Reversible lanes (morning peak)

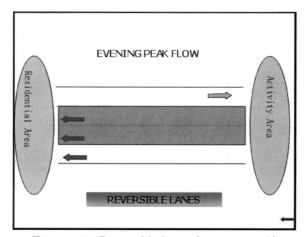

Figure 7.5: Reversible lanes (evening peak)

f) Traffic channelization

Channelization is a process of directing traffic into defined paths on roadways (Figure 7.6). It can reduce or eliminate potential hazards to motorists and pedestrians and avoid confusion in traffic flow. Generally it requires islands, pavement markings, or other suitable means of facilitating traffic flow to separate potential areas of conflict. If properly designed and executed, it improves safety and provides for maximum utilization of available space. It regulates movements and speeds of vehicles, and can increase the speed up to 15kmph.

Where turning volumes are heavy, specially designated turning lanes can promote smooth vehicular flow by removing turning movements from through lanes. Right turn lanes when accompanied by separate turn signal indicators are highly effective in decreasing the right turn vehicle exposure to oncoming through traffic. Left turn on red provision and special turning signals can increase the effectiveness of right turn lanes. Most of the cities have introduced channelization projects. They are noncapital intensive, but costs vary between raised barrier and painted islands.

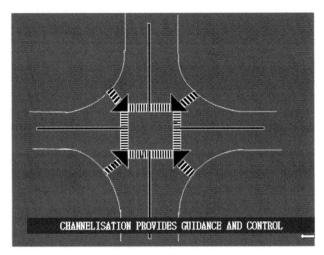

Figure 7.6: Channelization at junctions

g) Turn restrictions

When turning movements conflict with through traffic, turn restrictions may provide a suitable solution. Basically turning bans on left minimizes vehicle pedestrian conflicts while right turn minimizes vehicle to vehicle conflicts. Part time turn restrictions can be effective during peak periods. However public compliance is reportedly better where turn restrictions are maintained full time.

Following are the warrants for turn restrictions:

1. The right turn volume exceeds 20% of total approach volume.

2. Right turn constitutes 10% of total movement on a given street.

3. Right turn movements interfere with straight through movements of 1500 vph regardless of number of lanes.

4. A left/right movement interferes with pedestrian crosswalk volumes in excess of 2000 persons per hour.

5. 600 vehicles conflict with 1000 or more pedestrians per hour.

6. 7 vehicles turn per green interval for several successive signal changes.

7. More than three intersection accidents that involve turning vehicles occur within a 12-month period.

8. The number of traffic lanes available at the intersection will accommodate only a single movement in each direction, and there is an appreciable demand for right turns.

9. Periodic gaps in opposing traffic do not occur due to traffic signals ahead.

10. Drivers will observe right turn prohibition when an alternative route is available.

h) Off street loading

Although preventing curbside truck loading and unloading removes traffic impedance, providing off street loading facilities in CBDs is generally too costly to be included in the TSM plan. Thus many cities can only modify urban zoning ordinances to require that new developments provide facilities for off street loading and unloading and/or restrict or prohibit loading and unloading during peak hours.

i) Transit stop relocation

Curb side loading and unloading of transit and paratransit passengers especially at intersections can seriously impede traffic flow. Turnout bays near transit route junctions provide an ideal solution. However, in many situations, this solution may not be possible. In these cases relocating transit stops may provide an equally effective solution. Basically there are 5 places where transit stops can be located.

1. The near side of an intersection.
2. The far side across an intersection.
3. The far side of an intersection after left turn.
4. Midblocks.
5. Turnouts.

For the most part bus stops are located at intersections. However, where blocks are exceptionally long or where bus patrons are destined for midblock employment or residence relocation, the transit stop relocation to midblock would be a suitable alternative, especially when accompanied by a midblock cross walk. Due to visual obstructions created by the bus, motorists may find site conditions difficult at nearside stops. Also, it is hazardous for other vehicles when bypassing the loading bus. However, if the bus waits for a red light, nearside bus stops can reduce travel time. Farside stops are advantageous where:

1. Other buses may turn in either direction.
2. Turn movements especially left turns from the arterial in the direction being considered is heavy.
3. Cross traffic is heavy, and the curb lane and other lanes are needed for storage when signal is red.
4. Several streets meet at the intersection.
5. Site distance favor farside locations.
6. Left turn only lane effectiveness is increased with farside locations.

The experience has shown that simple changes in bus stop locations have improved travel times to a great extent (Figure 7.7 and Figure 7.8).

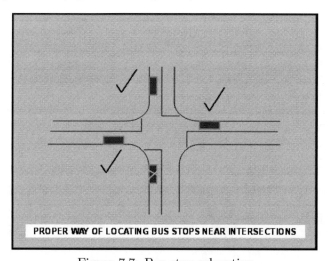

PROPER WAY OF LOCATING BUS STOPS NEAR INTERSECTIONS

Figure 7.7: Bus stop relocation

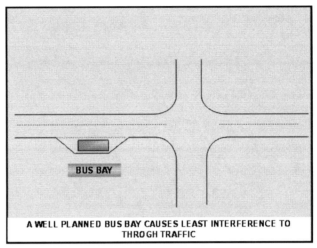

A WELL PLANNED BUS BAY CAUSES LEAST INTERFERENCE TO THROGH TRAFFIC

Figure 7.8: Bus bays

7.1.2.3 Preferential treatment of high occupancy vehicles

The following TSM actions improve the flow of high occupancy vehicles during peak travel periods.

a) Bus and car pool lanes on city streets and urban arterials.

b) Bus preemption of traffic signals.

c) Toll policies.

The time savings and improved transit service levels resulting from these actions enhance the attractiveness of high occupancy models. Ultimately if these actions are incorporated into other TSM actions to encourage high occupancy travel modes, significant shifts from low occupancy vehicles and overall improvement in vehicular flow can be expected.

1. Bus and car-pool lanes on city streets

Reserved lanes on city streets and urban arterials can expedite the movement of high occupancy vehicles through congested areas in or near the center of the city. When dedicated expressway lanes can be extended onto principle urban arterials and city streets the benefits of preferential treatment are optimized. Like dedicated expressway lanes, reserved lanes on city streets were first instituted for bus traffic. The following benefits have occurred due to these actions:

a) Improving travel time savings.

b) Increasing the utilization of existing facilities.

c) Improving bus service levels.

d) Reducing stop and go driving.

The following types of lanes have been experimented

a) With flow bus lane

Reserving the curb lane on city streets for bus traffic is relatively easy and inexpensive to implement and requires a minimum number of changes in established bus routes. However, it makes it easy for other vehicles to violate the lane restriction and thus enforcement of the reserved lane concept is necessary to maintain its effectiveness. In addition, unless left turn restrictions are instituted concurrently, conflicts with left turn vehicles result. This entails removal of on-street parking and prevention of curbside vehicle stops during the time when reserve lane restrictions apply.

b) Contra flow bus lanes
Reserving one lane of a one way street for buses moving in the opposite direction to normal traffic flow is proving to be an effective manifestation of the reserved lane concept. Contra flow lanes are virtually self-enforcing. They are usually installed on one way streets carrying the light flow direction of peak period travel, which minimizes delays at signalized intersections during peak periods. However, when contra flow bus lanes are installed on one way streets, a conflict with right turning traffic, which the implementation of the one way street had eliminated, is created. This type of contra flow lane will require the removal of on-street parking and the prevention of curbside vehicle stops during affected hours.

Figure 7.9: Contra flow bus lane

c) Median bus lanes
Median bus lanes are frequently instituted in the right-of-way, previously assigned to street-car traffic. While this practice constitutes an efficient use of roadway space, all passengers must cross traffic to board or leave buses. An interference with right turn traffic is also created.

Figure 7.10 Median bus lane in Ahmedabad (Janmarg)

d) Bus streets

Bus streets represent the full development of the urban roadway reserved bus lane concept. They are gaining acceptance in large cities. They provide relatively easy access to and egress from buses because buses are not competing for street space with autos. The bus streets are largely self-enforcing. The disadvantage is that auto and truck access to adjacent buildings is eliminated and, as such, alternate parallel traffic routes may be required.

Figure 7.11 : Bus only street in London

2. Bus preemption of traffic signals

About 10-20% of bus travel time in CBD routes is spent waiting at traffic signals. In order to reduce this delay, signal systems that allow the bus to preempt normal traffic signal timing patterns have been developed. Signals are equipped with optically or electronically actuated detectors that respond to signals transmitted from a device on the bus. This device causes the signal phase selector to lengthen the green interval or to shorten the red interval so that the bus can proceed uninterrupted through the intersection. Once the bus has passed the signal returns to normal position. The following advantages were noticed when installed.

I. Reduction in bus travel time.

II. Increased auto delay.

III. Impediment to auto traffic flow.

IV. Platoon preempting is better than 4-5 buses cross.

V. 10-15 buses per hour is warranted for installations.

VI. This is more effective with contra flow.

3. Toll policies

Preferential treatment at toll collection points can be accorded to high occupancy vehicles by permitting nonstop passage at tolls.

I. By differential tolls favoring high occupancy vehicles.

II. Preferential treatment at toll collection points can be accorded to high occupancy vehicles by permitting nonstop passage at tolls by displays.

7.1.2.4 Reduced peak period travel

The following TSM actions discussed can improve peak-period flow by reducing the number of vehicle kilometers traveled (VKT) during peak periods.

1. Work rescheduling.

2. Congestion pricing.

3. Peak period truck restrictions.

Altering work schedules would eliminate the need for some workers to travel during peak periods. Imposing higher charges during peak periods, e.g., tolls, transit fares, and roadway road fees would make it more costly and hence less desirable to travel at peak times. Finally restricting the times when trucks can pick up and deliver merchandise to off-peak periods would remove impedance to peak period traffic flow. Other complementary TSM actions could be:

I. Increased work trip occupancy through preferential treatment of high occupancy vehicles, ride sharing, important services, etc.

II. Instituting higher parking fees for long term parking (congestion, pricing).

III. Encouraging walking and bicycling for short work trips.

a) Work rescheduling

The rescheduling of work hours to reduce the amount of work-related peak period travel could be accomplished by:

I. Staggering or rearranging employee starting and quitting times to achieve a more even distribution of arrivals and departures over a longer period of time.

II. Reducing the work week to four days and, as is commonly practiced, increasing the number of hours worked per day, staggered or flexible work hour programs.

In the past, work reschedules were implemented primarily to reduce peak period congestion at company sites or on transit facilities. The cost of implementation is negligible. But some costs for data collection and processing of surveys are included in evaluation procedure can be implemented. The advantages are:

a) Readily implemented at relatively low cost.

b) Can be implemented on an area wide basis.

c) Peak hour reduction - need to construct new roads will be delayed.

d) At other places like restaurants, lobbies, elevators, and stores, queues can be reduced.

e) Employees experience shorter work trip travel times and more planned and better work conditions.

f) Flextime experience improves employee's morale since the employee is given some control over his/her work schedule.

g) An indirect benefit on energy consumption and/or air quality is observed.

Implementation considerations:

1. No difficulty in rescheduling working by 15 minutes by all companies.

2. 30 minutes per hour is reliable only by large firms or public agencies.

3. Riding pools may be affected.

4. The actions must be coordinated with local transit authority. Transit operators can themselves help identify the locations.

5. If traffic reduces drastically, then it may encourage, single occupancy auto-counter production.

6. Employees at close proximity to each other can be effective.

7. Predicting the effect on roads is complex due to trip length. This may increase congestion also.

8. Instituting regional citywide staggered work is found to be counter productive.

b) Peak period truck restrictions

Congestion charging is used as a measure to disincentivise use of private vehicle and encourage public transport and nonmotorized transport in busy areas of a city particularly during peak periods. This is done by cordoning the city centers and charging all private vehicles that are entering this area. While implementing congestion charging, it is important to provide good alternatives for private vehicles for this measure to be successful. This is another TSM action that can be implemented by:

1. Instituting truck roads.

2. Preventing truck travel on same routes.

3. Temporal restrictions are established to accommodate merchants desire 7 AM to 6.30 PM.

4. Restricting all truck pickups and deliveries to night time.

5. Permitting trucks only during off-peak periods.

6. Restrictions during peak periods are also a problem.

7.1.2.5 Promotion of high occupancy and nonvehicular travel modes

This TSM action is implemented through the following:

a) Ride sharing.

b) Encouraging human powered travel modes.

c) Auto restricted zones.

They improve the efficiency of existing transportation by reducing the number of vehicle - km traveled in congested areas or time periods without altering mobility.

1. Ridesharing

It is a form of paratransit that entails prearranging of shared rides for people travelling at similar times from approximately the same origin to approximately the same destination. In lightly populated areas transit efficiency is not profitable and resorting to ride sharing is found to be a feasible TSM action. The following are the variations:

a) Ridesharing: Car owners in turn drive others by rotation

b) Car pools: Organized system. No parking fee is charged in these cases (Figure 7.12).

c) Van pools: Over 10 miles distance, one-way trip distances are much cheaper than car pool system when 10-12 persons are carried.

Area wide pooling programs can also be considered by discussion with public transport companies, are the best suited program can be implemented.

Figure 7.12: Promotion of Car pooling

2. Human Powered Modes

Encouraging bicycles, etc. is found to have the following benefits:

a) Health.

b) Recreational.

c) Congestion reduction.

d) Prevention of air pollution.

To encourage bicycles bikeways can be constructed. They are classified as:

Class I: Completely separated right-of-way designated for exclusive use.

Class II: Restricted right-of-way exclusive use or semi exclusive use of bicycles. By signs and street markings vehicle parking may be allowed.

Class III: A shared right-of-way designated by signs placed on vertical posts and stenciled on the pavement.

Usually Class III is only feasible. In all these cases:

a) Convenient secure storage of parking is important.

b) Parking to be located near major trip generatora.

c) Change of mode terminals.

d) Bicycle lockers, racks at transit stops (Figure 7.13).

e) Transit/bicycle piggyback can be tried. Bike bus carries - second trailer carrying cycle onboard.

The transit vehicle, condition of street surface lighting, conflicts with MV, etc., are the major issues that are to be seriously managed.

Figure 7.13: Bicycle lane in Ahmadabad

Figure 7.14: Secured bicycle parking facility near bus stop

Improving the existing pedestrian circulation system can be achieved by the following actions:

a) Widening sidewalks.

b) Clearing of impediments to pedestrians.

c) Better lighting.

d) Midblock crossing arrangements.

e) Access to transit/parking garages.

f) Arcades.

g) Malls.

h) Plazas.

i) People mover system.

j) Only pedestrian streets for people by providing plants, fountains, kiosks, etc.

Generally it is recommended to provide 1.2m width for paths for residential streets and at least 1.8m for commercial areas. One can add +0.6m for obstructions on pedestrian paths.

7.1.2.6 Parking management

No other operational control can have as dramatic effect on traffic flow as the proper management of an area by parking supply controls. Decisions are important on:

a) Location.

b) Amount of on and off-street space allocated to parking.

c) The parking charges applied to the allocated space.

d) The length of time of parking permitted effect nearly all the TSM actions.

1. Parking regulations

These are meant:

a) To control the number and type of vehicles entering congested activity centers.

b) To be coupled with other TSM actions to improve transit and paratransit service, such as, preferential treatment for high occupancy vehicles. The number of vehicles entering an area can be reduced.

c) Since many cities have some form of parking restrictions, before instituting new regulations, more stringent enforcement may avoid the need to improve additional regulations.

2. Other point:

a) Long and short term parking - To discourage long term parking by commuters and to favor short term parkers

b) Parking taxes - Imposing a citywide tax. In Los Angeles for instance a 2 year 25% tax on all parking was imposed.

c) Parking surcharges - Surcharge on certain users of parking facilities is another way. Employees can levy parking surcharges on employees with single passenger vehicles.

d) Increased parking rates - General increase in rates can also control parking.

e) Interrelated effects - Mode shift is the after effect.

3. Implementation considerations

a) Should be implemented fully over a larger area otherwise spillover takes place.

b) These actions should encourage through traffic.

c) Other actions like CBD transit circulation, etc. are to be examined before implementation.

d) Parking charges do not reduce parking as only a shift takes place.

4. Limiting parking place

While increased parking charges represent an economic disincentive, limiting parking spaces restrict supply.

a) Not an encouraging experience for bigger cities.

b) By restriction of parking spaces up to 45-51% of the demand by zoning laws can discourage parking.

c) Effective in small urban areas.

d) Adequate alternatives are to be considered.

e) Extend to 1/3 mile beyond the parameter of activity center.

5. Park and ride facilities

Coupling fringe parking with express transit service can bring good effects (Figure 7.15). The space requirements for self-parks are about 350 sq. ft./vehicle.

Advantages:

a) Parking shifts to fringes.

b) Attractive/cheaper.

6. Guidelines

a) Parking area to be large enough for circulation and for pedestrian safety.

b) Close to activity center (1 mile).

c) Located on dense travel corridor, radial, etc.

d) Not to compete with other service area.

e) Adjoining areas not to be effected.

f) Convenient access/egress to buses.

g) Quick transit service, say 5 min. headway.

h) Free parking (if possible).

Figure 7.15: Commuter park-and-ride

7.1.2.7 Transit and para-transit service improvements

A number of aspects can be improved to enhance the level of service of transit/paratransit services through the following:

a) Transit marketing.

b) Security measures.

c) Transit shelters.

d) Transit terminals.

e) Transit fare policy and fare collection techniques.

In addition, the following facilities can help:

a) Extending the service provided by transit with paratransit operations on to a unified network of service.

1. Transit Terminals

These are the places where collection, distribution, and transfer functions are combined. There are a variety of designs, but basically they can be classified as:

a) Park and ride is designed for transfer function and is suitable for small and low density areas.

b) Mode transfer terminals are suitable for outlying areas.

c) Off-street terminals are useful for urban settings.

d) Central area transit terminals are interchange facilities.

2. Central Area Transit Terminals

Off-street passenger distribution is freed and curb lanes are liberated. Multiuse terminals can encourage buses and transit system.

a) Outlying terminal: Aids in consolidating routes. Reduces vehicular traffic destined to city.

b) Off-street terminal: Downtown curb loading capacity is limited. On-street loading/unloading is slow.

7.2 Data collection, retrieval, and analysis for effective management

7.2.1 Information files and data collection: survey and counts

Effective planning and management of transit operations, scheduling, and analysis of efficiency in general require accurate data about operations and usage of transit lines and networks. Transit agencies must therefore organize, maintain, and regularly update systematic information and data. These data files should include:

1. Data about lines and facilities, such as locations and equipment of bus stops on streets; designs and dimensions of rail transit right-of-way, track layouts, signals, stations, yards and workshops, etc.

2. Data about public transport vehicles, including body dimensions, design and performance data, age, condition, breakdowns, etc.

3. Types of service provided and schedules for all modes and lines.

4. Data about usage of services, such as, passenger boardings, alighting and volumes along the lines, their time fluctuations and their trip lengths, trip generation of different major activity areas, such as, shopping mall, stadiums, university campuses, medical complex's, and others.

5. Miscellaneous information on crime incidents, methods of fare collection and types of fares, train-dispatching efficiency, passenger preferences with respect to schedules, riding comfort, and other service parameters.

7.2.2 Organization of surveys

Good planning and continuity in data collection are necessary to obtain and maintain the current database. The frequency and comprehensiveness of field surveys must be determined based on a compromise between the need for accurate information and the cost of surveys. A good practice is to organize major, detailed surveys at longer intervals and supplement them by minor ones, often on a sampling basis, within these intervals. In other words, a comprehensive cross-sectional set of data, describing entire operations at one time, is combined with longitudinal or time data on key elements, such as passenger volumes on maximum load sections or peak-hour flows into the CBD.

7.2.3 Transit speed and delay surveys

The purpose of a speed-and-delay survey on street transit lines is to find the distribution of time a TU spends in travel, classified as running, dwells at passenger stops, and several categories of delays. It is also intended to record the locations, durations, and causes of the delays. The measured travel times and delays are used to compute operating speed and reliability of service during different periods of the day. This information is important for planning possible operational improvements.

7.2.4 Passenger volume and load count

The purpose of passenger counts is to determine the passenger volume on TUs over different sections of a line, the maximum TU load and the section on which that occurs, variations of volumes in time, analysis of service quality, i.e., all elements needed for scheduling of operations. A detailed survey should include TU passenger load counts at several points along each line, particularly focusing on the sections with heavy loads to find the maximum load sections (MLS). Minor annual surveys may be limited to MLSs and one or more additional sections on each line to verify the changes recorded on the MLS.

7.2.5 Passenger boarding and alighting counts

The most detailed information on passenger volumes on a transit line is obtained through the counts of boarding and alighting passengers at each stop or station along its entire length. This count provides the data on the number of passengers using each station, as well as TU loads at all points along the line. One can also compute the distribution of

192

passenger trip lengths and total work of the line in passenger-km for any hour or day. This represents virtually all the information, extending or shortening of the line, addition or abandonment of some stops, etc.

7.2.6 Other types of surveys

In addition to the above described rather standard surveys, many other surveys can be undertaken to obtain various types of data. Several examples of such surveys are described here.

1. Transfer counts.
2. Fare usage.
3. Passenger travel information.
4. Attitudinal and modal split survey.
5. Use of timetables.

7.3 Role of private sector in public transport management

7.3.1 Experience of private operators in India

Generally the service level provided by private operators are far from satisfactory, and there are frequent complaints of over-charging, rash driving, rude behavior of crew, nonadherence to scheduled time tables, not starting services until the vehicle was fully loaded, and very poor condition of buses. It is suggested that privatization has to be accompanied by appropriate regulatory frameworks and institutions. Table 7.1 shows the percent of public and private sector buses in India.

Table 7.1: Percent of public sector buses in different years

Year	Public Sector Buses	Private Buses	% of Public Sector Buses	% of Private Buses
1	2	3	4	5
1976	52200	62800	45.4	54.6
1981	69600	923000	43	47
1986	84000	143300	37	63
1991	104106	225000	31.4	68
1992	107100	251300	30	70
1993	109700	271500	28.8	71.2
1994	111200	282400	28.4	71.6
1995	111500	314600	26.2	74
1996	111100	338700	24.7	75.3
1997	113400	468803	19.4	80.3
1998	115200	401980	22.2	77.6
1999	116000	402000	22.3	77.3
2000	118100	407500	22.6	78
2001	115000	411980	21.9	78.4
2002	114700	420980	21.4	78.6
2003	114900	435980	21	79.8
2004	111400	450980	19.7	79.9
2005	113300	465000	20	81.9

7.3.2 Competitive advantages of STUs

In the present situation, it is obvious that the development of well-coordinated public transport services require both the state transport undertakings and the private sector bus operators to play a major role in the coming years. However, so far the country has not been able to develop any major players in the private sector to run coordinated bus transport services. This sector is still dominated by small ownership fleets with very little investment in terms of infrastructure needed for running reliable and responsible public transport services. The levels of training and the working conditions of labor in the unorganized private transport sector are extremely unsatisfactory. Finally, the road safety record of small fleet operators with ill-trained workers cannot be said to be satisfactory. In such an environment it is the state transport undertakings which give public transport an element of reliability and coordination. The STUs have much strength which needs to be built upon in the coming years. They have a vast pool of professional managerial talent with long experience in running public transport systems. They have also built up in most states extensive infrastructure facilities for bus operation on a large scale. The STUs have successfully operated uneconomical routes in rural areas cross subsidizing them with surpluses from the more remunerative routes. Indeed, there are examples of STUs in our country running some of the largest bus operation networks in the world. In spite of operating buses manufactured with outdated technology, STUs have achieved very high rates of vehicle productivity, fuel economy, and manpower productivity. They have succeeded in training and employing a huge work force of skilled manpower which is approaching the one million mark in terms of directly employed workers. They have also achieved one of the main objectives of nationalization, namely, ending exploitation of workers in the transport sector by providing terms of employment which conform to accepted norms of labor welfare and labor laws. The STUs are also playing an extremely valuable role in many states in promoting social and economic development. To cite but one example, the spread of education in rural areas (particularly among girl children) is greatly aided by the concessional travel facilities offered to students by the STUs. It is our view, therefore, that these strengths of the public undertakings in this sector should be profitably used for developing public transport services in the country in combination with the private sector bus operators.

7.3.3 Private transport operators' role in selected states

7.3.3.1 General

Private operators have been playing a complementary role, and they have been aggressively occupying the space vacated by state operators. They have developed a wide network of operations and run through all major centers of the country. It has lead to generation of large entrepreneurial groups, like the road cargo sector. If we also include the unauthorized operators like jeeps, maxi-cabs, and even trucks, the reach of private operators is even more. They run even in interior rural areas and hilly areas. The major lacuna of this development has been absence of organized large-scale players in the field. This field has been mostly occupied by unorganized small fleet operators barring some whom we can call at the most as medium-sized operators. The challenge to policy makers lies in reigning in these unorganized operators and making the sector attractive to large scale players. We present below the industrial structure of private operators and their operational characteristics.

7.3.3.2 Rajasthan

In 1979 the Rajasthan government issued 64 permits to private operators to operate bus services alongside RSRTC buses in Jaipur. In two years the private operator's share of buses increased to 122, which resulted in unhealthy competition forcing RSRTC to withdraw its services in 1984. Subsequently, to meet the increasing traffic demand, the state government issued permits to private operators to operate different kinds of services and as on 1990, Jaipur had 2750 auto-rickshaws, 223 vikram taxis, 700 tempos, and 289 mini buses.

The service level provided by private operators was far from satisfactory, and there were frequent complaints of over-charging, rash driving, rude behavior of crew, nonadherence to scheduled time tables, not starting services until the vehicle was fully loaded, and very poor condition of vehicles and the resultant breakdowns and overloading were almost twice the capacity of the vehicle, etc. This situation compelled the Rajasthan state government to convene a meeting and directed RSRTC to restart its services in Jaipur.

7.3.3.3 Orissa

During the later part of 1970s private operators owned and operated 2160 buses in Orissa state while the state-owned Orissa State Road Transport Corporation (OSRTC) had operated only 712 buses. Between the period 1978 and 1988 the fleet strength of the private operators doubled while of RTCs fleet declined. OSRTCs fleet utilization was one of the lowest in the country during 1991-92. With the major share of buses with the private operators, they were very powerful and influential. While the private operators cornered 91.3% of the total profitable routes in the state, OSRTC was forced to operate all other nonremunerative routes spread all over the state. Taking advantage of this situation, the private bus operators demanded a fare increase from 10.0 to 20.0 paise per passenger km which the government could not agree, forcing the private operators to go on strike.

7.3.3.4 Madhya Pradesh

In Bhopal city, largely private operators provided public transportation while the Madhya Pradesh State Road Transport Corporation (MPSRTC) was providing services only to government servants and school children at concessional rates. About 400 mini buses, 417 tempos, and 4600 auto-rickshaws were involved in providing public transport requirements in Bhopal city. Since the fare structure in respect of various modes differed, public interest was the first victim in the ensuing heavy cut throat competition. Major causes for the large number of accidents by private vehicles were rash driving, dangerous overtaking, and the poor quality of the drivers employed by the private operators.

7.3.3.5 Andhra Pradesh (Combined)

Private operators until 1978 provided the road passenger services in Vishakapatnam. They were operating 44 routes with 124 buses. The bus operation was found to be tardy, and there were frequent accidents involving private buses. During the year 1978, the Visakapatnam city witnessed a large-scale public agitation and law and order problems on account of the poor bus service in the city. The agitation compelled the state government to issue directions to the Andhra Pradesh State Road Transport Corporation (APSRTC) to introduce bus services in Visakapatnam. Ultimately APSRTC had to introduce 100 buses with effect from December 11 1978, which was subsequently increased to 129 by December 20 1978.

In Vijayawada private operators provided passenger services. The traveling public was not satisfied with the services provided by the private operators with the result Vijayawada witnessed a series of agitations leading to law and order problems. Thus, APSRTC introduced bus services in Vijayawada.

Prior to 1987, private operators were providing bus services in the district of Srikakulam. There were numerous public complaints about private operators that their services were not reliable, not safe, not punctual, inadequate, and of poor quality, and that they were only interested in making quick profits, etc. This situation forced the Andhra Pradesh government to nationalize the bus services in Srikakulam in 1987. After the nationalization, the fleet of buses in Srikakulam started increasing on an average of 15.1% compared to the 5% increase before nationalization. With appropriate scheduling and an increased fleet, APSRTC operated 1.08 lakh passenger kms daily compared to 53,311 passenger kms per day operated by private operators prior to nationalization. A random survey revealed that the public in Srikakulam district are happy with nationalized passenger services of APSRTC compared to private operations.

7.3.3.6 Kerala

In Kerala both the state-owned Kerala State Road Transport Corporation (KSRTC) and private operators provide passenger bus services side by side. While the private operators share of the total passenger buses in the state is around 89%, the KSRTCs share is only about 11%. Because of their major share in the total fleet of buses, the private operators are very much organized and are very influential. In the beginning of the 1990s the private operators in the state went on an indefinite strike pressing for an increase in the existing fare structure. The strike went on for a couple of days forcing the state government to increase the fare from 12.5 to 14.0 paise per passenger km.

7.3.4 Factors influencing private operators

The following factors in general are influencing most of the operators. These factors were identified based on discussions with a number of private operators located in Hyderabad, Bangalore, and Pune.

7.3.4.1 Easy entry/easy exit

The passenger road transport sector is characterized by free play for small time operators, if we leave out the state transport services. Anybody, even with one bus can start a service. They can almost operate at will. There are certain routes which have been denationalized in which they can operate. But they may just take license for one route and operate on some route which they find profitable. They start as contract carriers but operate more as stage carriers. They are also fleet footed. The moment they find a particular route unprofitable they shift to another route. They can cut frequency and change routes depending upon traffic flow. In fact, even the larger players in this industry complain about these small fleet operators. They are also threatened by substitutes. Just as state transport operators complain about private operators, these unauthorized bus operators complain about maxi cabs and autos that are also unauthorized.

7.3.4.2 Low investment/low technology

It is a low investment industry and bankers are willing to fund bus service operation. The performance of these buses should be good and that is why the bankers are willing to lend. The performance is good because these operators are not bound by any route restrictions or service obligations and pay lower taxes. The technology has been mostly stable excepting in recent times when Volvos started flooding the market. Maintenance is simple and can be outsourced. Often they do not even maintain a garage.

7.3.4.3 Faster pay back

Unlike other services, bus services start fetching returns from day one. It generates cash daily and if we consider passes, these are in fact advances. That is why debt servicing is also not a problem for them. Their operations can in fact be characterized as highly liquid by unviable. The main issue about these operators is that they lack any long-term stake in the sector. They are there to reap short-term gains. This attitude is antithetical to the management of public utilities.

7.3.4.4 Control

The dominance of small fleet operators has made any regulatory efforts a big failure. It is very difficult to monitor and track these operators. There is a complete lack of any information about their operations. That is why it is difficult to monitor their schedules, frequencies, and traffic patterns. Most of these operators are proprietary concerns, and they maintain little physical or financial data. This nullified practically any critical analysis of their revenue model or their cost structure from our study point of view.

7.3.4.5 Revenue model

It emerges from a study that organized operators mostly prefer interstate operations as that is the most profitable. Very few organized players are in the intrastate segment. They are very adept in identifying profitable routes and are flexible in scheduling. They are also aggressive in their pricing. They follow different pricing depending upon the peak hours and peak days. They also work through a network of booking agents. There are some states like Karnataka which have denationalized intradistrict routes. Here they are expected to operate on scheduled routes and frequencies.

It also emerges that these operators also operate on a thin margin. In Karnataka it was found that the moment KSRTC allowed flexi-fare to its divisional controllers, the private operators could not face the stiff competition from them. Similarly, they again found that the moment KSRTC introduced new buses, the private operators found it difficult to compete with them. Many of the operators simply moved away to other routes. They also could not cope with the recent fuel hikes, as the RTCs did not follow it up with fare hikes. It also emerges that in each state there are very few operators with more than 50 buses. They all mostly own in the range of 5 to 10 buses. This may be because recent hikes in fuel costs and RTCs stubbornness in not hiking fares has made many of these services unviable even for private operators. This again establishes the point that this sector is still unattractive for organized players. Even in cargo movement we find organized players like TCI, TVS, etc., but in bus services we hardly find any organized players. They try to complement their earnings through revenues from unaccompanied luggage. This is especially lucrative in the case of interstate movement. The contribution from this source can range from 15% to 25% depending upon the aggressiveness of the operators. They work on the principle of earnings per bus and as long as it covers the cost of running, they are satisfied with it. Their earnings per km may work out like this. Their average VU per month is about 600-625 km/day. They also assume revenue from lugguage to the tune of 15% to 25% of the traffic revenue. Many operators opine that the latest high technology buses may not be viable on many routes. The business model of these high tech buses is yet to be established. These may succeed as long distance interstate operations or as tourist buses.

7.3.4.6 Cost structure

The study sought to construct the cost structure of private operators but found it extremely difficult. It was observed that the operators hardly maintain any physical or financial information. Also, since these are proprietorship, they do not have to disclose financial information. They work with basic information like average vehicle utilization in a month, earnings per bus per trip, earnings through luggage, crew salaries, fuel efficiency, bus cost, etc.

We tried to normatively construct their cost structure. They provide for double crews on long distances. They are engaged beyond normal hours. They may not have conductors on these trips. Their fuel efficiency is low as they are not so much focused on this as their maintenance is not professionally managed like RTCs. Excepting the large operators, rarely do they own any maintenance depots. Their overheads are low as they are mostly owner managed. They do not maintain huge office infrastructure. They maintain meager infrastructure for maintenance. They are at an advantage when it comes to MV tax as they pay per seat per quarter.

The cost per kilometer of Volvo and luxury bus has been worked out as presented in Table 7.2. We constructed this cost structure normatively based on the information supplied by some operators. On an average the cost structure is expected to behave on the pattern depicted in the Table. It is based on the assumption that Volvo will be running 500 km per day and luxury bus 350 km per day.

Table 7.2: Economics of private operators

Component	Volvo Rs / Km	Share of cost %	Luxury Rs / km	Share of cost %
Fuel	12.60	44.06	8.00	46.51
Personnel	2.10	7.34	2.50	14.53
Maintenance	2.80	9.79	1.75	10.17
Depreciation	5.60	19.58	1.85	10.76
Interest Cost	3.40	11.89	1.50	8.72
Misc	2.10	7.34	1.60	9.30
Total	28.60	100.00	17.20	100.00
Earning per km	36.00		21.00	
Profit per km	7.40		3.80	

They try to manage cost by controlling personnel cost, maintenance, and overheads. Their cost of buses and depreciation has been going up as competition is getting severe. They are competing on bus brands like Volvo, and interiors and facilities. The cost structure of organized operators is slightly different as they maintain a marketing office and have better maintenance infrastructure. Of course they are not under any obligation to build any infrastructure for passenger amenities or bus stands or depots.

7.3.4.7 Quality parameters

The stress on bringing in organized players is to usher in professionalism and concerns for quality. It may be fashionable to say that the market will determine the quality aspects of service. The absence of a credible alternative public mode, has left the public with no option except to go for any service that is in operation. For example, they may not even have a spare bus in case of breakdown or accidents. They fail miserably on quality parameters like:

1. Bus conditions.
2. Reliability of service.
3. Crew behavior.
4. Accident rates.
5. Passenger amenities.
6. Maintenance infrastructure.

The services provided by private operators are a far cry, excepting select leading operators in each state as pointed out by the survey conducted by IIM Bangalore.

7.3.4.8 Competitive edge

The competitive advantage of private operators is very clear. They are entrepreneurial and market driven. This they are able to adopt because as of now they are not burdened by any social service obligations. They are cost effective. Because these are entrepreneurial, they are cost conscious and try to control build up of overhead. The share of personnel cost is quite low compared to STUs. They may lose some of these advantages if they are brought under regulation and are asked to follow labor laws, quality parameters, and service obligations.

7.3.5 Policy issues confronting private operators

Discussions with them indicate that they are equally concerned about policy dilemmas. The large players among them feel that they are also providing a useful service, which goes unrecognized. They would like to have clarity on their role and what is going to be the policy on privatization of routes. They feel piecemeal privatization will not help. In the absence of clarity on this, they are not definitely willing to commit resources to this sector. They are open to operating on intradistrict routes and intrastate routes if they are provided with appropriate policy and tax support. This is discussed under USO under policy section. They also would like to see a strong regulatory body, as within their group, organized operators face difficulties with unorganized operators. They feel they should control the number of players who can operate in each segment. Too many players can spoil the case. They are wary of concessional segment though they are willing to cater to them as long as the subsidy is compensated. They agree that they cannot provide infrastructure the way STUs have built up. They also opine that they should be given access to bus stands for which they can be charged a fee. They quote the Chennai model as the case.

7.3.6 A relook at privatization options

The primary objectives of privatization in this sector will be to encourage competition and to encourage large scale organized players to enter the field. This can only ensure economy of operations, fresh injection of funds in the sector and professionalism in the field. Otherwise it will be RTCs at one end of the spectrum and a host of small fleet operators at the other end of the spectrum. Both groups are difficult to manage through government control mechanisms. It is important to expose the RTCs to competition but at the same time ensure a level playing field. These also need to be freed of controls if they have to face competition. One group alone cannot have unbridled freedom.

The privatization has to be thought segment wise. The segments prescribed for policy making are:

1. Interstate.
2. Interdistrict.
3. Intradistrict.
4. Urban.
5. Interior rural and hilly.

Each one of these segments would require a tailor-made approach and solution. Privatization also has to proceed keeping this segmentation in mind.

Of course, in all cases of participation by private parties, the governments should prescribe a minimum number of fleets that should be owned by them and corresponding infrastructure. It should specify quality parameters and labor requirements. It should also specify the maximum number of players who can operate in a segment. We suggest three to four players in each segment of which one should be a government operator. This helps to control if they tend to operate as oligopolists and will also help to set benchmarks. While privatizing routes, an exercise has to be taken to assess the traffic needs. This should be in fact a continuous exercise. It should avoid excessive competition or lack of service.

Small fleet operators can join together under a banner and compete. One can as such prescribe that each operator should have at least 50 buses which can be scaled up later. They can have it either on their own or come together. This will ensure some economy for them also. This will also ensure that they maintain a certain level of infrastructure. The policy should have sufficient entry barriers so that everybody cannot enter the field at their will. It should also depend upon due diligence of the operators. They should exhibit better management practices in terms of crew training, information systems and accounting, compliance, and engineering.

The licensing will be based on agreed upon norms for fare fixation, traffic flow, and productivity, like it has been implemented in the highway sector.

Interstate routes are the most lucrative ones. These routes can be auctioned and the surplus from this can be put into a fund which can help subsidize operators who work in loss-making routes. They can be auctioned on the basis of rent which they are willing to pay for the quarter. It can be per bus or per schedule.

Intrastate or interdistrict are also fairly profit making operations. Here also it can be auctioned. Alternatively, interdistrict and intradistrict can be combined as these run parallel in many segments. The government can form blocks of these routes and can auction the entire block. As mentioned before each block can have three players of which one will be RTC. The blocks should be formed such that it should include also loss-making routes. The operators are expected to cross subsidize and still return a surplus to the government.

Purely loss-making routes like interior rural routes or routes covering remote areas or hilly areas can be treated separately. These would form the universal service obligations. These can be auctioned on what kind of support would be needed. They can ask for tax waivers or for financial support. This is supposed to be met through generated from profit making routes.

In urban sectors again some support may be needed. Here again they can form blocks and auction these. Here the operations may not be viable as it will have huge concessional segments, low vehicle utilization, and off-peak operations.

Alternatively, each route can be auctioned. Here if a route is identified as profitable it should be on the basis of license fees that an operator is willing to pay. If it is expected to be a loss-making route, then it should be based on the support that they would require. This principle is followed in London transport. Here again it will lead to proliferation of operators.

Another alternative which can be pursed is that RTCs should increasingly outsource their operations. They can hire buses instead of owning all the buses. They can easily hire up to 25% of their fleet strength. This will also meet the objective of involving private entrepreneurs in this sector. There are various practices for compensating these bus owners. Each RTC can device its own practice. It can also outsource maintenance activities which are noncritical. It can even outsource its existing maintenance infrastructure which has huge excess capacities. O and M can be left to private operators. This will also help in reducing costs. In fact, many states have their own tire rethreading units also.

Privatizing operations and allowing private parties will in fact lead to better tax realization as they are now operating illegally.

In privatization, globally the experience has been that it is equally necessary for governments to ensure viability of both state run corporations and private operators. Initial responses will be towards curtailing RTCs, but it should take care that it does not lead to sickness of

RTCs. One suggestion that is made is that RTCs themselves can act as the licensing body. It can decide which routes are to be privatized and the license fees. It is felt this might lead to conflict of interest, and it may not lead to the desired result of aggressive privatization. Here RTC itself is a stakeholder, and, so, they may be viewed always suspiciously both by the private operators and general public.

7.4 The global trend

The policies of government have been going against global trends and local needs. The global trend is to treat public transport as a public utility and as a contributor to overall development. Public transport services whether provided by state or private operators, are subsidized in most countries. For example, in European countries like the U.K., France, Sweden, and Switzerland, the cost of operation of public transport buses is subsidized by the states from about 40% to 75%. In some European countries there is a practice of imposing taxes on private vehicles or on firms employing more than a minimum number of people to raise resources for subsidizing public transport facilities as bus transport is treated more as a public utility service than as a commercial undertaking. The global trend is also to encourage public transport and discourage privately owned vehicles. In India the policy appears to be working against both these propositions. It encourages privately owned vehicles by offering tax exemptions/reductions and is punitive in its taxation of public transport. Within public transport, it is more supportive of private than state-owned providers.

7.5 Assessment of user satisfaction

The commuters in any urban area are quite in their demands and perceptions. For example, commuters using their own vehicles for work trips will be very happy if the speeds of operations even during peak periods is nearer to the design speed of the roads, enjoy free parking, and do not encounter any difficulty in finding a parking place at any point in time at all the places they visit. Cyclists will be very happy if they could enjoy an exclusive right-of-way and proper arrangements for easy manoeuvrability at junctions. Pedestrians very much desire to have adequate quality footpaths and opportunities for safe crossing facilities on all busy corridors. The city officials need to conduct periodic perception surveys of commuters using the facilities at least once a year. This data is very useful in developing appropriate improvement measures to maximize commuter perception.

There is another large section of commuters (about 50 to 60%) using mass public transportation systems (bus, suburban rail, and metro systems) in major metropolitan cities. There is an urgent necessity that their satisfaction levels be given serious importance in order to enhance the use of public mass transportation facilities. Primary surveys need to be undertaken to gauge their perceptions and their views on areas of improvement. The stakeholders belonging to this category could be broadly divided into three groups, namely:

1. Service providers of mass public transport facilities (employees, drivers, etc.).

2. Commuters using the facilities.

3. Opinion makers (knowledgeable individuals who can influence both service providers and commuters using the facilities).

The primary data collection schedules for obtaining the views are given in the Appendix of this chapter. The Indian Institute of Management is involved in collecting this primary data from about 60,000 persons in the state of Karnataka, Andhra Pradesh (combined). The findings of these primary surveys are used in developing appropriate strategies for enhancing the ridership of mass transportation facilities.

Summary

This chapter mainly discusses the importance, problems, and efficient use of the public transport management infrastructure. It also highlights the improved vehicular flow at different conflict intervals, reversible lanes, channelized sections, and also of high occupancy vehicles in vehicular and nonvehicular modes.

It also gives the information about the data collection and analysis for effective transport planning and shows some light on the role of private sectors in some selected states and also says how government policies affect the global trend and user satisfaction

Appendix

Respondent Category:
Public Transport Company Opinion Makers

Please circle the most appropriate single alternative, unless it is clearly specified that you can choose more than one alternative. Your responses will help us evolve means to enhance the functioning of PUBLIC TRANSPORT COMPANY. At no instance will your answers be identified with you.

1. Name of the interviewer:
2. Date of the interview:
3. Quality checks: Field Supervisor to circle and sign.
4. Guided interview, Training **1**, Scrutiny **2**, Back Check **3**
5. Signature:——————— Name:————————
6. ZONE

   Hyderabad **1**, Telengana **2**, Rayalaseema **3**, Andhra **4**
7. Location: (place of interview)

   Home / School / Office / Shop **1**

   City/Town/Village name **2**

   District:
8. Name of the respondent:
9. Address:

Instructions to Interviewers: Please record response as specified (Circle / Tick / Write, etc.) for each question. Use dark pencil or blue color ballpoint pen. Be courteous to respondents and interview only those people who wish to be part of the survey by answering all questions.

QUESTIONNAIRE OPINION MAKERS

1. Gender: (Circle response) Male **1** Female **2**
2. Please tell me your age (in years): (Circle response)

   <20 **1**, TERMINATE >65 **5**, TERMINATE

   21 - 35 **2**, 36 - 50 **3**, 51 - 65 **4**
3. Residential status: (Circle response) Urban **1**, Rural **2**
4. Please tell me your educational qualification: (Circle response)

   Illiterate **1**, Literate Primary School **2**, High School **3**

   Graduation **4**, Post Graduation **5**

5. Please tell me your occupation. Specify designation for 3, 4, 8, 9, 11 and circle response code.

   1 Student

   2 Housewife

   3 Govt. Servant Central

   4 Govt. Servant State

5 Business Person

6 Social Worker /NGO

7 Teacher

8 Community Leader

9 Private Company

10 Agriculture

11 Elected Representative

12 Others

6. Please tell me your average family monthly income (in rupees): (Circle response)

<5000 **1**, 5001 - 10000 **2** , 10001 - 15000 **3**, >15000 **4**

7. Are you a bus pass holder? (Circle response) Yes **1** (Continue) No **2** (GO TO Q. 8)
If Yes, specify category of PASS HOLDER:

1) Concession Bus Pass: Student **1**, Employee **2**, Any other **3**

2) NonConcession Bus Pass: Daily **1**, Monthly **2**

3) Since when are you using the bus pass: (specify years/months)

8. Current number of bus pass holders in your family: (Circle response)

0, 1, 2, 3, 4, More than **5**

9. Duration of experience as a bus-passenger (in years): (Circle response)

Less than 1, 2, 3, 4, 5, More than 5

10. As a bus-passenger, the travel has been mostly in:
(Circle ONE response only for each type of travel)

1. City
Ordinary **1**, Metro Express **2**, Metro Liner **3**, Veera **4**

2. Intercity
Ordinary **1**, Express **2**, Semi-luxury **3**, Hitech **4**, Volvo **5**

11. Do you own any of the following (tick as many as appropriate):

Sl. No	. Ownership of Vehicle	Tick your response
1	2 Wheeler	
2	Car	
3	Auto	
4	Taxi	
5	Maxicab / Matador / Trax / Minibus	
6	Bus	

12. Have you ever traveled in buses other than PUBLIC TRANSPORT COMPANY?
(Circle response) Yes **1**, No **2**

13. People travel in PUBLIC TRANSPORT COMPANY buses because (tick as many as appropriate):

Sl. No.	Reasons to travel in PUBLIC TRANSPORT COMPANY	Tick Your Opinion
1	They have no better alternative	
2	It is the safest	
3	It is the most comfortable	
4	It is the most convenient in terms of timing	
5	It is the cheapest	
6	It is run by a government corporation	
7	It is meant for common good of society	
8	It offers concessions to the needy	

14. Share your opinion on the following statement using the scale:

1 = Strongly Disagree, **2** = Disagree, **3** = Uncertain/Neutral,

4 = Agree, **5**= Strongly Agree

SL.No	Statement	Scale Agree / Disagree				
1	Public should be encouraged to use personalized vehicles than relying on PUBLIC TRANSPORT COMPANY	1	2	3	4	5
2	The condition of roads in my area are pathetic	1	2	3	4	5
3	There is a heavy misuse of bus passes	1	2	3	4	5
4	Smaller vehicles are better suited than normal buses	1	2	3	4	5
5	Because of shortage of buses from PUBLIC TRANSPORT COMPANY, people are forced to use personalized vehicles	1	2	3	4	5

15. Denote your preferences on the below given various travel attributes for PUBLIC TRANSPORT COMPANY as per the rating scale: Refer to scale and circle one response for each attribute.

1 = Not at all Important, **2** = Less Important, **3** = Important,

4 = Very Important, **5** = Most Important

SL. No	Statement	Rating Scale				
1	Time of the schedule	1	2	3	4	5
2	Fare (cost of the ticket)	1	2	3	4	5
3	Comfort in the bus	1	2	3	4	5
4	Facilities in bus shelter/stand/terminus	1	2	3	4	5
5	Reliability of service	1	2	3	4	5
6	Safety of the journey	1	2	3	4	5
7	Travel duration (journey time)	1	2	3	4	5
	NON-PUBLIC TRANSPORT COMPANY travel attribute	Rating Scale				
8	Passenger friendly behavior of the staff	1	2	3	4	5
9	Balance of speed with safety	1	2	3	4	5
10	Balance of punctuality and customer needs	1	2	3	4	5

16. Denote your judgment regarding the quality of PUBLIC TRANSPORT COMPANY service on the various attributes given below, as per the rating scale:

Refer to scale and circle one response for each attribute.

1 = Very Poor, **2** = Poor, **3** = Average, **4** = Good, **5** = Very Good

SL. No	Quality of PUBLIC TRANSPORT COMPANY Service	Rating Scale				
1	Punctuality	1	2	3	4	5
2	Speed	1	2	3	4	5
3	Frequency	1	2	3	4	5
4	Seat Availability	1	2	3	4	5
5	Fare (cost of the ticket)	1	2	3	4	5
6	Reliability	1	2	3	4	5
7	Convenient timings	1	2	3	4	5
8	Comfort in the bus	1	2	3	4	5
9	Facilities in bus shelter/stand/terminus	1	2	3	4	5
10	Number of stops during the journey	1	2	3	4	5
11	Handling of luggage	1	2	3	4	5

17. Describe the behavior of PUBLIC TRANSPORT COMPANY staff on the various attributes given below, as per the rating scale. Refer to scale and circle one response for each attribute.

1 = Very Poor, **2** = Poor, **3** = Average, **4** = Good, **5** = Very Good

SL.No	PUBLIC TRANSPORT COMPANY Staff Behavior Rating	Rating Scale				
1	Courtesy	1	2	3	4	5
2	Honesty: (returning small change)	1	2	3	4	5
3	Honesty: (diligently issuing tickets)	1	2	3	4	5
4	Helpful to: (women, elderly, children)	1	2	3	4	5
5	Discipline in stopping when required	1	2	3	4	5

18. Have you ever noticed breakdown of buses? Yes **1** No **2**

(If the answer is Yes continue; otherwise, go to question number 19).

18.1 The vehicles you noticed were mostly of:

1 PUBLIC TRANSPORT COMPANY

2 Non-PUBLIC TRANSPORT COMPANY

3 BOTH

19. Did any time the bus you were on traveling break down? Yes **1** No **2**

(If the answer is Yes continue; otherwise, go to question number 22)

20. The bus belonged to: **1** PUBLIC TRANSPORT COMPANY, **2** NonPUBLIC TRANSPORT COMPANY, **3** BOTH

The reasons attributable for the breakdown are (Tick as many as appropriate):

SL. No.	Reasons for Bus Breakdown Tick Your Opinion
1	Poor maintenance of vehicle
2	Bad conditions of road
3	Aged vehicle
4	Rude handling by driver
5	Any other

21. Describe your overall post breakdown experience as:

SL. No.	Post Breakdown Experience Tick Your Opinion
1	Best available alternative was arranged quickly
2	Taken care of well, until the alternatives were made available
3	Left to ourselves/not at all cared for

22. Compare PUBLIC TRANSPORT COMPANY with private buses (Non-PUBLIC TRANSPORT COMPANY) on the following various parameters as per the rating scale. Refer to scale and circle one response for each attribute.

1 = Worse than private, **2** = Equal to private,
3 = Slightly better than private,
4 = Much better than private, **5** = Excellent

SL.No	Service Comparison PUBLIC TRANSPORT COMPANY vs. Private Operators	Circle Response				
1	Timing of the schedule	1	2	3	4	5
2	Fare (cost of the ticket)	1	2	3	4	5
3	Comfort in the bus	1	2	3	4	5
4	Facilities in bus shelter/stand/terminus	1	2	3	4	5
5	Reliability of service	1	2	3	4	5
6	Safety of the journey	1	2	3	4	5
7	Travel duration	1	2	3	4	5
8	Passenger friendly behavior of the staff	1	2	3	4	5
9	Balance of speed with safety	1	2	3	4	5
10	Balance of punctuality and customer needs	1	2	3	4	5

23. List the best practices of private (Non-PUBLIC TRANSPORT COMPANY) buses, which could be emulated by PUBLIC TRANSPORT COMPANY. (Please tick as many as appropriate):

Best Service Quality by PUBLIC TRANSPORT COMPANY **1**,
Best Service Quality by NON-PUBLIC TRANSPORT COMPANY **2**,
Both Are Same **3**

SL. NO.	Service Quality	Service Required		
		PUBLIC TRANSPORT COMPANY	Non - PUBLIC TRANSPORT COMPANY	Both are Same
1	Comfortable seating	1	2	3
2	Leg room between seats	1	2	3
3	Convenient places for boarding	1	2	3
4	Convenient places for alighting	1	2	3
5	Convenient stops during the journey for snacks/coffee/lunch/dinner	1	2	3
6	Passenger need based stops for relaxation and attending toilet requirements	1	2	3
7	Better quality entertainment like music/video	1	2	3
8	Easy ticketing facility	1	2	3
9	Cost effectiveness	1	2	3
10	Less travel time	1	2	3
11	Convenient departure and arrival timings	1	2	3
12	Cleanliness of exterior	1	2	3
13	Easy placement of luggage	1	2	3
14	Less rash driving	1	2	3
15	Empathic behavior by staff	1	2	3

24. To make PUBLIC TRANSPORT COMPANY continue to provide efficient and cost-effective transport service, it should enjoy functional freedom and autonomy in: (Please tick as many as appropriate.)
Functional Freedom Tick Your Opinion

1 Increasing fares for reasons beyond its control like hike in diesel price/input costs
2 Deciding the routes and their frequencies
3 Having differentiated services for various customer segments
4 Deciding different fares for off-peak and other special services
5 Cancellation of schedules/trips/services when there is no patronage

25. If there is a hike in fare, I shall: (Circle any one response only.)
Fare Hike My opinion (Circle any one response only)
1 Grudgingly continue to travel in PUBLIC TRANSPORT COMPANY
2 As a responsible citizen, empathize with PUBLIC TRANSPORT COMPANY and continue to travel
3 Go for alternative modes
4 Join agitation if someone gives a call

26. Share your impressions about PUBLIC TRANSPORT COMPANY, by using the scale: (Circle any one response.)
1 = Strongly Disagree, **2** = Disagree, **3** = Uncertain/Neutral,
4 = Agree, **5** = Strongly Agree

SL. NO.	Your Impressions about PUBLIC TRANS-PORT COMPANY	Scale Agree / Disagree				
1	Is providing best services to public	1	2	3	4	5
2	Needs support from government to do better	1	2	3	4	5
3	Should be privatized	1	2	3	4	5
4	Has grown too big, hence needs to be bifur-cated	1	2	3	4	5
5	Should be freed from governmental control	1	2	3	4	5
6	What ever is done, still there is always short-age of buses experienced by public	1	2	3	4	5

27. Is there a need to increase number of services in your area? YES **1** NO **2**
If Yes: Could you provide details of starting point and ending point?
Route——— From——— To
Route 1 —————————
Route 2 —————————
Route 3 —————————

28. Is there a need to decrease number of services in your area? YES **1** NO **2**
If Yes: Could you provide details of starting point & ending point?
Route——— From——— To
Route 1—————————
Route 2 —————————
Route 3—————————
Thank you!

Stake Holders Opinion Survey Format for Commuters

Please circle the most appropriate single alternative, unless it is clearly specified that you can choose more than one alternative. Your responses will help us evolve means to enhance the functioning of Bus Company. At no instance will your answers be identified with you.
Name of the interviewer: ——— Date of the interview:————————-
2005 Quality checks: Field Supervisor to circle and sign. ———
Guided interview: training **1**, Scrutiny **2**, Back Check **3**
Signature: ——— Name: ———
Name of the District:————————
Location: (Place of interview)————————
On board (fm——————— to———————) **1**
Bus Stand——— **2**
(City/Town/Village name) ———————
District:———————
Name of the passenger (respondent):————————
Address:————————

Instructions to Interviewers:
Please record response as specified (Circle/Tick/Write, etc.) for each question. Use dark pencil or blue color ballpoint pen. Be courteous to respondents and interview only those people who wish to be part of the survey by answering all questions. Do not interview any person without obtaining their full consent for the interview.

QUESTIONNAIRE PUBLIC TRANSPORT COMPANY COMMUTERS

1. Gender: (Circle response) Male **1**, Female **2**

2. Please tell me your age (in years): (Circle response)
<20 **1** TERMINATE, >65 **5** TERMINATE
21 - 35 **2**, 36 - 50 **3**, 51- 65 **4**

3. Residential status: (Circle response) Urban **1**, Rural **2**

4. Please tell me your educational qualification: (Circle response)
Illiterate **1**, Literate Primary School **2**, High School **3**
Graduation **4**, Post Graduation **5**

5. Please tell me your occupation: (Circle response)
Student **1**, Housewife **2**, Govt. Servant **3**, Business Person **4**, Others **5**

6. Please tell me your average family monthly income (in rupees): (Circle response)

    <5000 **1**, 5001 - 10000 **2**, 10001 - 15000 **3**, >15000 **4**
7. Are you a bus pass holder? (Circle response) Yes **1** (Continue), No **2** (Go to Q. 8)
If Yes, specify category of PASS HOLDER:

    1) Concession bus pass: Student **1**, Employee **2**, Any other **3**
    2) NonConcession bus pass: Daily **1**, Monthly **2**
    3) Since when are you using the bus pass: ——————— (specify years/months)

8. Current number of bus pass holders in your family: (Circle response)
0, 1, 2, 3, 4, More than **5**

9. Duration of experience as a bus passenger (in years): (Circle response)
<**1, 2, 3, 4, 5**, >**5**

10. As a bus-passenger, the travel has been mostly in:
(Circle ONE response only for each type of travel)

    1. City
Ordinary **1**, Metro Express **2**, Metro Liner **3**, Veera **4**
    2. Intercity
Ordinary **1**, Express **2**, Semi-luxury **3**, Hitech **4**, Volvo **5**

11. Have you ever traveled in buses other than PUBLIC TRANSPORT COMPANY?
(Circle response) Yes **1** No **2**

12. People travel in PUBLIC TRANSPORT COMPANY buses because (Tick as many as appropriate):

Sl. No.	Reasons to travel in PUBLIC TRANSPORT COMPANY	Tick Your Opinion
1	They have no better alternative	
2	It is the safest	
3	It is the most comfortable	
4	It is the most convenient in terms of timing	
5	It is the cheapest	
6	It is run by a government corporation	
7	It is meant for common good of society	
8	It offers concessions to the needy	

13. Compare PUBLIC TRANSPORT COMPANY with private buses (Non-PUBLIC TRANSPORT COMPANY) on the following various parameters as per the rating scale. Refer to scale and circle one response for each attribute.
1 = Worse than private, **2** = Equal to private,
3 = Slightly better than private,
4 = Much better than private, **5** = Excellent

SL. No	Service Comparison PUBLIC TRANSPORT COMPANY vs. Private Operators	Circle Response				
1	Timing of the schedule	1	2	3	4	5
2	Fare (cost of the ticket)	1	2	3	4	5
3	Comfort in the bus	1	2	3	4	5
4	Facilities in bus shelter/stand/terminus	1	2	3	4	5
5	Reliability of service	1	2	3	4	5
6	Safety of the journey	1	2	3	4	5
7	Travel duration	1	2	3	4	5
8	Passenger friendly behavior of the staff	1	2	3	4	5
9	Balance of speed with safety	1	2	3	4	5
10	Balance of punctuality and customer needs	1	2	3	4	5

14. Denote your judgment regarding the quality of PUBLIC TRANSPORT COMPANY service on the various attributes given below, as per the rating scale:

Refer to scale and circle one response for each attribute.

1 = Very Poor, **2** = Poor, **3** = Average, **4** = Good, **5** = Very Good

SL. No	Quality of PUBLIC TRANSPORT COMPANY Service	Rating Scale				
1	Punctuality	1	2	3	4	5
2	Speed	1	2	3	4	5
3	Frequency	1	2	3	4	5
4	Seat Availability	1	2	3	4	5
5	Fare (cost of the ticket)	1	2	3	4	5
6	Reliability	1	2	3	4	5
7	Convenient timings	1	2	3	4	5
8	Comfort in the bus	1	2	3	4	5
9	Facilities in bus shelter/stand/terminus	1	2	3	4	55
10	Number of stops during the journey	1	2	3	4	5
11	Handling of luggage	1	2	3	4	5

15. Describe the behavior of PUBLIC TRANSPORT COMPANY staff on the various attributes given below, as per the rating scale. Refer to scale and circle one response for each attribute.

1 = Very Poor; 2 = Poor; 3 = Average; 4 = Good; 5 = Very Good

SL.No	PUBLIC TRANSPORT COMPANY Staff Behavior Rating	Rating Scale				
1	Courtesy	1	2	3	4	5
2	Honesty: (returning small change)	1	2	3	4	5
3	Honesty: (diligently issuing tickets)	1	2	3	4	5
4	Helpful to: (women, elderly, children)	1	2	3	4	5
5	Discipline in stopping when required	1	2	3	4	5

16. Have you ever noticed breakdown of buses? Yes No

(If the answer is Yes continue; otherwise, go to question number 19).

17. If yes, the vehicles you have noticed were mostly: 1-of PUBLIC TRANSPORT COMPANY, 2-of Non-PUBLIC TRANSPORT COMPANY

18. Did at any time the bus you were traveling on breakdown? Yes, No
(If the answer is Yes continue; otherwise, go to question number 22)

19. The bus belonged to: 1- PUBLIC TRANSPORT COMPANY, 2 - Non-PUBLIC TRANSPORT COMPANY

The reasons attributable for the breakdown are (Tick as many as appropriate):
Reasons for Bus breakdown———- Tick Your Opinion

1	Poor maintenance of vehicle
2	Bad conditions of road
3	Aged vehicle
4	Rude handling by driver
5	Any other: ———————

20. Describe the overall post breakdown experience as:

Post break down experience ——— Tick Your Opinion	
1	Best available alternative was arranged quickly
2	Taken care of well, until the alternatives were made available
3	Left to ourselves/not at all cared for

21. Compare PUBLIC TRANSPORT COMPANY with private buses (Non-PUBLIC TRANSPORT COMPANY) on the following various parameters as per the rating scale. Refer to scale and circle one response for each attribute.

1 = Worse than Private, 2 = Equal to Private,

3 = Slightly Better than Private,
4 = Much Better than Private, **5** = Excellent

SL.No	Service Comparison PUBLIC TRANSPORT COMPANY vs. Private Operators	Circle Response				
1	Timing of the schedule	1	2	3	4	5
2	Fare (cost of the ticket)	1	2	3	4	5
3	Comfort in the bus	1	2	3	4	5
4	Facilities in bus shelter/stand/terminus	1	2	3	4	5
5	Reliability of service	1	2	3	4	5
6	Safety of the journey	1	2	3	4	5
7	Travel duration	1	2	3	4	5
8	Passenger friendly behavior of the staff	1	2	3	4	5
9	Balance of speed with safety	1	2	3	4	5
10	Balance of punctuality and customer needs	1	2	3	4	5

22. List the best practices of private (non-PUBLIC TRANSPORT COMPANY) buses, which could be emulated by PUBLIC TRANSPORT COMPANY. (Please tick as many as appropriate.)

Best Service Quality by PUBLIC TRANSPORT COMPANY **1**

Best Service Quality by NON-PUBLIC TRANSPORT COMPANY **2**

Both Are Same **3**

SL. NO.	Service Quality	Service Required		
		PUBLIC TRANSPORT COMPANY	Non - PUBLIC TRANSPORT COMPANY	Both Are Same
1	Comfortable seating	1	2	3
2	Leg room between seats	1	2	3
3	Convenient places for boarding	1	2	3
4	Convenient places for alighting	1	2	3
5	Convenient stops during the journey for snacks/coffee/lunch/dinner	1	2	3
6	Passenger need based stops for relaxation and attending toilet requirements	1	2	3
7	Better quality entertainment like music/video	1	2	3
8	Easy ticketing facility	1	2	3
9	Cost effectiveness	1	2	3
10	Less travel time	1	2	3
11	Convenient departure and arrival timings	1	2	3
SL. NO.	Service quality	Service Required		
13	Cleanliness of exterior	1	2	3
14	Easy placement of luggage	1	2	3
15	Less rash driving	1	2	3
16	Empathic behavior by staff	1	2	3

23. To make PUBLIC TRANSPORT COMPANY continue to provide efficient and cost-effective transport service, it should enjoy functional freedom and autonomy in: (Please tick as many as appropriate.)

Functional Freedom ————— Tick Your Opinion
1 Increasing fares for reasons beyond its control like hike in diesel price/input costs
2 Deciding the routes and their frequencies
3 Having differentiated services for various customer segments
4 Deciding different fares for off-peak and other special services
5 Cancellation of schedules/trips/services when there is no patronage

24. If there is a hike in fare, I shall: (Circle any one response only.)
Fare Hike My opinion————— (Circle any one response only.)
1 Grudgingly continue to travel in PUBLIC TRANSPORT COMPANY
2 As a responsible citizen, empathize with PUBLIC TRANSPORT COMPANY and continue to travel
3 Go for alternative modes
4 Join agitation if someone gives a call

25. Share your impressions about PUBLIC TRANSPORT COMPANY, by using the scale: (Circle any one response.)
1 = Strongly Disagree, **2** = Disagree, **3** = Uncertain/Neutral,
4 = Agree, **5** = Strongly Agree

SL. NO.	Your Impressions about PUBLIC TRANSPORT COMPANY	Scale Agree / Disagree				
1	Is providing best services to public	1	2	3	4	5
2	Needs support from government to do better	1	2	3	4	5
3	Should be privatized	1	2	3	4	5
4	Has grown too big, hence needs to be bifurcated	1	2	3	4	5
5	Should be freed from governmental control	1	2	3	4	5
6	What ever is done, still there is always shortage of buses experienced by public	1	2	3	4	5

26. Is there a need to increase number of services in your area? YES **1**, NO **2**
If Yes: Could you provide details of starting point and ending point?
Route———— From———— To———— and
Route 1 ————
Route 2 ————
Route 3 ————

27. Is there a need to decrease number of service in your area? YES 1 NO 2
If Yes: Could you provide details of starting point & ending point?
Route———— From———— To
Route 1————
Route 2 ————
Route 3————
Thank you!

Respondent Category: PUBLIC TRANSPORT COMPANY Employees

Please circle the most appropriate single alternative, unless it is clearly specified that you can choose more than one alternative. Your responses will help us evolve means to enhance the functioning of PUBLIC TRANSPORT COMPANY. At no instance will your answers be identified with you.

Name of the interviewer: ———— Date of the interview:

Quality checks: Field Supervisor to circle and sign.

Guided interview: training **1**, Scrutiny **2**, Back Check **3**

Signature:———— Name: ———— Name of the District: ————

Location: (Place of interview) On board (fm ———— to ————) **1**

Bus Stand———————— **2** (City/Town/Village name)

District: ————————

Name of the employee (respondent):———————— Badge No.:————————

Designation:

Driver **1**, Conductor **2**, Supervisor **3**, Admin. Staff **4**, Officer **5**

Address:————

Instructions to Interviewers:

Please record response as specified (Circle / Tick / Write, etc.) for each question. Use dark pencil or blue color ballpoint pen. Be courteous to respondents and interview only those people who wish to be part of the survey by answering all questions. Do not interview any person without obtaining their full consent for the interview.

QUESTIONNAIRE PUBLIC TRANSPORT COMPANY EMPLOYEES

1. Gender: (Circle response) Male **1**, Female **2**

2. Please tell me your age (in years): (Circle response)
   <20 **1** TERMINATE , >65 **5** TERMINATE,
   21-35 **2**, 36-50 **3**, 51-65 **4**

3. Residential status: (Circle response) Urban **1**, Rural **2**

4. Please tell me your educational qualification: (Circle response)
   Illiterate **1**, Literate Primary School **2**, High School **3**,
   Graduation **4**, Post Graduation **5**

5. Please tell me your average family monthly income (in rupees): (Circle response) <7000 =**1**, 7001-15000 = **2**, 15001-25000= **3**, >25000 = **4**

6. Work experience (write response in no. of years): Total ————
   At PUBLIC TRANSPORT COMPANY at the current position: ————

7. Please tell me the number of promotions received so far during your tenure at PUBLIC TRANSPORT COMPANY.
   (Circle response) **0, 1, 2, 3, 4, >5**

8. Have you ever traveled in buses other than PUBLIC TRANSPORT COMPANY? Yes, No

9. Do you own a vehicle? Yes **1** (Continue), No **2** (Go To Q.10)

9.(1) If yes, please specify the type of vehicle owned by you.
   Two-wheeler = **1**, Car = **2**, Auto = **3**, Maxi cab = **4**,
   Matador = **5**, Minibus = **6**, Tempo-Trax = **7**, Lorry = **8**, Bus = **9**.

10. Please use the 5-point scale to answer this question: Circle ONE response only.

1 Strongly Disagree, **2** Disagree, **3** Uncertain, **4** Agree, **5** Strongly Agree

To make PUBLIC TRANSPORT COMPANY provide better service to people, in terms of its governance, it should be:

SL. NO.	Your Impressions about PUBLIC TRANSPORT COMPANY	Scale Agree / Disagree				
1	Completely privatized	1	2	3	4	5
2	Partially privatized	1	2	3	4	5
3	Better controlled by state government	1	2	3	4	5
4	Enjoy better patronage by state govt.	1	2	3	4	5
5	Least control and interference by state govt.	1	2	3	4	5
6	Given unconditional autonomy	1	2	3	4	5
7	Ban completely the services of private operators thus providing monopoly and larger scale of operations.	1	2	3	4	5

11. Please use the 5-point scale to answer this question: Circle ONE response only.

1 Strongly Disagree, **2** Disagree, **3** Uncertain, **4** Agree, **5** Strongly Agree

The best option to help PUBLIC TRANSPORT COMPANY come out of the present financial crisis is to:

SL. NO.	OPTIONS TO SOLVE THE FINANCIAL CRISIS AT PUBLIC TRANSPORT COMPANY SCALE	Scale Agree / Disagree				
1	Allow PUBLIC TRANSPORT COMPANY to freely borrow from lending organizations.	1	2	3	4	5
2	Sanction subsidies more liberally to shield from the impact of fuel hikes and concessional passes.	1	2	3	4	5
3	Pump in more funds in the form of government equity with conditions of performance.	1	2	3	4	5
4	Closing of some DEPOTS and/or merging with adjacent depots.	1	2	3	4	5

12. Please use the 5-point scale to answer this question: Circle ONE response only.

1 Strongly Disagree, **2** Disagree, **3** Uncertain, **4** Agree, **5** Strongly Agree

Please specify your opinion on the Major drawback of PUBLIC TRANSPORT COMPANY.

SL. NO.	Major Drawback of PUBLIC TRANSPORT COMPANY SCALE	Scale Agree / Disagree				
1	Government interference	1	2	3	4	5
2	Absence of professionalism at the policy making level (Board)	1	2	3	4	5
3	Forced to offer services at rates lower than cost	1	2	3	4	5
4	Functioning of private operators	1	2	3	4	5
5	Lack of control on illegal operations	1	2	3	4	5

13. Please use the 5-point scale to answer this question: Circle ONE response only.
    1 Strongly Disagree, **2** Disagree, **3** Uncertain, **4** Agree, **5** Strongly Agree
People travel in PUBLIC TRANSPORT COMPANY bus because:

SL. NO.	Reasons to Travel in PUBLIC TRANSPORT COMPANY Bus	Scale Agree / Disagree				
1	They have no better alternative	1	2	3	4	5
2	It is the safest	1	2	3	4	5
3	It is the cheapest	1	2	3	4	5
4	It is run by government	1	2	3	4	5
5	It is meant for common good of society	1	2	3	4	5

14. Please use the 5-point scale to answer this question: Circle ONE response only.
    1 Strongly Disagree, **2** Disagree, **3** Uncertain, **4** Agree, **5** Strongly Agree
Share your agreement / disagreement on public transport opinion statements

SL. NO.	Opinion on Public Transport	Scale Agree / Disagree				
1	Public should be encouraged to use two/four wheeler rather than relying on PUBLIC TRANSPORT COMPANY	1	2	3	4	5
2	The conditions of roads in my area are pathetic	1	2	3	4	5
3	Until roads are improved, public should use their own transport rather than asking for PUBLIC TRANSPORT COMPANY buses	1	2	3	4	5
4	There is a heavy misuse of bus passes	1	2	3	4	5
5	Smaller vehicles are better suited than normal buses	1	2	3	4	5

15. Please use the 5-point scale to answer this question: Circle ONE response only.
    1 = Not at all important, **2** = Less important,
    3 = Important, **4** = Very important, **5** = Most important
Denote your preferences on the below given travel attribute as per the rating scale.

SL. No	Service Comparison PUBLIC TRANSPORT COMPANY vs. Private Operators	Circle Response				
1	Timing of the schedule	1	2	3	4	5
2	Fare (cost of the ticket)	1	2	3	4	5
3	Comfort in the bus	1	2	3	4	5
4	Facilities in bus shelter/stand/terminus	1	2	3	4	5
5	Reliability of service	1	2	3	4	5
6	Safety of the journey	1	2	3	4	5
7	Travel duration	1	2	3	4	5
8	Passenger friendly behavior of the staff	1	2	3	4	5
9	Balance of speed with safety	1	2	3	4	5

16. Denote your judgment regarding the quality of PUBLIC TRANSPORT COMPANY service on the various attributes given below, as per the rating scale.

Refer to scale and circle one response for each attribute.

1 = Very Poor, **2** = Poor, **3** = Average, **4** = Good, **5** = Very Good

SL.No	Quality of PUBLIC TRANSPORT COMPANY Service	Rating Scale				
1	Punctuality	1	2	3	4	5
2	Speed	1	2	3	4	5
3	Frequency	1	2	3	4	5
4	Seat availability	1	2	3	4	5
5	Fare (cost of the ticket)	1	2	3	4	5
6	Reliability	1	2	3	4	5
7	Convenient timings	1	2	3	4	5
8	Comfort in the bus	1	2	3	4	5
9	Facilities in bus shelter/stand/terminus	1	2	3	4	55
10	Number of stops during the journey	1	2	3	4	5
11	Handling of luggage	1	2	3	4	5

17. Describe the behavior of PUBLIC TRANSPORT COMPANY staff on the various attributes given below, as per the rating scale. Refer to scale and circle one response for each attribute.

1 = Very Poor, **2** = Poor, **3** = Average, **4** = Good, **5** = Very Good

SL. No	PUBLIC TRANSPORT COMPANY Staff Behavior Rating	Rating Scale				
1	Courtesy	1	2	3	4	5
2	Honesty: (returning small change)	1	2	3	4	5
3	Honesty: (diligently issuing tickets)	1	2	3	4	5
4	Helpful to: (women, elderly, children)	1	2	3	4	5
5	Discipline in stopping when required	1	2	3	4	5

18. Have you ever experienced a breakdown of buses en-route when you TRAVELED IN PUBLIC TRANSPORT COMPANY bus?

Yes **1** (CONTINUE), No **2** (GO TO Q. 20)

18.1 If Yes, the reasons attributed for it are:

Please use the 5-point scale to answer this question: Circle ONE response only.

1 Strongly Disagree, **2** Disagree, **3** Uncertain, **4** Agree, **5** Strongly Agree

SL. No	Reasons for Breakdown	Rating Scale				
1	Poor maintenance (of vehicle)	1	2	3	4	5
2	Bad conditions of road	1	2	3	4	5
3	Aged vehicle	1	2	3	4	5
4	Rude handling by driver	1	2	3	4	5
5	Any other	1	2	3	4	5

19. How was the post-breakdown experience?

Best available alternative was arranged quickly — Yes **1**, No **2**

Taken care of well until the alternatives were made available— Yes **1**, No **2**

We were left to ourselves, no one helped us —— Yes **1**, No **2**

20. Compare PUBLIC TRANSPORT COMPANY with private buses (non-PUBLIC TRANSPORT COMPANY) on the following parameters as per the rating scale.

1 = Worse than Private, **2** = Equal to Private,

3 = Slightly Better than Private,

4 = Much Better than Private, **5** = Excellent

218

SL.No	Service Comparison PUBLIC TRANSPORT COMPANY vs. Private Operators	Circle Response				
1	Timing of the bus	1	2	3	4	5
2	Fare (cost of the ticket)	1	2	3	4	5
3	Comfort in the bus	1	2	3	4	5
4	Facilities in bus shelter/stand/terminus	1	2	3	4	5
5	Reliability of service	1	2	3	4	5
6	Safety of the journey	1	2	3	4	5
7	Travel duration	1	2	3	4	5
8	Passenger friendly behavior of the staff	1	2	3	4	5
9	Balance of speed with safety	1	2	3	4	5
10	Balance of punctuality and customer needs	1	2	3	4	5

21. List the best practices of Private (Non-PUBLIC TRANSPORT COMPANY) buses, which could be emulated by PUBLIC TRANSPORT COMPANY: (Please tick as many as appropriate.)

Best Service Quality by PUBLIC TRANSPORT COMPANY **1**,

Best Service Quality by NON-PUBLIC TRANSPORT COMPANY **2**,

Both are Same **3**

SL. No.	Service Quality	Service Required		
		PUBLIC TRANS-PORT COM-PANY	Non - PUBLIC TRANS-PORT COM-PANY	Both are Same
1	Comfortable seating	1	2	3
2	Leg room between seats	1	2	3
3	Convenient places for boarding	1	2	3
4	Convenient places for alighting	1	2	3
5	Convenient stops during the journey for snacks/coffee/lunch/dinner	1	2	3
6	Passenger need based stops for relaxation and attending toilet requirements	1	2	3
7	Better quality entertainment like music/video	1	2	3
8	Easy ticketing facility	1	2	3
9	Cost effectiveness	1	2	3
10	Less travel time	1	2	3
11	Convenient departure and arrival timings	1	2	3
12	Cleanliness of interior	1	2	3
13	Cleanliness of exterior	1	2	3
14	Easy placement of luggage	1	2	3
15	Less rash driving	1	2	3
16	Empathic behavior by staff	1	2	3

22. To make PUBLIC TRANSPORT COMPANY continue to provide efficient and cost-effective transport service, it should enjoy freedom and autonomy: (Please tick as many as appropriate.)

SCOPE OF FREEDOM and AUTONOMY Tick Your Opinion

1 In increasing fares for reasons beyond its control like diesel price increase ——

2 In deciding the routes and their frequencies ——

3 In having differentiated services for various customer segments ————

4 In deciding different fares for differentiated services ————

5 In managing its own finances and assets ————

6 In evolving its own policies and procedures in enhancing customer satisfaction ————

25. Share your impressions about PUBLIC TRANSPORT COMPANY, by using the scale: (Circle any one response.)

1 = Strongly Disagree, **2** = Disagree, **3** = Uncertain/Neutral,

4 = Agree, **5** = Strongly Agree

Sl. No.	Your Impressions about PUBLIC TRANS-PORT COMPANY	Scale Agree / Disagree				
1	Is providing best services to public	1	2	3	4	5
2	Needs support from government to do better	1	2	3	4	5
3	Should be privatized	1	2	3	4	5
4	Has grown too big, hence needs to be bifur-cated	1	2	3	4	5
5	Should be freed from governmental control	1	2	3	4	5
6	What ever is done, still there is always short-age of buses experienced by public	1	2	3	4	5

26. Is there a need to increase number of services in your area? YES **1**, NO **2**

If Yes: Could you provide details of starting point and ending point?

Route———— From———————— To —————

Route 1 ————————————

Route 2 ————————————

Route 3 ————————————

27. Is there a need to decrease number of services in your area? YES **1** NO **2**

If Yes: Could you provide details of starting point and ending point?

Route———— From ———————— To —————

Route 1 ————————————

Route 2 ————————————

Route 3 ————————————

Thank you!

Chapter 8

Resource Needs for Public Transport

8.1 Financial performance of public transport organizations

Financial performance of any public transport organization depends upon the revenue it generates on the basis of operations and how much it needs to spend on various inputs in running the organization. The revenue stream of bus undertakings mainly include two sources namely ticket sales and advertisement revenue on buses and other bus-related infrastructure. However the major share to the extent of 96 to 97 percent is contributed by ticket sales. The cost stream includes capital costs associated with buses, maintenance, fuel costs, and manpower costs. In addition, the organizations incur expenditure in creating infrastructure like bus stands, stops, etc. In India for quite some time the government of India and respective state governments provided some financial assistance to consolidate the working of these organizations. In India it is normal practice that whenever some financial assistance is provided a number of social obligations are also tied with it. Bus undertakings are no exception to this phenomenon. Running buses in cities with very low demand during off peak hour and student concessions are some of the examples of this phenomenon. For sustainable growth in the fleet to take care of demand increase and replacement needs of old stock, the undertakings must enjoy surplus revenue or profits. The following paragraph details the financial performance bus undertakings in India.

8.1.1 Financial performance: Turnover of STUs.

The financial performance of STUs does not truly reflect their physical performance. Currently the total revenue earned by them is in the range of about Rs.$20*10^4$ million per year on which they make a loss of Rs. $2*10^4$ million per annum. Some STUs like Karnataka SRTC, Bangalore Metropolitan Transport Corporation (BMTC), UPSRTC, some Tamil Nadu STUs, etc. have been showing profits in recent times. Also, STUs have been consistently adding to physical infrastructure in spite of poor earnings. Even though the capital base of STUs is estimated to be around Rs.$8*10^4$ million, the value of the assets owned by all the STUs in the country may exceed about Rs.$15*10^4$ million taking into account the rolling stock, the lands, buildings, and other items of infrastructure owned by them.

The poor financial performance of STUs in spite of their robust physical performance is more due to the impact of rising input prices relating to motor vehicle taxes, concessions and universal service obligations, unviable fare structures, and fuel prices. The following paragraphs analyze these factors. The main causes are:

1. Motor vehicle taxes

2. Cost of concessions

3. Uneconomic fare structure

8.1.2 Motor vehicles tax

STUs pay substantial amounts of motor vehicle taxes to state governments, usually as a percentage of traffic revenue. The nomenclature, incidence, and method of calculation of the taxes vary from state to state. The amount of MV taxes paid over the years by STUs as a group at the All India level is shown in Table 8.1 below. The total tax paid in 2004-05 by 36 STUs for which data is available was about Rs.$1.516*10^4$ million which represented 11% percent of their traffic revenue. For all the STUs together it is estimated to be around Rs.$2*10^4$ million per annum presently. It is rather significant that the financial losses suffered by the STUs annually roughly equals the MV tax. This point is illustrated in Table 8.1 below.

Table 8.1: MV Tax - All India

Year	Total Revenue	MV Tax	MV Tax Rate %	Losses of STUs (in Millions)
1995-96	9499	1135.22	12	10600
2000-01	15325	1620.93	10.6	19460
2001-02	16040	1635.2	10.2	21930
2002-03	16618	1640.6	9.9	15250
2003-04	10605	1240	11.7	14700
2004-05	14325	1516	10.6	17390
2005-06	17072	1731	10.1	26600
2006-07	16491	1661	10.1	7890

Source: STU from 1995-2007

Thus it may be seen that the states have usually treated STUs as an important source of revenue while at the same time expecting them to provide inexpensive transport services to the people. This runs counter to public policy prescriptions of encouraging the development of affordable public transport.

A bus during its lifetime (over a 10-year period) pays a much higher amount than any other mode of transport towards tax. It is a matter of concern that environmental friendly congestion and reduction oriented transport should pay higher taxes than others.

8.1.3 Cost of concessions

Another factor that significantly affects the revenues of STUs is concessions granted by state governments to various categories of users of STU services. According to statistics available with the CIRT, the cost of these concessions to the STUs amounted to Rs.1.137*104 million in 2000-01 and Rs.1.482*104 million in 2004-05 (Table 8.2). While some states reimburse the losses from concessions to STUs partly, in most cases such compensation by way of reimbursement is grossly inadequate. The following statement compares the cost of concessions to STUs with the overall losses sustained by them in their operations. It should be mentioned here that while the STUs are expected to provide affordable transport to students they cannot be expected to bear the full burden of the costs.

Table 8.2: Trend of Concessions All India (Rs in millions)

Year	Revenue	Losses	Concessions	MV Tax	Surplus	Losses Net of Concessions
			Million			
2000-01	153250	-19460	11370	16200	7110	-8090
2001-02	160400	-21930	13130	16350	7550	-8800
2002-03	166180	-15250	15250	16400	16400	00
2003-04	106050	-14700	12730	12400	17090	-1970
2004-05	143250	-17390	14820	15160	14400	-2570
2005-06	170720	-26600	15480	17310	-11520	-11120
2006-07	164910	-7890	16250	16610	11160	8360

Source: STU from 2000-2007

8.1.4 Uneconomic fare structure

The rising operational costs, taxes, and the burden of concessional travel schemes introduced by state governments are seldom adequately compensated in the fare structure of STUs which is determined by the state governments. For political and other considerations the state governments are reluctant to allow STUs to revise the fares with the periodicity that it requires. This situation was noted by the National Transport Policy Committee as far back as 1980 when they noted that "many State Transport Undertakings are presently operating at a loss, mainly on account of uneconomic fares which have been kept low as a deliberate policy of Governments. Such low fares are not in conformity with the principle of covering short term marginal costs. We therefore strongly recommend that fare structure of State Transport Undertakings should be revised and brought in line with costs structure. We also urge that within the broad policy frame which may be laid down by the proposed National Transport Commission, each Public Sector Undertaking should have the freedom and flexibility to revise and adjust its fare structure."

Thus, the fare structure of STUs in most cases is always found to be lagging behind their operational costs thereby forcing the STUs to operate at negative margins. This is in spite of the fact that the operational costs of STUs were increasing at a much higher rate than the consumer price index or wholesale price index mainly on account of the steep increase in the prices of HSD. Therefore, the earnings per km. (EPKM) of STUs as a group were lower than their cost per km. (CPKM) as shown in Table 8.3 below:

Table 8.3: Profit/Loss per Km (All India)

Years	EPKM(ps/km)	CPKM(ps/km)	Profit/Loss(ps/km)
1995-96	886.20	985.10	-98.90
2000-01	1280.70	1443.30	-162.60
2001-02	1335.40	1518.00	-182.60
2002-03	1419.60	1549.90	-130.30
2003-04	1561.20	1751.00	-189.80
2004-05	1574.8	1766.0	-191.20
2005-06	1687.3	1950.20	-262.90
2006-07	1836.1	1923.9	-87.80

Source: STU from 1995-2007

Also, they are expected to operate on interior rural routes, hilly, and remote areas which are highly subsidized. The STUs seek to cross subsidize such operations with the revenue generated on bus routes with better load factor. The scope for cross subsidization got eroded as the state governments permitted private operators to operate in the profitable routes with no compensating service obligations.

8.1.5 Manpower costs in STUs

STUs being seen as state's own agencies also employ their workers on terms similar to those of government employees besides complying with the provisions of law relating to welfare of labor. The personnel costs of STU operations have steadily increased over the years from 395 ps/km during 1995-96 to 687 ps/km in 2004-05 at an annual compounded average increase of 5.69%. This increase is mainly the result of the periodical revision of wages to the workers, which is necessitated when the state governments revise the rates of dearness allowance to their employees. The personnel cost across different sectors of rural, hilly, and urban transport services is presented in Table 8.4.

Table 8.4: Personnel Costs in STUs

Type of Operations	Year	Personal Costs	Total Costs	Share of Personnel Costs (%)
Rural	2000-01	529.96	1343.07	39.50
	2003-04	592.32	1569.38	37.70
	2006-07	454.53	1786.90	25.44
Hilly	2000-01	997.85	1963.83	50.80
	2003-04	1049.74	2166.96	48.40
	2006-07	3289.08	5001.10	65.77
Urban	2000-01	1248.11	2221.58	56.20
	2003-04	1524.50	3167.34	48.10
	2006-07	1444.44	3106.90	46.49
Total	2000-01	611.42	1443.32	42.40
	2003-04	686.93	1729.32	39.70
	2006-07	540.55	1923.90	28.10

Source: CIRT, Pune

In spite of the frequent wage revisions, the proportion of personnel costs in the total costs of STUs has declined over the years. The share of personnel costs in the total costs at the All India level was 42.4% in 2000-01 and 39.7% in 2004-05. The reduction in the personnel costs as a proportion of total costs has been due to productivity improvement of STU fleets as mentioned above and due to the reduction achieved in the staff per bus ratio. It is also partly due to a steep increase in fuel costs in recent years, which has increased the share of fuel costs relative to personnel costs.

8.1.6 Fuel efficiency and fuel costs

The fuel price pressure has made STUs critical to the possibilities of savings through better fuel efficiency. STUs have managed to control the impact of price hikes of fuel to some extent through fuel efficiency. They are adopting various strategies for achieving fuel efficiency. Earlier the belief was that fuel efficiency was technologically determined and maintenance dependent. In recent years the emphasis has shifted towards better driving practices. This has shown tremendous improvements in fuel efficiency.

Overall fuel efficiency in STUs improved from 4.41 km per liter (kmpl) to 4.78 kmpl during 1995-96 to 2004-05. (Table 8.5). This represents about 8% saving in fuel costs. The STUs which have achieved a fuel efficiency of over 5.00 kmpl include the following: Andhra Pradesh SRTC 5.29, Karnataka SRTC 5.28, Gujarat SRTC 5.19, UPSRTC 5.03, Rajastan SRTC 5.00, NW Karnataka RTC 5.36, and NE Karnataka RTC 5.44. It is significant to note that several STUs are now focusing their attention on the use of biodiesel or CNG.

Table 8.5: Diesel Prices, Fuel Efficiency, and Cost per Km Compared to Whole Price Index

Year	Diesel Price Rs/Lt	(Kms/Litre)	Cost per Km	WPI
1995-96	8.86	4.41	2.01	121.6
2000-01	19.66	4.55	4.32	155.7
2001-02	21.96	4.55	4.53	161.3
2002-03	25.2	4.69	5.37	166.8
2004-05	30.86	4.73	6.52	175.9
2005-06	35.66	4.78	7.46	187.3
2006-07	38.76	4.97	6.96	194.9

Source: CIRT, Pune

In spite of substantial improvement in the fuel efficiency of STUs operations in recent years, fuel costs have increased tremendously posing a major threat to the viability of STU operations. The share of the fuel costs at the All India level has increased from 25.20% in 2000-01 to 30.48% in 2004-05. In 2005-06 its share has 35.66% (Table 8.5). The share of fuel cost in rural, hilly, and urban areas in 2000-01 and 2004-05 along with the kmpl is given in Table 8.6.

Table 8.6: Percentage Variation in Fuel Costs

	2000-01 (Ps/Km)	2005-06 (Ps/Km)	As in April 2006 (kmpl)
Rural	26.60	32.39	5.79
Urban	18.30	21.80	3.5
Hilly	12.84	29.50	5.66
Overall	25.20	30.48	5.28

The growth rate of fuel prices during the last ten years has been high at 14.94% per annum compared to the growth rate of WPI at 4.41%. From less than Rs.9 per liter in 1995-96 to about Rs.20 per liter in 2001 and about Rs.35 per liter in 2006. Table 8.5 gives the trend of increase in the price of HSD in comparison with the increase in the wholesale price index. It shows that HSD prices have been increasing at much higher rate than WPI and fuel forms the main component of cost of bus operations.

The steep increase in the price of diesel is also accentuated by the taxes levied on it by the Center and the states. While the central government levies an excise duty of about 16% ad volerum on diesel, the states levy sales tax up to 33%. This is shown in the cost structure of HSD given in Table 8.7 below. It can be seen from Table 8.7 that the share of the basic value of diesel ranges from 58% in Mumbai to 71% in New Delhi. The implication of this is that every time there is a hike in the base price, there is a cascading effect on the overall price due to an automatic increase in the taxes levied on diesel.

Table 8.7: HSD Retail Selling Price Rs/KL

	Mumbai		New Delhi		Kolkata		Chennai	
Basic Value	22,966	0.58	22,966	0.71	22,966	0.66	22,966	0.65
Excise & Cess	5,684	0.14	5,343	0.17	5,561	0.16	5,342	0.15
Value + Excise	28,650	0.72	28,309	0.88	28,527	0.82	28,308	0.80
Sales tax rate	33%		12.5%		17%		23.43%	
Sales Tax Amount	10,469	0.26	3,384	0.10	5,859	0.17	6,643	0.19
Selling Price	39,672		32,246		34,952		35,504	

Table 8.7.a: Share of Duties and Taxes in Retail Selling Price of diesel

S. No	Particulars	Delhi	Mumbai	Chennai	Kolkata
1	Price without customs duty, excise duty and sales tax components	21.01	20.89	20.89	20.93
2	Custom duty (Based on 1st FN of March '07)	1.38 (5%)	1.38 (4%)	1.38 (4%)	1.38 (4%)
3	Excise duty (levied @ 6% + Rs. 13.00/liter plus 3% education cess)	4.70 (16%)	4.72 (14%)	4.70 (14%)	4.71 (14%)
4	Sales tax (including irrecoverable taxes)	3.16 (10%)	7.97 (23%)	6.34 (19%)	5.86 (18%)
5	Total of customs duty, excise duty and sales tax components (2+3+4)	9.24 (31%)	14.07 (40%)	12.42 (37%)	11.95 (36%)
6	Retail selling price (1+5)	30.25	34.96	33.31	32.88

Source: Ramanayya (2005a, 2005b)

8.1.7 Replacement and augmentation of rolling stock

The cost of rolling stock, spare parts, tires and tubes, etc. has been steadily increasing over the years. Given the operating conditions in India the buses need to be replaced over a much shorter period than is the case in other countries. The STUs therefore find it necessary to replace about 12 of their rolling stock every year to ensure that the over aged vehicles are phased out from their fleet. Further, there is also the need to augment their rolling stock at the rate of at least about 10% every year to meet the demand for increased passenger services. Thus, the STUs need to acquire new rolling stock every year to the extent of about 20-25% of their current fleet strength if they are to provide satisfactory service. The demands of long distance bus users and the urban commuters for buses of superior design and comfort have made it necessary for the STUs to invest substantial amounts to acquire new rolling stock of better quality.

The above factors go to show that the STUs need to invest in acquiring about 25,000 to 30,000 new buses every year to sustain efficient operations. These resources have to be generated annually out of their depreciation reserves and profits. A significant part of the cost of the rolling stock is accounted for by central and state taxes. The excise duty levied by the central government at 16% on the bus chassis and the sales tax/VAT levied by the state governments on the chassis as well as the bus bodies amounts to about 25% of the total cost of a bus acquired by an STU.

8.1.8 Investment in infrastructure

While the state transport undertakings operate only about 20-25% of the bus services in most states (in states like Andhra Pradesh, Tamilnadu, Karnataka, Maharashtra, STUs operate more than 50% of bus services), they are involved in providing the bulk of infrastructure facilities like bus stations, bus shelters, and other passenger amenities. The STUs are usually required to meet these obligations out of the revenues generated by their operations. In addition, the STUs have also to invest on the construction of bus depots in different parts of the state and provide workshop facilities in order to be able to provide reliable transport services to the people. This is in contrast with the private bus operators who are not expected to invest on bus stations, bus depots, etc. owing to the small size of their fleets in most cases. While there are no reliable estimates of the investments made by STUs in respect of infrastructure, it may be reasonable to assume that such investments account for at least 20% of the value of the rolling stock owned by the STUs or about Rs.2.5*10^4 millions. The STUs in many cases have borrowed funds or used their own revenues for making such investments on infrastructure, and they incur substantial debts on such investments made for the benefit of the traveling public.

8.2 Inter STU comparison

In this section, we discuss performance of select STUs on the parameters discussed above for a deeper understanding. The STUs were chosen to represent different categories of operations: APSRTC, KSRTC, Gurajat RTC, Rajashthan RTC, and Uttar Pradesh RTC were studied as representatives of state wide corporations. DTC, BEST, Chennai Transport Corporation, and Ahmedabad Transport Corporation were chosen as cases of urban transport corporations. Uttranchal and Himachal Pradesh were chosen as cases of hilly areas. Tamilnadu State Express Transport Corporation is included as a case of long distance operations.

In all the state level corporations it can be observed that the fleet strength has remained stagnant or actually came down. It is to be expected that passenger traffic would have been growing at a higher rate, which means the lost traffic has been weaned away by the private operators. Each state has its own policy but there will be an equal number of unauthorized operators. So privatization has been happening more by default, and it is difficult to say this is due to the result of encouragement given to private operators as there is no tangible support given to private operators either. STUs suffered in terms of occupancy rate and this is happening irrespective of the segments.

At state level all corporations made losses excepting Karnataka, Punjab, and UP which managed to break even. Pepsu incurred a nominal loss. This is more or less a repetition of the All India level story. The physical parameters in areas like fleet utilization, vehicle utilization, and fuel efficiency are reasonably good. There is wide variation in the cost per km (cpkm) with some states showing cost Rs.21.42 (Punjab) and Rs.17.65 (Pepsu). The high cpkm could be due to lower vehicle utilization as much as due to higher cost structure. One general observation that can be made is that a ban on augmentation itself could have acted as the cost driver. A ban on augmentation without a VRS scheme would have only resulted in higher BSR and administrative expenditures per bus or per km which are committed expenditures. In urban operations BMTC is the only profit making corporation. It has been on an expansion path and has been able to keep costs down. Its BSR is among the lowest. In fact the statistics on BSR is quite revealing. The BSR in Delhi, Mumbai, Ahmedabad are very high indeed. The share of the personnel cost is also very high. The personnel cost in urban centers are bound to be high because of higher emoluments, but this should be controlled through leveraging on high-density traffic and time management. These are also the corporations, which remained stagnant in terms of fleet strength.

In fact, the losses and extent of losses defy predictions. Himachal Pradesh STC operating in the hilly terrain is making losses only marginally at Rs.270 million in 2003-04. Its fleet utilization is high but occupancy rate is low at 46%. Its BSR is quite impressive at 4.89. Its fuel efficiency is low and that may be because of the terrain. But we find that its fuel efficiency is same as the one in urban centers, though it is common to blame fuel cost for uneconomic operations on hilly terrain. The fuel efficiency of Uttaranchal is quite good at 4.74 km pl. Its losses are also only marginal.

8.2.1 Interstate variation in MV tax

There are wide variations in MV tax rates among atates ranging from 17.35% (Uttar Pradesh SRTC) to 5.5% (BMTC) as of 2004-05. In states like Gujarat and Maharashtra also the motor vehicles tax is as high as 17% of the turnover of the STUs. In Rajasthan, motor vehicles tax is assessed as 2.1 percent of the current cost of the bus chassis to be paid on a monthly basis. This works out to about 25% of the cost of the chassis per annum. Thus, over a span of eight to ten years the RSRTC pays more than four times the cost of the chassis on each bus. It is reported by the Rajasthan STU that due to an unscientific formula used for assessing M.V. tax on the basis of reported vehicle utilization, the motor vehicles tax of private operators is assessed at about 25% of the rate applicable to buses operated by the Rajasthan STU. Most private operators report a low vehicle utilization of less than 100 to 150 Km/day and pay M.V. tax at very low rates. The RSRTC on the other hand, has to pay M.V. tax at a much higher rate as it reports a higher actual rate of vehicle utilization. Such differential rates of tax discriminating against STUs are to be found in other states also. In Uttar Pradesh, the average passenger tax levied on the UPSRTC was about Rs.2.35 lakh per bus in 2004-05 while during the same year the private bus operators had to pay only an average of Rs.0.85 lakh. Also, in Haryana, the passenger tax is levied at 60% of the basic fare while in Punjab the state collects M.V. tax at Rs.650 per seat per annum in addition to a special road tax of 5 paise per km. per seat which together works out to an average tax liability of Rs.3.93 lakh per bus owned by the STU in the year 2005 06. During the same year private operators had to pay Rs.2.80 lakh per bus which was 29 percent lower than the tax paid by the STU.

8.2.2 Quality of service provided by the STUs

The perception of passengers about service quality of the public transport system is brought out in a study conducted by the Indian Institute of Management, Bangalore in the states of Karnataka and Andhra Pradesh. The STUs are rated higher than private bus operators in the matter of quality of service in many states. The study by IIM Bangalore carried out an extensive field survey spread across 16 districts in the state of Andhra Pradesh and Karnataka in the year 2005. It covered 20,000 samples consisting of commuters, opinion makers, and employees. The attributes of the service quality on which the opinion of commuters was surveyed in the study were comfort, convenience, overloading, seating arrangements, travel time, etc. It emerged from the study that the public rated state owned transport corporations higher than private operators on all the service attributes. The analysis of the responses point out that the expectations of the public are growing, and that they are expecting better buses, infrastructure, and amenities. The growing expectation cuts across all segments. It is not just urban travelers who are expecting better services but also the rural segment. The public is willing to pay more for better services if the services can be improved. The study also pointed out that the stakeholders rate public operators higher than private operators. Their preference is for both public and private operators combined to encourage competition, but they are not in favor of only private operators being given exclusive rights.

STUs have an appreciable record in controlling the rate of accidents. At the All India level accidents involving STU operations came down from 0.39 accidents per lakh km in 1995-96 to 0.18 accidents in 2004-05. Their record in reducing breakdowns and cancellations of services is also commendable. The STUs also have an advantage in providing backup service in case of breakdowns and accidents in view of their huge fleet strength which private operators lack.

8.3 Review of the existing funding pattern

8.3.1 Capital structure and investments of STUs

These organizations have been investing in infrastructure in spite of the absence of a clear policy to strengthen the capital structure of the STUs. They have not been augmenting their buses, but they have been trying to upgrade their bus stands due to political compulsions. The more profitable STUs are in the forefront of modernizing their fleets, which is indicative of a strategy for improving profitability. It is also noteworthy that the STUs have been consistently providing for depreciation reserves of substantial amounts, ranging from Rs.900 crores to Rs.960 crores during the period between 2000-01 and 2004-05.

8.3.2 Capital contribution to STUs

In the wake of the formation of state road transport corporations, the central government introduced a provision for making capital contributions to the STUs to strengthen their capital base. Under the scheme, the state governments also had to extend corresponding budgetary support towards the equity of the corporations. There was no capital infusion coming after the initial burst of contributions. Unfortunately, the state governments too found it convenient to discontinue their capital contributions to STUs. This coupled with the losses sustained by the STUs due to the factors discussed above completely eroded the capital base of STUs in the country. The STUs carry huge accumulated losses on their balance sheets, and they are managing the deficits with borrowed funds and compensations from state governments. Borrowing of funds by the STUs with their negative net worth has proved to be difficult and expensive. The combined outstanding borrowings of all the STUs for the year 2004-05 stood at about Rs.8*10^4 millions with a debt servicing liability estimated at Rs.8550 millions.

8.4 Estimation of resource requirements

The overall financial implications for the center, states, and STUs are discussed in this section. This follows from the discussion in the previous sections on demand forecast and policy initiatives prescribed to enable the states to meet demand.

8.4.1 Infusion of capital

The first step towards revitalizing STUs will be to create clean balance sheets. STUs carry huge accumulated losses on their balance sheets for reasons discussed so far. These losses are more than their net worth and this seriously erodes their financial strength. It makes borrowing much more difficult. Government as promoter needs to inject funds to inspire confidence among banks and financial institutions. Infusion of equity capital in the form of capital contribution from the state and the central governments is a measure, which needs to be initiated immediately. The earlier plan of capital contributions to STUs should be resumed immediately. The capital infusion needs of each STU should be assessed keeping in view their long term viability. This would enable the state governments to prepare a long term investment plan for each of the STUs and provide the required funds accordingly. This can be achieved by handling the debt burden of the STUs.

8.4.2 Policy towards debt burden

The STUs have been primarily financing their deficits through borrowings in the absence of support from governments. This has now grown to be quite huge, and they have reached the stage when most of their borrowings go into debt servicing itself. This cycle has to be broken. Debt servicing is one of the important items of cost for STUs after considering major costs like fuel and personnel. It is therefore necessary to reduce the debt burden of the STUs, currently estimated at a total of about Rs.9,000 crores as shown in Table 8.8 below:

Table 8.8: Outstanding Debts (Estimated)

Year	Interest	Estimated Outstanding Debts (Rs Million)
2000-01	570	40710
2001-02	767	59000
2002-03	741	61750
2003-04	819	74450
2004-05	855	85500

It is recommended that 50% of the outstanding loans of the STUs should be taken over by the central and the state governments. Financial relief through debt taken over by the government has in the past been given as in the case of state electricity boards to enable them to participate in a program of power sector reforms. The balance of 50% would be serviced by the STUs.

8.4.3 Motor vehicle tax

In the policy, it has been suggested that MV tax should move towards a rate 5.5% from the present level of 11%. The financial implication of this is shown in Table 8.9 below:

Table 8.9: Financial Impact of Introducing Standard MV Tax Rate of 5.5 % (Rs million)

Year	Revenue	Tax Collected	Current MV Tax Rate	Benchmark Rate (5.5%)	Loss in Collection
	1	2	3	4	(2-4)
2000-01	15326	1621	0.106	842.93	7780.7
2001-02	16041	1635	0.102	882.25	7527.5
2002-03	16618	1641	0.099	913.99	7270.1
2003-04	18112	1810	0.100	996.16	8138.4
2004-05	19509	1845	0.095	1072.99	7720.1
Average Loss in Collection per Year					7687.3
Average Loss in Collection per Year					

Source: CIRT, Pune.

States see this as a major source of revenue. So, the center should consider compensating the states for the loss for the first three years, and the states should bear it in the subsequent years. The collections will go up substantially subsequently given the buoyancy of this sector.

8.4.4 Students concessions

The implications of students concessions have been discussed in the previous sections. It has also been suggested under the policy section that the fare should be equally shared by the users (students), STUs, and state governments, as this primarily a state governments decision. This would require an annual outlay of about Rs.1, 500 crores from all states put together.

8.4.5 Universal service obligations

Service obligations in terms of uneconomic services like rural and urban services need to be spelled out. It is expected that 20% to 30% of routes are expected to fall under this category. STUs or private operators should be given benchmarks for cost per km and earnings per km, and the balance will be met through compensation from a pool. This pool will be created through cess or deficit charges on the lines of telecommunications, from luxury services, and other profit making routes or sectors. If the states are unwilling to do this, it should be prepared to meet the deficit. States should take steps to reduce their share of a number of these routes.

8.4.6 Fleet augmentation

In the section on demand forecast, the total number of additional buses is estimated around 130,000. This would require an outlay of Rs.20,000 over the five year plan. It is recommended the center should bear 50% of this burden apart from reducing duties on bus chassis. States should bear 25% of the investment and also reduce sales tax on spare parts and bus body building. STUs should bear the balance of the 25% investment. Enable the STUs to meet about 50% of the cost of the new buses to be procured to replace their overaged rolling stock. The STUs will raise the balance of 50% by borrowing from institutional sources or by using their depreciation reserves.

8.4.7 Summary of financial implications for governments and STUs

The policy should specify the type of financial support that is to be extended to STUs and private operators. It can be in the form of equity support, access to financial institutions, tax subsidy, and through categorizing it as priority sector. A comprehensive financial package has to be devised to improve the viability of both public and private operators. The center should also indicate the extent of support that it would be willing to extend to the states. The center should also insist on certain governance mechanisms and operational performance including VRS for the support that it would be extending to the state.

The financial implications of suggestions made above for the center and the states governments and STUs for XI Plan is summarized below in Table 8.9a. This will indicate the extent of financial support that would be required from various governments. The above measures will go a long way in developing public transport facilities to play their assigned role in speeding up the economic and social development of the country.

The financial implications of all the measures proposed above do not add up to more than Rs.20,000 crores for the entire period of the XI Five Year Plan for the central government. Similarly the commitment from all state governments put together will come to Rs. 30,000 crores for the entire plan period. Thus the annual commitment from the central government is only Rs.4000 crores and from all the state governments about Rs.6000 crores annually. Investment of this amount for improving the public transport system is completely justified in view of the benefits that would accrue to over 20 million passengers using STU services on any given day. This is also a most cost effective investment compared to the investment of about Rs.12,000 crores to Rs.15,000 crores required for building one metro rail system in a single metro in the country which would probably cater to only about one million passenger trips per day.

Table 8.9a: Implications of Financial Restructure Pl Format

Items	Suggestions	Financial Implications	Contribution from Centre	Contribution from States	STUs
MV tax	Benchmark MV tax rate above this govenment has to bear	Rs.800 crores per year	Loses to be compensated by centre of 3 years	States to bear the loss after 3 years	To pay 5.5% MV tax
Student concessions	Policy for revision of fares, no indiscriminate issue of passes	Rs. 1500 crores annually	No obligation	States to bear 1/3rd of the cost	STUs to bear 1/3rd of the costs. Students to pay 1/3rd
USOs	Service goals to be specified	20% of the losses of all corporations can be attributed to this	To prescribe national bench marks to support urban service	States to compensate STUs for losses incurred on this. It can collect cess on luxury and express services buses for this.	STUs will be compensated only based on achieving some benchmark performance standards
Fleet Augmentation	Fleet Augmentation plan to be made	Rs. 20000 crores total for 5 years	Centre to bear 50% of this. Also to reduce duties and excise on bus chassiss	States to bear 25%. Also to reduce ST on bus body building and spare parts. States to guarantee loan	STUs to raise from FIs
Capital support	To create clean balance sheet	Aggregate cumulative borrowings of all states Rs. 9000 crores	Centre to share 25% of the accumulatd borrowings	States to share 25% of the accumulated borrowings	STUs to service 50% balance borrowings.

8.5 Institutional finance for STUs

Presently, the STUs as well as private bus operators depend upon the commercial banks for their borrowing needs where the terms of credit are quite stiff. This would require an accelerated infusion of funds, which requires establishment of a special institutional arrangement for funding public transport. We would like to recommend the establishment of a fund on the lines of infrastructure or highways sector. This fund can be backed and administered by a public sector financial institution like the IDBI, HUDCO, or the UTI. Currently, NABARD funds a number of infrastructural projects in the states through RIDF. Public transport provision is to be considered as a basic infrastructure and RIDF funds may be made available to the rural sector.

8.5.1 Institutional strengthening of STUs

Apart from extending financial support and reducing the impact of certain liabilities mentioned above, the state transport undertakings need to be given greater functional autonomy than is available in some states. Strategic and operational freedom is an essential ingredient of a successful corporation. To ensure this freedom combined with accountability, we suggest the adoption of the mechanism of well conceived MOUs between STUs and state governments. The MOU will spell out specific commitments from the state governments in matters relating to financial support and regulatory environment. These will include policy on reimbursement of cost of concessions, formula for revision of fares, capital contributions, universal service obligation payments, etc. The MOU will also spell out the financial and operational performance expected from STUs including quantitative and qualitative aspects of services, technology upgradation, development of infrastructure, etc. The financial support of the government can be tied to the STUs achieving specified milestones in respect of their performance parameters. It is felt that such an arrangement between the STUs and the government will go a long way in removing the uncertainty and arbitrariness in the policy environment for STUs. This will in turn encourage them to strive hard to reach the milestones.

8.6 Innovative methods to generate revenue surpluses

There is an urgent need to market the concept of effective and efficient public bus systems in all million plus cities to minimize environmental degradation, to conserve the usage of petroleum products, and reduce traffic congestion especially in metropolitan cities. It is well known that if a bus runs half empty (load factor 50%) the revenue for the empty seats are lost once for all. Load factor could be improved through scientific study of demand and reviewing the current routing and scheduling once in two years to enhance ridership. It is common knowledge that during off peak hours the load factor will be definitely less and adjust the fares accordingly to meet at least the operating cost during off peak hour. Another innovative way is to provide a variety of services (air conditioned, limited halt, express, and delux services) during peak hours with different fare structures to cater to the needs of different classes of people. In India there is a perception that bus transport is meant for workers, school children, housewives, and people belonging to low income groups. This perception need to be changed through the provision of different types of services mentioned above. In order to retain the ridership some sort points (similar to frequent flier mileage points of airline companies) may be followed. In order to encourage the use of public transport all the organizations employing more than 250 people may be persuaded to contribute annually at the rate of Rs. 250 per employee. The governments need to contribute to equity capital of these undertakings at least to the tune of concessions provided by these organizations. For all the monthly pass holders in addition to concessional fare accident insurance, reimbursement of medical expenses due to bus accidents could be conceived and marked vigorously. All these strategies improve the ridership and revenue for the organization. It has been noticed that decrease in congestion normally brings in the reduction in accident rates and consequently the out go from insurance companies. They may be persuaded to part with 1 to 2 percent of revenue annually for improving the public transport system in urban agglomerations.

Summary

This chapter mainly highlights the financial issues of public transport organizations, interms of motor vehicle tax, fuel cost, fuel efficiency, rolling stocks, turnover of STUs, and mainly investment in infrastructure. It also shows some light on existing funding pattern of STUs and how these terms affect the running status of the government organization.

Chapter 9

Economics of Public Transport

9.1 Cost of public transport services

Public transport in India is considered as a means of transport for the labor class and mostly used by middle class sections of the society and to some extent by school going children due to the subsidy provided to this section of society. This perception need to be changed in order to plan and operate services required for different sections of public living in urban areas. A scientific evaluation of economics of different categories of public bus services helps in proper planning and provision of different categories of public bus services. This could be comprehensively achieved through the various subheads discussed in this chapter. The urban areas in India could be broadly divided into different categories based on the functionality of the city for the purpose of urban bus services.

a. State Capitals

b. District Headquarters

c. Other Business centers in a state

The requirements of bus services are quite different in each of these urban areas. For example the services in a state capital could be comprised of:

a. Air Conditioned Bus Services

b. Express Services

c. Limited Halt Services

d. City Services

e. Suburban Services

While in the case of the other two categories, the services could be limited to:

a. Limited Halt Services

b. City Services

c. Suburban Services

Thus the cost of services needs to be developed in each case separately. What is more important is developing a template for different cost elements in general and evaluating them with current data of urban operations in India. The following Table 9.1 provides data on different cost elements for selected public bus operations in different cities. It may be noticed that there are wide variations across different cost elements among these cities. For example personal cost as a percentage of total cost varies from a high of 61.29% in the case of Ahmedabad Metropolitan Transport Service (AMTS) STU to a low of 28.53% in the case of Delhi Transport Corporation (DTC) organization. The same is the case with respect to fuel cost as a percentage of total cost from a high of 35.93% of Bangalore Metropolitan Transport Corporation (BMTC) to the low of 13.36% of DTC organization.

Table 9.1: Details of Cost Elements for Sample Urban Public Transport Services in India in 2013

Sl No	Description	Urban (India)		BEST		DTC (City)		BMTC STU		AMTS STU	
A	Financial (Rs in million)										
1	Traffic Revenue	60176.004		13067.986		15244.17		15244.17		969.554	
2	Other Revenue	4397.383		1188.852		834.325		1160.687		100.95	
3	Total Revenue	65191.514		14256.838		12355.375		16404.857		1070.504	
	Total Revenue Ps/Km	3916.11		537.59		371.07		354.38		302.8	
B	Cost (Rs in million)	Value	%	Value	%	Value	%	Value	%	Value	%
1	Personal	45433.53	41.9	12138.13	59.1	11469.45	28.5	7049.5	41.2	1504.37	61.3
2	Fuel and Lubricants	45433.53	41.9	12138.13	59.1	11469.45	28.5	7049.55	41.2	1504.37	61.3
	Paise/Km	134.79		146.48		161.35		132.99		148.47	
3	Tyres and Tubes	1201.42	1.1	262.01	1.3	85.922	0.21	333.37	1.9	18.27	0.74
	Paise/Km	7.22		9.88		2.58		7.2		5.16	
4	Spare parts	2216.63	2.1	714.635	3.5	248.11	0.62	509.51	2.9	45.52	1.85
	Paise/Km	13.32		26.95		7.45		11.01		12.88	
5	Interest	23164.87	21.4	1611.85	7.84	18885.0	46.9	272.27	1.59	64.33	2.62
6	Depreciation	5041.746	4.65	674.91	3.28	1713.34	4.26	1185.78	6.92	-	-
7	M.V.Tax	1152.57	1.06	39.838	0.19	145.407	0.36	838.427	4.89	4.621	0.19
8	Passenger Tax	267.035	0.25	-	-	-	-	-	-	10.561	0.43
9	Other Tax	295.195	0.27	221.77	1.08	26.33	0.07	-	0.00	-	0.00
10	Total Tax	1714.80	1.58	261.608	1.27	171.737	0.43	838.427	4.89	15.182	0.62
11	Others	7207.625	6.65	1013.371	4.93	2260.669	5.62	791.283	4.62	282.034	11.5
12	Total cost	108418.4	100	20561.1	100	40206.7	100	17136.6	100	2454.5	100
	Paise/Km	651.28		775.31		1207.52		370.19		694.28	
C	Operating Cost	83538.779		18687.7		21149.928		16025.929		2375.054	
D	Operating Ratio (%)	138.82		143		183.58		105.13		244.96	
E	Surplus before Tax	-41512.14		-6042.714		-27679.61		106.657		-1368.887	
	(Paise/Km)	-249.37		-227.85		-831.29		2.3		-387.19	
F	Net profit/ loss (Rs in million)	-43226.94		-6304.322		-27851.347		-731.77		-1384.069	

Source: State Transport Undertakings by Central Institute of Road Transport, pune 2013

BEST - Bombay Public Transport

DTC - Delhi Transport Corporation

BMTC - Bangalore Metropolitan Transport Corporation

AMTS - Ahmedabad Metropolitan Transport Service

It may be noted from Table 9.1 that revenue in rupees per km operated is highest in the case of BEST, i.e., at Rs. 53.76 and least in the case of AMTS at Rs. 30.28. However, revenue is a function of load factor and the fare structure. The total cost of providing bus service per km work out to a high of Rs.120.75 per km in the case of DTC, while it is a minimum at Rs 37.01 per km in case of BMTC. This wide variation needs a comprehensive review of operations. The cost could be broadly divided into fixed cost and variable cost. Fixed cost includes all the cost items such as salaries, depreciation, office maintenance, and other overheads. Variable costs the ones which relate to fuel, maintenance, and other operational costs.

The details of cost elements for sample urban public transport services in India for the last 5 years is given below in Table 9.2 to Table 9.4.

Table 9.2: Details of Cost Elements for Sample Urban Public Transport Services in India in 2005-06

(Million)	India (Urban)	BEST	DTC (UR-BAN)	BMTC (STU)	AMTS
Financial cost	31178.4	8476.554	3178.473	6202.094	851.165
Revenue (ps/km)	244.86	353.03	183.34	225.09	-
Total (personal, material, taxes)	427.211	10982.330	9214.481	5178.098	1142.217
in paise/km	335.52	457.39	531.52	187.93	-
Operating ratio%	-	132.69	198.24	83.01	154.57
Surplus before tax	-101.202	-2090.274	-5967.374	1326.338	-281.001
in ps/km	-79.48	-87.06	-344.22	48.14	-
Net profit/loss	-115.427	-2505.776	-6036.008	1023.996	-291.052
in ps/km	-90.65	-104.36	-348.18	37.16	-

Source: Ramanayya (2005a, 2005b)

Table 9.3: Details of Cost Elements for Sample Urban Public Transport Services in India in 2008-09

(Million)	India (Urban)	BEST	DTC (UR-BAN)	BMTC (STU)	AMTS
Financial cost	3839.69	8939.873	3684.040	9909.9	1165.386
Revenue (ps/km)	273.44	376.73	268.88	246.6	-
Total (personal, material, taxes)	618.024	13048.096	17568.540	9336.966	2190.819
in paise/km	440.12	549.89	1282.24	232.34	-
Operating ratio%	-	148.96	317.80	98.20	195.19
Surplus before tax	-218.474	-3679.78	-13788.7	1070.406	-1011.04
in ps/km	-155.78	-155.07	-1006.37	26.64	-
Net profit/loss	-115.427	-2505.77	-6036.00	1023.996	-291.052
in ps/km	-166.68	-173.16	-1013.36	14.26	-

Source: Ramanayya (2005a, 2005b)

Table 9.4: Details of Cost Elements for Sample Urban Public Transport Services in India in 2010-11

(Million)	India (urban)	BEST	DTC (UR-BAN)	BMTC (STU)	AMTS
Financial cost	51504.7	11127.817	9079.310	13192.689	1089.058
Revenue (ps/km)	318.22	425.51	344.76	290.29	-
Total (Personal, material, taxes)	841.992	14941.642	29830.461	12693.246	2300.869
in paise/km	520.23	571.34	1132.74	279.320	-
Operating ratio%	-	135.73	187.34	94.64	220.29
Surplus before tax	-307.959	-3231.61	-20612.2	1165.920	-1196.90
in ps/km	-190.27	-123.57	-7827.0	25.65	-
Net profit/loss	-326.945	-3813.82	-20612.2	499.443	-1211.81
in ps/km	-202.0	-145.83	-7827.0	10.99	-

Source: Ramanayya (2005a, 2005b)

Table 9.5: Comparing the Total Profit and Loss of Different Organization in Past Few Years

Net Profit/Loss (in millions)	BEST	DTC	BMTC	AMTS
2005-06	-2505.776	-6036.008	1023.996	-291.052
2008-09	-4109.033	-13884.5	272.934	-1025.433
2010-11	-3813.825	-20612.197	499.443	-1211.811
2013	-6304.322	-27851.347	-731.77	-1384.069

Source: Ramanayya (2005a, 2005b)

As shown in the tables the BMTC is the only organization that has recorded profits for many years and the same BMTC in the year 2013 incurred a loss of Rs.731.7 million. All the other organizations trend is a continuous loss, and it increases with time.Thus there is an urgent need to look into the viability of public bus organizations as a whole and the current tax liability as well as subsidies to be absorbed by these organizations. Any loop holes in the functioning of these organizations should be considered and corrected; otherwise, they will be become a great loss to the governments and the society at large. On the other hand, if these undertakings do not expand with time and reduce their services on the basis of profitability, public patronage and interest in using them may be affected and the public may shift to personal vehicles.

9.2 Manpower requirements

In all major urban areas of India, city bus services are in operation for a period of 14 to 16 hours a day, then only it is possible to attract more patronage to bus system; otherwise, people may prefer their own personal modes. Operating 14 to 16 hours in a day requires two sets of crew per bus operated. The number of buses operated and the staff involved in various operations in running the services in urban operations are tabulated below. It may be noted that there is no uniformity in the manpower needs across organizations. Since the crew expenditure comprises of about 40% of the total expenditure optimum number to be employed is essential. Each organization has to work out what is optimum as per their field conditions. It is worthwhile to outsource any activity which will bring economy to the organization.

Table 9.6 to Table 9.8 provides manpower data of different organizations in India in the last few years. The maximum productivity per person works out to a maximum of 51.45km/day in the case of the BMTC organization and a minimum in the case of BEST of 28.79km/day in the year 2005-06.

Table 9.6: Urban Undertaking for Staff Positioning in 2005-06

	India (Urban)	BEST	DTC (Total)	BMTC (STU)	AMTS
Total staff	124896	34470	28460	18150	3886
Staff per bus on road	8.45	11.21	9.07	5.51	10.12
Manpower productivity per day limits kms	27.80	19.10	25.03	41.59	20.39
Effective kms per crew/day	27.80	28.79	41.76	51.45	31.27

Table 9.7: Urban Undertaking for Staff Positioning in 2008-09

	India (Urban)	BEST	DTC (Total)	BMTC (STU)	AMTS
Total staff	134470	3184	29164	27559	5729
Staff per bus on road	7.35	8.50	9.06	4.99	4.29
Manpower productivity per day limits kms	27.03	21.54	17.19	39.95	31.25
Effective kms per crew/day	-	31.68	26.53	49.13	39.37

Table 9.8: Urban Undertaking for Staff Positioning in 2010-11

	India (Urban)	BEST	DTC (Total)	BMTC (STU)	AMTS
Total staff	149037	30183	35557	32875	5274
Staff per bus on road	7	7.39	6.67	5.84	7.82
Manpower productivity per day limits kms	29.23	23.74	22.52	37.87	27.28
Effective kms per crew/day	-	31.83	30.37	46.60	-

The above tables give the total staff, staff per bus values, and effective kms per employee for different bus undertakings. Every organization presents different staffing rates compared and in order to give the optimum BSR values its impact on total cost, passenger satisfaction, and patronage should be given due consideration. A national strategy may be more appropriate in the development of norms for different cost items.

9.3 Estimation of social, economic, and environmental benefits

There is an urgent necessity in India to provide an efficient public transport system such that the society can derive optimum social and environmental benefits. These two aspects need to be given serious consideration:

1. Optimum fleet size for a given urban area such that more people can use the bus system as shown in Table 9.9.

2. Estimating the economic and social benefits due to that policy.

3. Unfortunately there is no systematic study undertaken to assess the fleet requirements with relation to population size of an urban area. The limited research undertaken by the author at IIM Bangalore provided the guidelines which are given below.

Table 9.9: Norms for Bus Fleet Based on Population

Population Range (million)	Buses Required per Million Population	
	Desirable (Scenario 1)	Minimum (Scenario 2)
1-2	400	300
2-4	500	400
4-6	600	500
6-8	800	060
>8	1000	800

Applying these criteria, the fleet strength needed in different cities of India for three different time periods is presented below.

The buses required for million plus urban areas by 2011 varies from a minimum of 84,728 to a desirable number of 106,500. By 2016, the demand for buses range from 111,978 to 152,677. Moreover, some more cities might reach a million plus by the year 2016, and the bus fleet requirement could go up. Data is not available about the number of buses in operation in different cities of India. The requirement of buses for metropolitan cities of India is separately tabulated in Table 9.11 to Table 9.13. These tables also present the additional fleet needed by 2011 and 2016 on the basis of fleet in operation in 2006.

A bus on an average provides mobility to about 1000 people in a day and the average distance travelled is about 6 to 7 kms per person. Thus, if the same travel, i.e., 6000 to 7000 person kms is to be accomplished by personal mode the resources (fuel and environmental degradation) spent is 3 to 5 times higher than bus travel.

Table 9.10: Fleet Requirements in Different Urban Centers of India

Sl. No.	Name of Cities	As per 2001 Census		2006		2011		2016	
		Scen. 1	Scen. 2	Scen. 1	Scen. 2	Scen. 1	Scen. 2	Scen. 1	Scen. 2
01	G.Mumbai	8184	6547	10203	8184	12788	10230	15984	12788
02	Kolkata	9257	10573	11564	9252	14456	11564	180689	14456
03	Delhi	10223	8186	12791	10233	15989	12791	19987	15989
04	Chennai	5140	3855	5622	4497	7027	5622	8784	7027
05	Bangalore	3412	2843	5687	4265	8886	7109	11107	8886
06	Hyderabad	3320	2767	5534	4150	8646	6917	10808	8646
07	Ahmedabad	2712	2260	3389	2825	5649	4237	8827	7061
08	Pune	1878	1502	2817	2347	3521	2934	5868	4401
09	Surat	1406	1125	1757	1406	2636	2196	3295	2746
10	Kanpur	1345	1076	1682	1345	2522	2102	3153	2627
11	Jaipur	1162	930	1453	1162	1816	1453	2724	2270
12	Lucknow	1133	907	1417	1133	17771	1417	2657	2214
13	Nagpur	1061	849	1327	1061	1659	1327	2488	2073
14	Patna	512	341	1067	854	1334	1067	1667	1334
15	Indore	492	328	1024	820	1281	1024	1601	1281
16	Vadodara	448	298	560	373	1166	933	1457	1166
17	Bhopal	436	291	546	364	1137	909	14211	1137
18	Coimbatore	434	289	542	362	1130	904	1412	1130
19	Ludhiana	419	279	523	349	1090	872	1362	1090
20	Kochi	407	271	508	339	1059	847	1324	1059
21	Vishakapatnam	399	266	499	332	1039	831	1298	1039
22	Agra	396	264	496	330	1032	826	1290	1032
23	Varanasi	364	232	454	303	757	568	1183	947
24	Madurai	358	239	448	299	747	560	1167	933
25	Meerut	350	233	438	292	730	547	1140	912
26	Nasik	346	230	432	288	720	540	1125	900
27	Jablarpur	335	223	419	279	698	524	1091	873
28	Jamshedpur	331	220	413	275	689	516	1076	861
29	Anansol	327	218	409	273	681	511	1065	852
30	Dhanbad	319	213	399	266	665	499	1039	832
31	Faridabad	316	211	396	264	659	495	1030	824
32	Allahabad	315	210	394	262	656	492	1025	820
33	Amritsar	303	202	379	253	632	474	790	593
34	Vijayawad	303	202	379	253	632	474	790	892
35	Rajkot	301	200	376	251	626	470	783	587
	Total	58444	45708	76345	59541	106526	84728	152677	111978

Table 9.11: Requirement of Buses for Metropolitan Cities in India 2006

Name of City	Buses as on 2006	Requirement		Correc-tion for Rail Network	Net Requirement		Deficit	
		Scen.1	Scen.2	%	Scen.1	Scen.2	Scen.1	Scen.2
Ahmedabad	540	3389	2825	0	3389	2825	2849	2285
Bangalore	3925	5687	4265	0	5687	4265	1762	340
Chennai	2737	8031	6425	30	5622	4497	2885	1760
Delhi	2434	15989	12791	20	12791	10233	10357	7799
Mumbai	3391	20460	16368	50	10230	8184	6839	4793
Hyderabad	2838	5534	4150	0	5534	4150	2696	1312
Kolkatta	1144	16521	13217	30	11564	9252	10420	8108
Total	17009	75611	60041		54817	43406	37808	26397

The fleet required by 2011 and 2016 are presented in Table 9.12 and Table 9.13. By 2016, the deficit increases between 58,000 to 76,500 based on this scenario.

Table 9.12: Requirement of Buses for Metropolitan Cities in India 2011

Name of City	Buses as on 2006	Requirement		Correct-ion for Rail Network	Net Requirement		Deficit	
		Scen.1	Scen.2	%	Scen.1	Scen.2	Scen.1	Scen.2
Ahmedabad	540	5649	4237	0	5649	4237	5109	3697
Bangalore	3925	8886	7109	0	8886	7109	4961	3184
Chennai	2737	10038	8031	30	7027	5622	4290	2885
Delhi	2434	19987	15989	20	15989	12791	13555	10357
Mumbai	3391	25575	20460	50	12788	10230	9397	6839
Hyderabad	2838	8646	6917	0	8646	6917	5808	4079
Kolkatta	1144	20651	16521	30	14456	11564	13312	10420
Total	17009	99432	79263		73441	58470	56432	41461

Table 9.13: Requirement of Buses for Metropolitan Cities in India 2016

Name of City	Buses as on 2006	Requirement		Correct-ion for Rail Network	Net Requirement		Deficit	
		Scen.1	Scen.2	%	Scen.1	Scen.2	Scen.1	Scen.2
Ahmedabad	540	8827	7061	0	8827	7061	8287	6521
Bangalore	3925	11107	8886	0	11107	8886	7182	4961
Chennai	2737	12548	10038	30	8784	7027	6047	4290
Delhi	2434	24983	19987	20	19987	15989	17553	13555
Mumbai	3391	31969	25575	50	15984	12788	12593	9397
Hyderabad	2838	10808	8646	0	10808	8646	7970	5808
Kolkatta	1144	25814	20651	30	18069	14456	16925	13312
Total	17009	126056	100844		93566	74853	76557	57844

There is no authentic data about the number of buses in operation by private operators in different cities of India. The information presented in Table 9.11 to Table 9.13 indicate that the current scenario in metropolitan cities is very dismal and needs urgent remedial action. This partly explains the congestion problems of commuters in metropolitan cities. Due to this shortage of bus fleet many commuters who may be interested in using public transport were forced to use their personal modes.

Some statistical data provided by CIRT (Central Institute of Road Transport, Pune) as reported by individual undertakings. The information is already presented in Table 9.1.

Table 9.14: Comparison of Fleet Size to Urban Populace in Major Indian Cities

City (STUs)	Population (Millions) (1-3-2001)	No of Buses in SRTUs (Sep 2005)	Bus to Population Ratio
Banglore (BMTC)	5.69	3977	1:1430
Chennai (CNI)	6.42	2733	1:2315
Delhi (DTC)	12.79	2585	1:4948
Mumbai (BEST)	16.37	3391	1:4827
Ahmedabad (AMTC)	4.52	510	1:8863
Hyderabad	5.6	2424	1:2310

As per the information provided in Table 9.14 above, and the norms of bus fleet based on population shown in Table 9.9, it is clear that all the bus undertakings are incurring losses except BMTC. Thus public bus undertakings have become really white elephants on public money. Both state and central governments stopped funding this organization, thus the process is really complicated as far as resource mobilization is concerned. But at the same time, the state government imposes a lot of constraints in their functioning which impinge on their revenue such as:

1. Student concessions

2. Passenger taxes for doing business.

This is best illustrated from the data of APSRTC of India which is shown in the below table. The state is divided into 3 regions. In each zone the loss making and the total loss making routes are presented.

It is impossible for any organization to be in business in such a situation. As a matter of fact, the customer surveys indicate that the people are very happy about the services, thus in analyzing the functions of bus services, a new criteria called economic value added (EVA) may be adapted. Application of this in the case of APSRTC is presented in next section.

Table 9.15: Number of Routes and Loss Making Routes

Year	2001			2003			2005		
	SBU1	SBU2	SBU3	SBU1	SBU2	SBU3	SBU1	SBU2	SBU3
Number of routes	847	383	68	860	310	37	922	270	33
Number of loss making routes	583	294	64	711	302	97.42	709	270	33
% of loss making routes	68.83	76.76	94.12	82.67	97.42	100	76.90	100	100
Total % of loss making routes	79.90			93.36			92.30		

From the above Table 9.15 it is clear that the different areas of SBUs show the highest % of loss making routes which is a great loss to the government, and it also failed in the matter of reaching public satisfaction.

9.3.1 Application of EVA methodology for evaluating the financial performance of the corporation and responsibility centers

In a country like India the transport undertakings are not allowed to operate buses on cost plus principle, the state government directs them to operate services to the needs of the society irrespective of load factors (demand for services) or return on investment. In addition the transport services are to provide service at the concessional price to some sections of society especially school going children. As such, evaluating the performance of transport undertaking solely on the basis of financial performance is not proper or desired. A new concept of EVA methodology is suggested in lieu of financial analysis. This concept of EVA is being followed by many corporates. However, this methodology needs to be adjusted to take care of the components of transport operations.

9.3.2 Economic value added (EVA) methodology

The objective of applying EVA is to develop a common financial performance evaluation template which can be used across depots and divisions, as well as, organization as a whole. EVA can be calculated as:

EVA = Net Operating Profit After Tax Capital Charges (Invested Capital X Cost of Cap)

EVA formula for APSRTC can be:

Profit + Opportunity Cost of Concessions + Differential MV Tax Adjustment-

Less (Opportunity Cost of Equity by Government and Actual Interest Charges)

EVA is used in the private sector to make adjustments to profit and loss to adjust for accounting. In a passenger road transport system context, it can be used for incorporating the opportunity cost of meeting socio economic services. Here the profits can be adjusted for an unreimbursed amount of concessions, differential MV taxes, and cost of providing uneconomical services.

a. The cost of capital of both equity and borrowings is then deducted from the adjusted profit to arrive at EVA.

b. Deducting cost of capital will make the responsibility center managers conscious of asset cost.

EVA enables financial comparison at division and depot levels as the impact of external factors are ironed out. The purpose of this application will be to evaluate if the operations are efficient after meeting these obligations. The responsibility center in-charge cannot take refuge under the argument of incomparability. It also helps to point out the corporation's contribution to other sectors in financial terms.

9.3.3 Economic value added (EVA) computation

EVA valuation of APSRTC for the years 2000-01 to 2005-06 are provided

Three adjustments were considered:

a. Unreimbursed amount of concessions

b. Difference between actual MV tax paid and benchmark rate of MV tax of 6.25%

c. Losses from providing interior rural routes

Valuation by two methods are provided:

a. After adjusting for only the unreimbursed amount of concessions and MV tax differential

b. After adjusting for the above plus losses incurred on interior rural routes.

Table 9.16: Economic Value Added Method 1

Years	Profit	Unreimbursed Student Concession	Differential MV Taxes	Adjusted Earnings	Capital Charges (Millions)	EVA
2000-01	-2099	2028	2157	2086	834	1252
2001-02	-2720	1512	1867	659	1071	-412
2002-03	-1817	1398	1567	1148	1175	-27
2003-04	-420	1520	1660	2760	1253	1507
2004-05	-2248	1675	1783	1210	1231	-21
2005-06	-521	0	718	197	1120	-923

Table 9.17: Economic Value Added Method 2

Year	Profit	Interior Rural Losses	Unreimbursed Student Concession	Differential MV Taxes	Adjusted Earnings	Capital Charges (Millions)	EVA
2000-01	-2099	2028	1508	2157	4225.46	834	3391
2001-02	-2720	1512	1121	1867	2648.86	1071	1578
2002-03	-1817	1398	1724	1567	3845.74	1175	2671
2003-04	-420	1520	1694	1660	5504.95	1253	4252
2004-05	-2248	1675	2072	1783	4310.72	1231	3080
2005-06	-521	0	1948	718	3063.37	1120	1943

9.3.4 EVA results – observations

a. It can be seen from the tables that EVA helps to capture the net impact of external factors

b. It can be observed from the table that even though profits have been fluctuating, EVA has been showing a steady trend and is significantly positive

c. In the last year, EVA has fallen even though operational performance improved because of oil price hike and salary hike.

9.3.5 EVA results – Hyderabad city region

a. The templates can be extended to SBU levels and depot levels

b. A model computation undertaken on Hyderabad city region is provided for illustration

c. For Hyderabad, profits were adjusted for unreimbursed amount of student concessions and MV tax differential

d. Buses with Re.1 written down value were valued at saleable value and land at guideline value

e. Interest charges are assumed at 8%.

Table 9.18: EVA: Hyderabad City Region

Year	Profit Before Interest	Unreim-bursed Conces-sion	MV Tax Adj	Adj Profit	Total Assets	Capital Charge (int@ 8%) in 0.1 million	EVA
2000-01	-1487	2839	2895	4247	30608	2448	1799
2001-02	-1394	2737	2424	3767	30282	2422	1345
2002-03	901	3716	1671	6288	28842	2307	3981
2003-04	1261	4489	1827	8677	31306	2504	6173
2004-05	2332	4626	1961	8919	33245	2660	6259

9.3.6 Financial and economic scenario

The revenue and profitability of any bus undertaking is influenced by many factors. What is really needed is a template combining all these factors over a number of time periods and changing each of the variables will estimate the financial position of the organization. A macro developed by IIM for APSRTC is used for purposes of illustrations and from that it is clear, if the organization is able to increase the load factor by a small value over a number of years and reduces the bus staff ratio to some extent, it would result in profitability as well as wiping out the accumulated loses.

This macro will provide the areas of improvement and its impact on profitability. Thus, if the authorities bestow attention, it is not difficult to make their profit over a five year period. It is ascertained from the concerned officials that the load factor and staff ratio values are achievable. Some undertakings were able to reach these targets. Thus, what is lacking is the will to achieve these targets.

9.3.7 Environmental benefits of public transport

9.3.7.1 Urban passenger transport

In the case of urban passenger transport needs, the current scenario of Bangalore is discussed in detail. Detailed information for other cities is not well documented for undertaking a comprehensive analysis. The trip rates could be used for assessing the needs but not to identify the locations where specific improvements are needed to avoid congestion and minimize environmental problems.

9.3.7.2 The current scenario in Bangalore

Bangalore has become a true cosmopolitan city and is witnessing a tremendous activity in industry, trade, and commerce leading to an exponential growth in population. Bangalore has 5.7 million population as per 2001 census records and is expected to reach around 11 and 22 million in 2021 and 2041, respectively. This unprecedented growth has created severe strain on the infrastructure like the urban water and sewerage system, transport network, telecommunication systems, etc. The public transport needs are met by BMTC to a large extent but not to the satisfaction of growing needs of commuters.

The road network of any city consists of arterial and nonarterial roads. Arterial roads are normally designed to the standards of state highways. Bangalore has a total network of 4,300 km of road out of which only 252 km are arterial roads. National and state highways entering the city add another 100 km to the arterial roads carrying most of the vehicular traffic. The road networking has not been scientifically planned, as the city did not expect the unprecedented growth of population and economic activity. There is no provision for expansion or for widening of the existing roads. The recent development of outer, inner, and satellite ring roads are expected to provide some respite to the current traffic woes. Traffic planning is left with the only choice of one-way systems. The construction of underpasses and flyovers may provide some relief to the high-density traffic of city roads. The present road network consists of ring roads and major radial corridors. A number of proposals have already been included in the Master Plan 2015. It is necessary to integrate/superimpose all these proposals in the light of projected travel demand for road traffic and in conformity with each other and there is neither conflict nor duplication. For decongestion of traffic in Bangalore city, the government has constructed flyovers and construction work still going on in some junctions. Vehicle emissions in India from the transport sector contribute 51,221 ton of carbon monoxide (CO) and about 2,467 ton of particulate matter (PM) annually. Baseline environmental studies are conducted to assess the current parameters.

i) Ambient air quality

ii) Water quality

iii) Identification of project affected persons (PAPs)

iv) Soil erosion details

v) Noise levels, etc.

The urban air pollution is contributed generally by a variety of sources such as industrial, commercial, and transportation sectors. However, at Bangalore air pollution problems which are quite severe are mainly compounded by the transportation sector while the other sources such as industrial, etc. are contributing less. As the core transportation sector presently consists mainly of petrol and diesel driven vehicles operating throughout the city, the major air pollutant components are contributed by the automobile exhaust emissions, which consist of suspended particulate matter (SPM), respirable suspended particulate matter (RSPM), oxides of nitrogen and sulphur, carbon monoxide, etc. and are monitored by the Karnataka State Pollution Control Board (KSPCB) at some locations and by the Central Pollution Control Board (CPCB) at some selected important intersections of the city. Air quality index less than 50 is permissible; 51 to 75 moderate; 75 to 100 heavy, and above 100 is considered severe air pollution. The following (refer to Table 9.19) localities are experiencing severe air pollution.

Table 9.19: Air Quality Levels at Selected Metro Corridor Locations

S. No	Location	Air Quality Index	Result
1	Yeshwanthpur	256	Serious Air Pollution
2	Navarang Junction (Rajajinagar)	148	Serious Air Pollution
3	Seshadripuram / Swastik Cirlc	140	Serious Air Pollution
4	Anand Rao Circle	189	Serious Air Pollution
5	National College / Vanivilas Circle	238	Serious Air Pollution
6	South End Cirlce	173	Serious Air Pollution
7	KIMS Circle	146	Serious Air Pollution
8	Sri. Aurobindo Circle/ Jayanagar 5th Block	178	Serious Air Pollution
9	Depot Mysore Road	256	Serious Air Pollution
10	Magadi Junction	140	Serious Air Pollution
11	Okalipuram	310	Serious Air Pollution
12	Shanthala Silks (Majestic)	314	Serious Air Pollution
13	Trinity Circle	232	Serious Air Pollution
14	Cauvery Bhavan (Mysore Bank Circle)	241	Serious Air Pollution
15	Old Madras Road	184	Serious Air Pollution

In addition, many locations are experiencing moderate to heavy air pollution levels. This clearly implies that urgent remedial measures are needed. Noise pollution is another health hazard of urban life and together with the air pollution problem needs a thorough evaluation as part of baseline environmental studies. About 16 junctions (refer to Table 9.20) are experiencing noise levels above permissible limits of 65 dB. For the purpose of understanding noise levels over a day the time is divided into three observation periods (Morning Peak - 08.30 to 11.30; Lean Period - 14.30 to 17.00 and Evening Peak - 17.00 to 20.00). During each of the three selected periods maximum and minimum dB (A) values are recorded.

Table 9.20: Noise Level Values at Selected Locations in Bangalore

S. No	Location	Morning Peak		Lean Period		Evening Peak	
		Max	Min	Max	Min	Max	Min
1	Kimco Junction/ Deepanjali Nagar	93.90	72.20	98.68	62.75	86.98	68.10
2	Vijayanagar / Toll Gate	95.79	68.40	94.37	63.80	95.46	64.96
3	Okalipuram Junction	98.90	67.98	97.98	66.48	98.15	67.82
4	Shantala Silks/ Majestic	85.46	67.23	96.06	67.94	92.95	68.87
5	Cauvery Bhavan / Mysore Bank Circle	97.72	64.28	99.43	65.30	96.54	66.56
6	Anil Kumble Circle	91.79	61.81	86.15	60.13	94.53	68.24
7	Trinity Circle / MG Road	96.43	67.57	95.58	67.54	96.25	68.72
8	Old Madras Road / Indira Nagar	100.68	67.04	98.68	62.75	100.27	66.86
9	Yeshwantpur Circle	97.19	64.86	92.25	62.42	92.92	64.78
10	Navarang Circle	98.14	64.16	96.06	69.80	95.11	68.87
11	Seshadripuram Circle	94.16	63.18	97.05	66.22	98.74	67.50
12	Ananda Rao Circle	97.41	66.06	100.56	66.16	86.98	68.10
13	National College Vani Vilas Circle	94.72	65.39	94.37	63.80	92.03	65.52
14	South End Circle	92.59	65.64	93.66	65.40	95.46	64.96
15	KIMS Circle	94.53	68.24	95.18	68.95	96.39	68.44
16	Jayanagar 5th Block / Sri Aurobindo Circle	96.07	69.88	96.18	69.12	94.43	71.21

It may be observed that at all the locations Lmax and Lmin values are higher than the permissible value of 65dB. Even during the off peak period the values recorded are above the permissible value. If a continuous recording is made at these locations throughout the day, one may understand that for about 16 to 18 hours these localities are experiencing noise levels above permissible limits. It is expected that with the completion of the metro in Bangalore city these noise levels are likely to be reduced by thirty percent.

9.3.7.3 Emission standards

The emission standards adopted in the state of Karnataka for petrol driven vehicles are presented in Table 9.21. Emission limits of petrol vehicles adopted in Bangalore are:

Table 9.21: Emission Standards for Petrol Vehicles

Limits	Vehicle Class	CO in (g/Km)	HC in (g/Km)	NOx in (G/Km)
Prior to July 2007	Displacement <150 cc	2	0.8	0.15
	Displacement >150 cc	2	0.3	0.15
Since July 2007	Vmax <130 km/h	2.62	0.75	0.17
	Vmax >130 km/h	2.62	0.33	0.22

CO in Mtld	NOx in Mtld	HC in Mtld	PM in Mtld
207.0	29.7	117.4	8.1

Field studies reveal that a ten-year old bus pollutes hundred times more than a new bus (Volvo report at Sustainable Mobility Conference on 04-02-2008). This clearly brings out that just not running any bus fleet will serve the purpose of minimizing the environmental pollution. It is essential that public transport undertakings (BMTC) in Bangalore need to update their fleet strength in tune with the requirements. The study undertaken by IIMB (T. V. Ramanayya and G. Ramesh) clearly brings out the need for additional fleet in different periods of time.

In order to minimize pollution levels the following observations are to be considered in developing appropriate policy and also enhancing monitoring strategies.

a. Auto rickshaws continue to pollute as they use poor quality/adulterated lubricants.

b. The auto giants have not made sustained efforts to develop renewable alternate fuels like biofuels, fuel cell technology, and electric vehicles

9.3.7.4 Transport and noise

The serious effects of transport noise have been recognized since 1970. Transport noise impacts include sleep disturbance, cardiovascular disease, elevated hormone levels, and psychological problems. But very little effort went on in collecting transport noise data even in developed countries. The situation is fast changing since the adoption of the Environmental Noise Directive in 2002 and the EEAs recent TERM report in 2008 has focused on EU wide noise data. The study highlights that 55 percent of those living in urban areas with more than 250,000 are enduring noise levels above the lower limit of the EU bench mark of 55 Lden for excess exposure. In India the problem is not that serious due to low levels of vehicle ownership. However, this problem persists in certain busy corridors of urban areas and at international airports with many flights. In the state of Karnataka, the problem areas are the international airport and some busy corridorors in the city of Bangalore.

A car traveling at 20 kilometers per hour emits 55 decibels of rolling noise, at 40 kilometers per hour 65 decibels, at 80 kilometers per hour 75 decibels, and at 100 kilometers per hour 80 decibels. Noise pollution increases with traffic congestion, as irritated drivers lean on their horns. Under the Central Motor Vehicles (Amendment) Rules 1999 the government has banned the use of shrill horns and multitoned horns. But some vehicle owners continue to use them. In the year 2003, 844 vehicles were booked by the transport department for noise pollution. Another cause of noise pollution arises from auto rickshaw drivers removing mufflers from their vehicles with the belief that this improves their pickup. Removal of mufflers increases the noise levels. Autorickshaws rolling out of manufacturing units comply with noise emission norms. But some auto rickshaw owners replace the silencers with cheap ones manufactured locally. These silencers referred to as 'dolly silencers', are easily available. Overall, noise pollution is a result of cumulative effects, both of the number of vehicles on the road and the ambient noise from industrial sources and other sources like electric generators. Therefore, individual vehicle-oriented standards may be limited in terms of helping to mitigate excessive noise levels.

Some of the measures that may be initiated to minimize noise impacts are:

1. Technological improvements to vehicles and air craft aerodynamics, low noise tires, etc.

2. Improvements to infrastructure with low noise road surfaces and rail tracks

3. Higher standards of offset distance from roads and railway lines for buildings

4. Traffic management techniques such as traffic calming, speed control of vehicles, and low noise operational procedures for aircraft

5. Noise barriers and sound proofing of dwellings if there is no other way

6. Create public awareness on the unnecessary use of the horn and on the ill effects of noise caused by auto rickshaws. Promote the use of silencers in autos.

7. Book those who alter bikes and other vehicles that roar through the streets and harm our eardrums.

8. Convince government regulators to implement the laws on noise pollution.

A similar comprehensive study needs to be undertaken in other cities of Karnataka especially in Mysore, Hubli-Dharward, and Mangalore. Only then is it possible to identify what measures need to be undertaken to minimize environmental related problems. Air pollution problems are severe where the number of vehicles and distance traveled is maximum. Increasing the two wheeler population leads to enhanced per capita emissions. The problem is severe in Bangalore, moderate in other major urban centers like Hubli-Dharwad, Mysore, Belgaum, Mangalore, and Gulbarga, and relatively less in other urban centers. Even in these cities, the problem will be concentrated in the city centers rather than in the extended suburbs. The main impacts of the air pollution are on the people who reside or work on the sides of arterial roads and in the city centers. The vulnerable parties are typically pedestrians, traffic police, and roadside shop owners.

9.3.7.5 Problems of automobile technology

Automobile technology has improved over the years by making the manufacturers adhere to stricter emission norms. These include improvements in combustion processes, treatment of exhaust gases (i.e., with catalytic converters), and use of cleaner burning fuels. However, the improved engine combustion and exhaust gas treatment will have virtually no effect on energy efficiency or greenhouse gas emissions. The use of natural gas, alcohol fuels, and propane in petrol engines will provide reductions of about 20 to 30 percent in greenhouse gas emissions, but their use in diesel engines will not reduce greenhouse gas emissions and may even slightly increase them. Efforts are underway by auto manufacturers in India to introduce improved technologies for engines running on alternative fuels. Even though, the number of four stroke vehicles is increasing, two wheelers still form a sizable amount of the total vehicle population plying on the roads with two stroke engines. Two stroke vehicles consume more fuel when compared to the four stroke ones and also cause relatively higher pollutant emissions. For two-wheelers and autorickshaws, conversion to four-stroke technology results in 35 percent improvement in fuel economy and reduction in hydrocarbon emissions. A Euro II compliant vehicle requires a multi-point fuel injection system. There are two basic types of engines: spark ignition and compression ignition engines. In the former, fuel ignition is triggered by an electric spark from a spark plug, while in the latter, atomized liquid fuel is injected with the help of a fuel pump and a nozzle into a cylinder full of hot compressed air, which results in ignition taking place. Larger cylinders which need more fuel require more than one injector, thus resulting in a multi-point fuel injection system. Even though battery driven cars have been introduced in the country, they have failed to garner a sizable proportion of the automobile market. This can be attributed to the cost of the vehicle and the shorter distance of travel per charging session. Vehicles running on a blend of ethanol and petrol are already plying on state roads. There is no need to modify the engine of the vehicles to run on a blend comprised of 5 percent ethanol. However, for vehicles to run on a 10 percent blend, the engine needs to be modified. Thus, it is seen that the automobile technology in India still needs to evolve in order to develop more energy efficient, eco friendly, and cost-effective vehicles. Unless these factors are addressed, it will be quite long before vehicles operating on clean technologies become popular.

Vehicles driven by electricity may gain more acceptance in the coming years due to changes in technology. Currently, the automobile manufacturers are working on advanced lead acid batteries, lithium ion, and nickel metal hydride batteries, which will increase the range to over 150 kilometers on a single charge and issues concerning integration and thermal and electric management are currently being addressed. The batteries are still expensive, but volume and time will bring this technology within the reach of consumer and solar charging is also a possibility which will increase the range by 10 to 15 percent. Thus more research and development work is needed to develop cost effective and eco friendly vehicles running from sources like batteries and fuel cells.

9.3.7.6 Recommendations and action plan of the expert committee on auto fuel policy, government of India

1. Grade separators to be provided wherever feasible in all urban centers without delay. This should become part and parcel of transport infrastructure development.

2. Reducing idling, stop time, and speed changes will considerably reduce pollution and improve the environment.

3. Develop a strategy to discourage the use of private vehicles (cars and two-wheelers) by levying a fee as well as for parking. The charges should reflect the true costs involved in traffic and transportation activities. This may positively influence the demand for public transportation.

4. Road pricing must reflect the true costs. This may reduce peak hour. The charges for using the roads during peak hours could be higher by 2-3 times than those other hours of the day.

5. Physical restrictions could be imposed on entry of vehicles either during part or the whole of the day into certain areas.

Summary

This chapter discusses the economic condition of the STUs of different states in terms of total revenue, different types of transport taxes, operating costs, and the net profit/loss. And it also deals with the manpower requirements like total staff ratio w.r.t the number of buses, total road length, and the population and how it effects the economic stability of STUs.

This chapter also gives the information about the bus fleet for populations of the different cities and discusses the EVA methodology for financial evaluation. Mainly it shows some highlights of environmental issues like emission standards, air quality index, noise levels, etc.

References and Bibliography

1. Assessment of Social and Economic Impact of Rural Roads Component, Sponsored by Government of Andhra Pradesh, May 2007, unpublished, IIM Banglore.

2. Anantharamaiah, K.M. and Ramanayya, T.V., Characteristics of vehicle ownership in rural areas, Indian Highways, *Journal of Indian Roads Congress*, New Delhi, September 1994.

3. Anantharamaiah, K.M. and Ramanayya, T.V., Rural passenger travel characteristics - a case study of southern India, Traffic Engineering, *Journal of Indian Roads Congress*, New Delhi, September 1994.

4. Anantharamaiah, K.M. and Ramanayya, T.V., Settlement connectivity and rural travel characteristics a case study of southern India, *Journal of Institution of Town Planners*, India, September 1994.

5. Anantharamaiah, K.M. and Ramanayya, T.V., Rural travel characteristics a case study of Ratnagiri district, *Moving Technology, Journal*, May 1991.

6. Anantharamaiah, K.M. and Ramanayya, T.V., Changes in rural travel characteristics in southern India published in the world conference on Transport Research, Lyons, France 1992.

7. Buchan, K (1992), Enhancing the Quality of Life. In Roberts, J., Cleary, J., Hamilton, K. and Hanna, J. (eds.), Travel Sickness: the need for a sustainable transport policy for Britain, Lawrence and Wishart.

8. Buehler, R. and Pucher, J. (2011) Making Public Transport Financially Sustainable. Transport Policy. 18(1), 126-138.

9. Casey Jr, H. J. (1955), The Law of Retail Gravitation Applied to Traffic Engineering, Traffic Quarterly, 9(3), pp. 313-321.

10. Chakroborty P., Recent Trends in Sustainable Transportation Planning, Lecture Notes, Jointly organized by CiSTUP and Dept. of Civil Eng., IISc Bangalore, 12th to 14th Dec. 2009.

11. Census of India (2011); RITES (2011); LDA (2005); MP Town & Country Planning Office (2008); Guwahati City Development Plan (2006); Government of NCT of Delhi (2009); Government of Uttar Pradesh (2006); Business Standard (2013); Directorate of Economics & Statistics, Karnataka; Directorate of Economics & Statistics, Uttar Pradesh; Directorate of Economics & Statistics, Madhya Pradesh; Directorate of Economics & Statistics, Assam (2013)

12. Census of India. (2011). Available at: http://www.censusindia.gov.in/

13. Central Institute of Road Transport (2000-2011), State Transport Undertakings - Profile and Performances.

14. Cervero, R. (1998). The Transit Metropolis, A Global Inquiry. Washington: Island Press.

15. CIRT (2007) Physical Performance of SRTU's for the year 1995-2007. Indian Journal of Transport Management, Central Institute for Road Transport, Pune, India

16. CIRT (2011); Delhi Metro Rail Corporation Limited; Bangalore Metropolitan Transport Corporation; Uttar Pradesh State Road Transport Corporation; RITES (2012); Assam State Road Transport Corporation; RITES (2011b).

17. Consulting Engineering Services India, Ltd. (CES), (2001), Proposed mass rapid transit for Thane city, Draft Final Report, MSRDC, Mumbai, India.

18. Daly, A. (1975), Measuring Accessibility in a Rural Context. Rural Transport Seminar, Polytechnic of Central London.

19. Delhi Metro Rail Corporation Limited; Bangalore Metro Rail Corporation Limited; Central Road Research Institute, Delhi; ifmo (2013).

20. Delhi Transport Corporation; Delhi Metro Rail Corporation; Uttar Pradesh State Road Transport Corporation; Atal Indore City Transport Services Ltd; Assam State Transport Corporation.

21. Directorate of Economics & Statistics, Delhi (2009); RITES (2011); Lucknow Municipal Corporation, DUDA; DMG Consultancy Services (2011); Guwahati Metropolitan Development Authority.

22. District level study of socio economic aspects of rural roads in the development of standards for planning rural roads in India (Ratnagiri in Maharshtra State) project sponsored jointly by Planning Commission, Ministry of Shipping and Transport, Government of India, and Maharashtra Government 1981-83, unpublished, IIM Banglore.

23. DMRC (2003). Detailed Project Report – Bangalore Metro (Phase I), Delhi Metro Rail Corporation Ltd., New Delhi, India.

24. Enoch, M., Potter, S., and Ison, S. (2005). Strategic approach to financing public transport through property values, *Public Money & Management*, 25(3), 247-154.

25. Furness K.P. (1965), Time function iteration, Traffic Engng. and Control, 7 (7) (1965), pp. 458–460

26. GOI (1987) Report of the Study Group on Alternative Systems of Urban Transport. Government of India, New Delhi, India.

27. GOM (2000) Mumbai Sky Bus Metro: Preliminary Engineering Cum Survey Report. Konkan Railway Corporation, Ltd., Govt. of Maharashatra, India.

28. Gould, P. (1969), Spatial Diffucion. Commission on College Geography, Association of Americal Geographers, Washington DC.

29. Gray, G.E. and Hoel, L.A. (1979) Public Transportation: Planning, Operations, and Management, Prentice-Hall Inc., Englewood Cliffs, New Jersey.

30. Harman, L. (1998) Technological Change and Public Transportation- Issues for the Year 2020. Draft Manuscript, Massachusetts Executive Office of Transportation and Construction, Boston, Massachusetts.

31. Hillman. M. et al. (1973). Personal Mobility and Transport Policy, Political and Economic Planning, Broadsheet 542, London.

32. Hills, P.J. (1996). What is induced traffic? Transportation, 23(1), 516.

33. http://www.censusindia.gov.in Census of India. (2001)(Government of India Ministry of Statistics and Programme Implementation Central Statistics Office Social Statistics Division. Census 2001).

34. http://www.moud.gov.in (Ministry of Urban Development).

35. http://www.Indiandemographics.weebly.com/settlement-patterns.

36. http://www.pmgsy.in (PMGSY site (project details state wise report) (data taken on -10-30-2013).

37. http://www.mapsofindia.com

38. http://www.gdpofindia.com

39. http://www.azadindia.com (Ministry of Urban development- Migration details).

40. http://www.slumdetailsofindia.com (primary census abstract for slum 2011, Office of the Registrar General & Census Commissioner, New Delhi India).

41. ifmo (2013). Megacity Mobility Culture– How Cities Move on in a Diverse World. Institute for Mobility Research, Munich, Germany.

42. INCCA (2007), Ministry of Environment and Forest, Govt. of India.

43. Innes JE and Booher DE (2000) Public Participation in Planning: New Strategies for the 21st Century. University of California at Berkley, Institute of Urban and Regional Development. University of California, USA.

44. International Transport Forum (2011) Road Safety Annual Report. http://internationaltransportforum.org/irtadpublic/pdf/11IrtadReport.pdf (Last accessed 25.05.2013)

45. Irwin N.A., von Cube H.G. (1962), Capacity restraint in multitravel mode assignment programs, Bull. Highw. Res. Bd, 347 (1962), pp. 258–289.

46. Kittleson Associates, Urbitran Associates, LKC Consulting Services, MORPACE International, Queensland University of Technology and Y. Nakanishi, 2003. A Guidebook for Developing a Transit Performance Measurement Systems, Transit Cooperative Research Program Report 88, Washington D. C., Transportation Research Board.

47. Lecture notes of Dr. Ashish Verma on Urban Transportation Systems Planning, IISc Bangalore.

48. Litman T. (2011), Transportation Elasticities - How Prices and Other Factors Affect Travel Behavior, Report, Victoria Transport Policy Institute.

49. Lohia, S.K. (2008). Urban Transport in India., Proc., Indo-US conference on Mass Transit Travel Behavior Research 08 (MTTBR-08). IIT Guwahati, India.

50. Mackay M. (2004) A Comparison of the Sample Survey and Open House Methods of Public Consultation for Transportation Issues in the City of Edmonton. Unpublished MSc Thesis, Department of Civil Engineering, University of Calgary.

51. Manuel, V.S., Perez, D.V., Ramon, M.R., and Tomas, S. (2009). Public transport funding policy in Madrid: is there room for improvement? *Transport Reviews*, 29(2), 261-278.

52. McKinsey & Company (2008), India's urban awakening: Building inclusive cities, sustaining economic growth. McKinsey Global Institute, McKinsey & Company

53. Mills, G. (1991). Commercial funding of transport infrastructure: lessons from some Australian cases, *Journal of Transport Economics and Policy*, 25(3), 279-298.

54. Ministry of Road Transport & Highways (2008-2011). Road accidents in India. Government of India, Ministry of Road Transport and Highways, Transport Research Wing, New Delhi

55. Ministry of Urban Development (2008); UMTC (2012); RITES (2012).

56. Mitchell, C and Town, S. (1976). Accessibility of various Cosial Groups to Differing Activities, Transport and Road Research Laboratory, Crowthorne, Berks.

57. Mumpower, J.L. (2001) Selecting and evaluating tools and methods for public participation. *International Journal of Technology, Policy, and Management.* 1(1): 66-77.

58. MMPG (1997), Techno-economic feasibility study of construction of Mumbai metro, Progress Report Submitted by MMPG to Govt. of Maharashtra, India.

59. Mumbai Metropolitan Region Development Authority (MMRDA). (2000), Selection of a mass rapid transit system for Mumbai, Final Report for Greater Mumbai: The Andheri-Ghatkopar Corridor, Mumbai, India.

60. MORTH (1999, 2000, 2003), Handbook on Transport Statistics in India. Transport Research Office, Ministry of Road Transport and Highways, Delhi, India.

61. MOUD (1998). "Traffic and Transportation Policies and Strategies in Urban Areas in India". Final Report. Ministry of Urban Development, Government of India, New Delhi.

62. MOUD (2008), Study on Traffic and Transportation Policies and Strategies in Urban Areas in India, Govt. of India.

63. Naganna, N. and Ramanayya, T.V. "A Critical Appraisal of Road Accessibility in Rural Areas" presented at National Seminar on Roads and Road Transport Rural Areas, Central Road Research Institute, New Delhi, 1985.

64. Ortuzar, J. de D. and Willumsen L.G., (1999), Modelling Transport, John Wiley and Sons.

65. PRC (1998), People Republic of China.

66. Papacostas, C.S. and Prevedouras, P.D. Transportation Engineering and Planning, Prentice Hall of India, New Delhi, 2002.

67. Parasuraman A., Zeithaml V A, Berry L L., 1985 A conceptual model of service quality and its implications for future research, Journal of Marketing 49: 41-50.

68. Planning for Non-motorized Transport in Cities- DIMTS-UITP Symposium, 2010; DDA (2007); Central Road Research Institute, Delhi; Bruhat Bengaluru Mahanagara Palike; Mobility Indicators, DULT, 2010-11; UMTC (2012); Indore Municipal Corporation; RITES (2012); Wilbur Smith Associates (2008); Guwahati Metropolitan Development Authority.

69. Planning Commission (2013) Recommendations of Working Group on Urban Transport for 12th Five Year Plan http://planningcommission.nic.in/aboutus/committee/wrkgrp12/hud/wg_%20urban%20Transport.pdf (last accessed 06.10.2013)

70. Pucher, J., Markstedt, A., & Hirschman, I. (1983). Impacts of Subsidies on the Costs of Urban Public Transport. Journal of Transport Economics and Policy, 17(2), 155-176.

71. Pucher, P., Korattyswaropam, N., Mittal, N., and Ittyerah, N. (2005). Urban transport crisis in India. Transport Policy, 12, 185–198.

72. Ramanayya T.V. (2005a), Strategies for Improving profitability of KSRTC, Project Report, IIM Bangalore, India

73. Ramanayya T.V. (2005b), Holistic Organisational Transformation Strategies (HOTS) for APSRTC, Project Report, IIM Bangalore, India

257

74. Ramanayya, T.V. and Anantharamaiah, K.M. Impact of Facility on Economic Development in Rural Areas, in Reddy, K.V.(Ed.), Transportation Systems: Tata McGraw Hill Publishing Company, Delhi, 1989.

75. Ramanayya T.V. and Anantharamaiah, K.M., Transportation Characteristics in Rural Areas of Southern India, proceedings of Third National Conference on Transportation Systems Study - Analysis and Policy, NCOTSS-1993, Andhra University, Visakhapatnam, December 1993.

76. Ramanayya T.V. and Anantharamaiah K.M. (2003). Database on Rural Travel Changes in Three Decades (A Case Study of Southern India), Presented at National Seminar on Integrated Development of Rural and Arterial Road Network for Socio- Economic Growth, 5 & 6 December 2003, New Delhi.

77. Rastogi R., Recent Practices in Transportation Planning and Traffic Engineering, Lecture Notes, MDONER Sponsored Short Term Course, IIT Guwahati, Jan. 15th to 19th, 2007.

78. Ramanayya, T.V. and Anantharamaiah, K.M. Changes in Rural Transport Scenario in South India (1978-1999), Presented in International workshop Providing Road Connectivity-The PMGSY Approach, A vision to transform Rural India Bhubaneswar, Orissa Feb 2002.

79. Ramanayya, T.V. and Anantharamaiah, K.M. Database on Rural Travel Changes in Three Decades (A Case Study of Southern India), Presented at National Seminar on Integrated Development of Rural and Arterial Road Network for Socio-Economic Growth 5 & 6 December 2003, New Delhi.

80. Reddy, B. and Balachandra, P. (2012). Urban Mobility: A comparative analysis of megacities of India. Transport Policy, 21, 152–164.

81. Reeven, P. Van (2008). Subsidisation and Urban Public Transport and Mohring Effect. Journal of Transport Economics and Policy, 42 (2), 349-359.

82. Rural Transportation Studies in Nine States of India funded by the Ministry of Surface Transport, Government of India 1986-89, unpublished, IIM Banglore.

83. Rural Infrastructure in Entire South India (9 States of India), Sponsored by Ministry of Transport, Government of India, 1996-98, unpublished, IIM Banglore.

84. Stokes G. and Cullinane, S. (1998), Rural Transport Policy, Pergamon, Netherlands.

85. Serebrisky, T. (2009). Affordability and subsidies in public urban transport: what do we mean, what can be done? Transport Reviews, 29(6), 715-739.

86. Shepherd, A. and Bowler, C. (1997) Beyond the requirements: improving public participation in environmental impact assessments. Journal of Environmental Planning and Management. 40(6): 725-738.

87. Schafer (1998). The global demand for motorized mobility. Transportation Research Part A, 32 (6), 455-477.

88. Singh, S.K. (2005). Review of urban transportation in India. Journal of Public Transportation. 8(1), 79-96.

89. Sulek, J. M., and M. R. Lind, 2000. A Systems Model for Evaluating Transit Performance, Journal of Public Transportation, 3 (1): 29-47.

90. Traditional and innovative ways of funding Public Transport: A review of literature, Manuscript Draft by International Journal of Environmental and Technology.

91. Transport Advisory Service (1997), Bus Services for Rural Communities – An audit of Villages in Engaland, TAS, Preston.

92. Ubbels, B & Nijkamp, P. (2002). Unconventional Funding of Urban Public Transport. Transportation Research Part D, 7(5), 317-329.

93. Ubbels, B., Nijkamp, P., Verhoef, E., Potter, S., and Enoch, M. (2001). Alternative ways of funding public transport: a case study assessment, European Journal of Transport and Infrastructure Research, 1(1), 73-89.

94. Vaca, E., and Kuzmyak, R. (2005). Parking Pricing and Fees, Chapter 13, TCRP Report 95, Transit Cooperative Research Program, Transportation Research Board, Federal Transit Administration.

95. Verma M., Verma A., Ajith P., and Sneha S., (2013). Urban Bus Transport Service Quality and Sustainable Development: Understanding the Gaps", 13th World Conference on Transport Research (WCTR), July 15-18, 2013 – Rio de Janeiro, Brazil.

96. Verma, A. and Dhingra, S.L.(2001), Suitability of alternative systems for urban mass transport for Indian cities, *Trasporti Europei, Quarterly Journal of Transport Law*, Economics and Engineering, Trieste, Italy, Anno VII, No.18, pp. 4-15.

97. Verma, A. and Dhingra, S.L. (2003), Urban rail transport corridor identification, GIS Development, *The Asian GIS Monthly*, India, Vol.-7, No.5, pp. 39-42.

98. Verma, A., and Dhingra, S.L. (2005) Optimal urban rail transit corridor identification within integrated framework using geographical information systems, *Journal of Urban Planning and Development*, A.S.C.E., 131(2), 98-111.

99. Verma, A. and Dhingra, S.L. (2006) Developing integrated schedules for urban rail and feeder bus operation, *Journal of Urban Planning and Development*, A.S.C.E., 132(3), 138-146.

100. Verma, A. and Dhingra, S.L. (2000) A Review of the State of Art of Metropolitan Transit Alternatives. All India Seminar on Urban Mass Transit Systems, The Institution of Engineers (I), Mumbai, India, pp.262-270.

101. Verma, A. (2010). Integrated Public Transportation System Planning and Modelling. VDM Publishing House Ltd., Mauritius.

102. Vuchic, V. (2005). Urban Transit: Operations, Planning and Economics. Hoboken, NJ: John Wiley and Sons.

103. Vuchic, V. R. 2005. Urban Transit Operation, Planning, and Economics. John Wiley & Sons, Inc., Hoboken, New Jersey.

104. Wetzel, D. (2006). Facing the Environmental Challenge: Innovative Methods of Financing Public Transportation. World Transport Policy & Practice, 12(1), 40-46.

105. White, P. (2002). Public Transport: its Planning, Management, and Operation, Spon Press, London.

106. WHO (2011). Global Health Observatory Data Repository - Road Safety: National Legislation. http://apps.who.int/gho/data/node.main.A999?lang=en (last accessed 06.05.2013)

107. World Bank (2011). http://data.worldbank.org/topic (last accessed 06.03.2013)

Index